Instant Pot Cookbook for Beginners

5-Ingredient Instant Pot Recipes - 550 Simple, Easy and Delicious Recipes for Your Electric Pressure Cooker

By Tracy Peterson

Tabel of Content

Chapter 4 Fish and Seafood Recipe 34

Chapter 5 Poultry Recipe..........49

Chapter 6 Vegan and Vegetarian Recipe 63

Chapter 7 Beef, Lamb and Pork Recipe 77

Chapter 8 Soups and Stews Recipe 96

Chapter 9 Snacks and Appetizers Recipe 110

Chapter 10 Broths and Sauces Recipe 122

Chapter 11 Beans, Grains and Legumes Recipe 125

Chapter 12 Pasta and Side Dishes Recipe 135

Introduction

Many individuals enjoy pressure-cooking. The instant pot is a multi-cooker that performs more than seven functions. The Instant Pot enables one to prepare a wide range of recipes, including meat, fish, eggs, beans, cakes, poultry, yogurt, vegetables, and many more. What makes the Instant Pot exceptional is because you can utilize various cooking programs like a steamer, rice cooker, and sauté pan, thus saving more money, time, and space as compared to purchasing the appliances separately.

This book has been carefully written to meet the needs of everyone who likes cooking and would like to save money, and the time they spend on cooking. The Instant Pot serves as a multi-use programmable piece of equipment that will ensure you prepare delicious meals quickly through multiple selections of cooking settings in a single pot. We give credit of the development to smart Canadian technology specialists aiming at having the appliance as the best device for the kitchen for multiple reasons like pressure-cooking, making cake and stir-frying, among others. It was created to serve as a one-stop-shop to allow home cooks to prepare a flavorful meal with the press of a button. With the help of the appliance, you can make nearly every meal you desire.

In this book, we will explore the variety of easy delicious dishes you can cook with your Instant Pot. We will explore a wide range of dishes, from breakfast to pasta, soups to stews, desserts to appetizers, meat to beef, side dishes to vegetables, and use a healthy ingredient in the process. Most recipes will require a maximum of five components. Each recipe contains the preparation time, nutritional information, cooking instructions, and ingredients that are necessary to prepare the dishes. Once you try these delicious dishes with our cookbook, you and your Instant Pot are sure to become inseparable too.
Read on and learn more!

Chapter 1: Instant Pot - An Instant Path to Health

The Instant Pot is a multifunctional cooker that acts as a slow and rice cooker, steamer, yogurt maker, and a pressure cooker. It is a single kitchen appliance or multi-cooker that performs the tasks of seven different machines ranging from an electric pressure cooker, steamer, yogurt machine, rice cooker, sauté pan to warming pot, etc. It functions with the amalgamation of pressure and steam, which enables your foods to cook at a faster rate and safer as compared to other kitchen devices. It is a programmable countertop multi-cooker, which speeds up cooking by 2~6 times using up to 70% less energy.

The Instant Pot can conveniently and consistently cook nutritious, healthy food, making everything from stews, rice pilaf, lentil, bacon, chicken to steamed veggies. The Instant Pot deserves a spot in your kitchen because you can rely on it more than any other kitchen devices.

The Instant Pot is a useful multi-cooker that can execute the functions of a pressure cooker, slow cooker, rice cooker, steamer, and more. It has many safety features that make it safer to use and comes in different models. It comes with preset programs that are specifically designed to cook your food to perfection, whether it be chicken, dessert, cheesecake, stew, soup, or porridge.

Why Instant Pot

The following is a shortlist of some great reasons to invest in an Instant Pot. No doubt, after you start using one regularly, you will be inventing your list, and the list will only keep growing from there.

◍ **Easy Way to Prepare Food** - Unlike the earlier pressure cooker incarnations, electric ones have timers that you can set, allowing for maximum cooking convenience. Beyond the standard settings such as high, medium, and low, you do not need to worry about temperature or pressure. Unlike a stove, the pressure cooker does it all for you, and much more safely, too. You will not have to check in on your meal every few seconds constantly. Once you have installed your pressure cooker in its designated spot and discovered how useful it is, you are likely to keep it at the ready for the next quick meal simply because of its convenience.

◉ **The Faster, the Better** - Let us face it; our lives are busy. No one needs to tell you that (although I just did). Cooking meals in the oven can take hours while using the stove requires a wary eye to keep dishes from overcooking. There is a reduction in cooking time by up to 70%. When it might have taken 24 hours before to make a pot of beans, a pressure cooker makes the task so time-efficient that you will no longer have to worry about watching the stove for hours on end.

◉ **Delicious Can Also Mean Nutritious** - Remember the days of boiling food (like chicken) for hours on end? Boiling washes away vital nutrients, whereas pressure-cooking locks in all those necessary minerals and vitamins. It leaves you wanting to use your pressure cooker more often because of the additional health benefits that are available by following this style of cooking.

◉ **Fewer Dishes to Clean -** Throw all your ingredients into the pressure cooker and lock the lid. It is the best version of a one-pot meal you have ever made. When it has finished cooking, the only dishes will be the pot and the plates (which will undoubtedly have been licked clean because of how great the recipes in this book will taste!)

Instant Pot Button Functions

The Instant Pot is a piece of incredible kitchen equipment with a beautiful design. It has several buttons whose aims are to achieve particular tasks to help cook your food better. The sensors are designed intelligently to avoid overcooking or burning of your food.

Some of the excellent cooking and safety features that you need to understand to make cooking with the pot easy for you include the following:

Keep Warm/Cancel
It stops any program that has been previously set, putting the cooker in standby. When the cooker is in this standby mode, pressing this key will set forth the KEEP WARM program, which can last as long as 100 hours. No secrets for this option since it will keep the temperature warm to about 145º F but can be adjusted. The KEEP WARM function automatically activates after the timer goes off. Unless the recipe specifies that you need to turn off the machine immediately after cooking, there is no need to rush back to the cooker. You can return to the kitchen whenever you want.

Soup
This setting aims at coming up with a variety of broths and soups. The default is set at 30 minutes of high pressure although this can be adjusted using the ADJUST or '+' and '-' buttons.

Porridge
It is for making oatmeal or porridge with various types of grains. The default here is high pressure for 20 minutes. Make sure you DO NOT use quick release for this setting, as it will result in a significant mess.

Poultry

The setting is used to make meals with poultry, and the default is at high pressure for 15 minutes.

Meat/Stew

The setting is for making meats or stew, and the default is at high pressure for 35 minutes. You can add time by selecting MORE if you want that bone stripping effect on your meat.

Bean/Chili

The setting is specifically for making chili or cooking beans. The default is high pressure for 30 minutes. But if you want well-done beans, then select MORE.

Rice

It is the setting that turns your Instant Pot into a rice cooker. It is a fantastic program for cooking either parboiled or regular rice. For excellent results, use the provided water measurements inside the pot and the rice-measuring cup. The default for this setting is automatic and cooks rice at low pressure.

For instance, the manual indicates that the cooking duration for the rice changes automatically depending on the food content. Cooking 2 cups of rice will take approximately 12 minutes, and more cups will take more time accordingly.

When one attains the working pressure, the pressure keeping time will be shown, but the total cooking time is not displayed. In this setting, the ADJUST key does not affect in whatsoever way.

Multigrain

The setting is for cooking a mixture of grains such as brown rice, mung beans, wild rice, etc. The set default for this setting is 40 minutes of high pressure while the LESS setting is 20 minutes of cooking time and the MORE setting involves 45 minutes of just warm water soaking, then 60 minutes of cooking time on high pressure.

Steam

The setting is for steaming seafood, veggies, or reheating foods. You should not NPR (natural pressure release) on this setting, as you will be likely to overcook your food. The default here is 10 minutes of high-pressure cooking. You will require about 1 to 2 cups of water for steaming and make sure you use a basket or a steamer rack as this setting can burn food which is in direct contact with the pot.

Manual

This button allows you to manually set your pressure and cooking time (the maximum time is 240 minutes). You can best apply the button when you have a recipe indicating that you should cook on high pressure for a specified number of minutes.

Sauté

This setting is for open lid browning, sautéing, or simmering.
- For regular browning: NORMAL - 160 degrees C (320 degrees F)
- For darker browning: MORE - 170 degrees C (338 degrees F)
- For light browning: LESS - 105 degrees C (221 degrees F)

Slow Cook

This setting converts your Instant Pot into a slow cooker, which can run to up to 40 hours. But the default is normal heat for 4 hours of cook time.

Yogurt

There are three programs on this setting: making yogurt, making Jiu Niang (fermented rice) and pasteurizing milk. The default of this setting is 8 hours of incubation. To pasteurize milk, adjust to MORE and to ferment rice or proof bread, adjust to LESS.

Timer (For Delayed Cooking)

Usually, many people confuse this setting with an actual cooking timer, which crushes their expectations regarding the cooker.

To Use this Setting the Right Way:

Start by selecting your cooking program (e.g. STEAM or any other function except the YOGURT and SAUTE) and then press on the TIMER button. Use the '+' and '-' for setting the delayed hours. Press on the TIMER setting again to change the minutes.

The time that you have set is the delayed time before the program begins. It is where you can set the pot to start cooking a few hours before arriving home or wake up so that you find freshly prepared dinner, lunch, or breakfast. You should allow for both sufficient cooking time and downtime before serving.

Top 5 Benefits of Instant Pot

Fast Cooking

The Instant Pot uses pressure to cook food, and instead of cooking beans for 3 hours, you can have bean soup or bean chili ready in 45 minutes. It means you will not have to stand over the kitchen counter and check the doneness of beans because, with the Instant Pot, you will always have perfectly cooked beans and legumes. You reduce the cooking time by 70%, which reduces the total preparation time as well.

Preserves Nutrients

Because you are cooking in a well-sealed container, the aroma, flavor, and nutrients remain within the food. Cooking with less amount of water or steam also helps the food retain their vitamins and minerals. In addition, you do not have to add water to prevent food from burning. Vegetables like broccoli and asparagus do not lose their bright color because they do not experience direct heat exposure. Meat has to cook to fall-off-the-bone tenderness. Beans and legumes are softer, and they taste better prepared in an Instant Pot.

Researchers have shown that when cooking with pressure, there is even distribution of heat, it all cooks at the same time, so no need for extension cooking.

Saves Energy

The Instant Pot is built in such a way that it does not require a gas or electric stove to cook for more extended periods. With slow cooker option in Instant Pot, you may prepare your food for a more extended period, but with little use of energy. Statistics show that Instant Pot saves energy up to 70% as compared to the other cooking appliances and methods.

Kills Harmful Microorganisms

The Instant Pot uses pressure cooking and temperatures higher than boiling water, which is useful in killing microorganisms. Therefore, another use of the Instant Pot includes acting as a sterilizer for baby bottles and jam pots. When speaking about harmful microorganisms, most people think about chicken and salmonella. Unfortunately, many ignore mycotoxins from the corn and beans. With high pressure cooking these microorganisms that may cause even liver cancer, a safe environment is created, and therefore foods from the Instant Pot is entirely safe to consume.

Safe To Use

Many think that Instant Pot is dangerous and that it may explode. It is entirely false, and with proper use of the Instant Pot, you will only experience positive things. The Instant Pot is easy and straightforward to use and just read your manual before operating.

Cheap

Yes, the Instant Pots are cheap although you may think otherwise. The Instant Pot is an appliance with different options; it can be used for stewing, as a rice cooker, a yogurt maker, a pressure cooker, a slow cooker, a steamer, and an option to keep the food warm. If you were to buy all these appliances one by one, you would go much over the Instant Pot price.

As you can see, the Instant Pot has many benefits, and if you do not own one, now it is the time.

FAQs of Instant Pot

Is the Instant Pot the Same As a Pressure Cooker?

No, it is not the same. While a pressure cooker only pressure cooks, the Instant Pot is a cooker with many functions like a pressure cooker, yogurt maker, slow cooker, warming pot, and rice cooker.

What Are the Drawbacks of Using Instant Pot to Cook?

The main drawback is that you cannot adjust, taste, or inspect the food when the cooking process starts. You have to wait for the set time to elapse.

Can I Pressure Fry with My Instant Pot?

Pressure frying is not recommended for electric pressure cookers because the splattering oil may melt the cooker gasket.

Is It Safe to Use the Instant Pot?
Yes, the Instant Pot is very safe to use. It has passed many UL certifications on safety.

Is the Cooking Process Faster When Using Instant Pot?
Using pressure to cook will always save you time. However, in some foods such as shrimps and broccoli, you may not notice this. When cooking foods such as pork, you will see that time is significantly cut.

What Is the Working Pressure of the Instant Pot?
It ranges from 10.15 to 11.6 psi.

What are the Accessories You Recommend for Instant Pot?
Some of the recommended accessories include steaming racks, meat thermometers, steamer baskets, trivets, etc.

How Do I Quick Release?
When cooking has finished, unseal the venting knob to the venting position. It will take just a short time (usually a few minutes) for the pressure to be released.

How Do I Natural Release?
When cooking has finished, you wait for the valve to drop completely before opening the cover. Turn the knob to vent, and the pressure will be released. It takes 10 to 25 minutes.

Do You Use the CHICKEN Button or the MANUAL Button for Chicken?
It depends. If your recipe calls for one, use it. If you are doing a whole huge chicken, it's best to use the MANUAL setting. To get a more particular flavor, try the POULTRY setting.

Are There Any Directions on How to Use the MANUAL Function?
The MANUAL function does what it says, and it will cook the food naturally for the desired time. Just set the time, and then press it, and it will cook the food once it has built up.

The Pot Isn't Heating Up on MANUAL. What Is Going on?
MANUAL adjusts the cooking time. However, if the contents are frozen, you will start to notice that the countdown will only happen when you attain the pressure. In addition, take a look at the liquid you have in the pot as well; it might cause the pressure to be lacking.

How Long Does It Take to Warm Up Before Cooking?
From 5 to 7 minutes. Use the warm liquid to help bring the pressure up faster.

Do You Need to Do an Initial Test Run?
Yes, it is lovely to do a test run, simply because you will understand how to use this better. Often, people do not understand, so try using the water to test how fast it heats up before it cooks.

How Do You Get Low-Pressure?
It is simple. There is a PRESSURE button, and first, you can press MANUAL, and then press the PRESSURE button until it's low. You can then press the TIMER button to adjust the time.

Can You Change the Heat on SAUTE Mode?
You sure can. You press the ADJUST button, and then choose the three levels of temperature. Most people use it on NORMAL, but occasionally, if you want to boil something, put it on MORE.

Chapter 2 Breakfast and Brunch Recipe

Apple Cinnamon Oatmeal

Prep Time: 6 mins, Cook Time: 8 mins, Servings: 4

Ingredients:

1 tsp. cinnamon powder
1 chopped apple
1 cup steel-cut oats
¼ tsp. ground nutmeg
3 cups water
Salt, to taste

Instructions:

1. Add all the ingredients to your Instant Pot and stir to combine.
2. Lock the lid. Select the Manual mode and set the cooking time for 8 minutes at High Pressure.
3. Once cooking is complete, do a natural pressure release for 5 minutes. Carefully open the lid.
4. Divide the oatmeal among four serving bowls and serve warm.

Nutritional info:

Calories 171, Fat 2.6g, Carbs 32.6g, Protein: 5.1g

Cashew and Mango Oatmeal

Prep Time: 8 mins, Cook Time: 3 mins, Servings: 2

Ingredients:

1 cup old-fashioned rolled oats
2 tbsps. unsweetened flaked coconut
2 tbsps. brown sugar
2 cups water
2 tbsps. chopped cashews
½ cup chopped mango

Instructions:

1. Put the oats and coconut in the Instant Pot, then sprinkle with the brown sugar. Pour in the water. Stir to mix well.
2. Lock the lid. Set to Manual mode, then set the timer for 3 minutes at High Pressure.
3. Once the timer goes off, perform a natural pressure release. Carefully open the lid.
4. Transfer the oatmeal in a serving bowl, then fold in the cashews and mango before serving.

Nutritional info:

Calories 276, Carbs 45.6g, Protein 7.1g, Fat 8.4g

Chocolate Oatmeal

Prep Time: 12 mins, Cook Time: 10 mins, Servings: 6

Ingredients:

2½ tbsps. cocoa powder
2 cups oatmeal
1 tsp. cinnamon powder
6 cups water
1 cup milk

Instructions:

1. In the Instant Pot, mix the milk, oatmeal, cocoa powder, cinnamon powder, and water.
2. Lock the lid. Select the Manual mode and cook for 10 minutes at High Pressure.
3. Once cooking is complete, do a natural pressure release for 10 minutes. Carefully open the lid.
4. Stir the oatmeal again and divide into bowls to serve.

Nutritional info:

Calories 110, Fat 4g, Carbs 8g, Protein 5g

Cauliflower and Barley Bowls

Prep Time: 12 mins, Cook Time: 30 mins, Servings: 4

Ingredients:

½ cup grated Parmesan cheese, divided
3 tbsps. extra virgin olive oil, divided
3 cups chicken stock
1 cup pearl barley
1 head cauliflower
Salt and pepper, to taste

Instructions:

1. Press the Sauté button on the Instant Pot and heat 2 tablespoons olive oil.
2. Add the cauliflower, salt and pepper, and sauté for 6 to 8 minutes, stirring occasionally.
3. Add half of the Parmesan cheese, stir, and cook for 3 to 4 minutes more.
4. Add the remaining olive oil, barley, and stock, and whisk well.
5. Lock the lid. Select the Manual mode and set the cooking time for 15 minutes at High Pressure.
6. Once cooking is complete, do a natural pressure release for 7 minutes, then release any remaining pressure. Carefully open the lid.
7. Sprinkle with the remaining Parmesan cheese. Divide into bowls and serve warm.

Nutritional info:

Calories 252, Fat 4g, Carbs 20g, Protein 6g

Espresso Oatmeal

Prep Time: 12 mins, Cook Time: 10 mins, Servings: 4

Ingredients:

1 tsp. espresso powder	2 tbsps. sugar
2½ cups water	1 cup milk
	1 cup steel-cut oats

Instructions:

1. Add all the ingredients to the Instant Pot and stir well.
2. Lock the lid. Select the Manual mode and cook for 6 minutes at High Pressure.
3. Once cooking is complete, do a natural pressure release for 5 minutes. Carefully open the lid.
4. Stir your oatmeal again, divide into bowls and serve warm.

Nutritional info:

Calories 120, Fat 2g, Carbs 10g, Protein 5g

Sweet Potato Hash

Prep Time: 12 mins, Cook Time: 10 mins, Servings: 4

Ingredients:

1 yellow onion, chopped	cubed
½ lb. ground pork sausage	1 tbsp. Italian seasoning
1 sweet potato,	6 eggs, beaten
	2 cups water

Instructions:

1. Set the Instant Pot to Sauté. Add the onion, sausage, and sweet potato to the pot, and stir to incorporate.
2. Cook for 5 minutes and transfer to a baking dish. Set aside.
3. In a bowl, mix the eggs with Italian seasoning, and whisk well. Pour the eggs over the sausage mixture.
4. Add 2 cups water and trivet to your Instant Pot. Place the baking dish on the trivet.
5. Lock the lid. Select the Manual mode and cook for 5 minutes at High Pressure.
6. Once cooking is complete, do a quick pressure release. Carefully open the lid.
7. Remove from the pot and serve hot.

Nutritional info:

Calories 216, Fat 6g, Carbs 12g, Protein 5g

Bread Pudding

Prep Time: 12 mins, Cook Time: 15 mins, Servings: 8

Ingredients:

½ cup maple syrup	2 cups coconut milk
1 bread loaf, cubed	4 eggs
½ cup butter	2 cups water

Instructions:

1. In a blender, blend the coconut milk with eggs, butter and maple syrup until smooth.
2. Transfer the mixture to a pudding pan and add the bread cubes. Cover the pan with tin foil.
3. Add 2 cups water and trivet to your Instant Pot. Place the pudding pan on the trivet.
4. Lock the lid. Select the Manual mode and cook for15 minutes at High Pressure.
5. Once cooking is complete, do a quick pressure release. Carefully open the lid.
6. Allow to cool for 5 minutes before serving.

Nutritional info:

Calories 271, Fat 4g, Carbs 12g, Protein 10g

Cheesy Bacon Quiche

Prep Time: 5 mins, Cook Time: 10 mins, Servings: 6

Ingredients:

2 tbsps. olive oil	2 cups Monterey Jack cheese, grated
6 eggs, lightly beaten	
1 cup milk	1 cup bacon, cooked and crumbled
Salt and pepper, to taste	

Instructions:

1. Grease the Instant Pot with olive oil.
2. Combine the eggs, milk, salt, and pepper in a large bowl. Stir to mix well.
3. Put the cheese and bacon in the pot, then pour the egg mixture over. Stir to mix well.
4. Lock the lid. Set to Manual mode, then set the timer for 10 minutes at High Pressure.
5. Once the timer goes off, perform a natural pressure release for 5 minutes. Carefully open the lid.
6. Transfer the quiche on a plate and serve.

Nutritional info:

Calories 396, Carbs 5.5g, Protein 23.7g, Fat 31.3g

Strawberry Oatmeal

Prep Time: 6 mins, Cook Time: 3 mins, Servings: 2

Ingredients:

1 tbsp. ground flaxseed	¼ cup sliced strawberries
3 cups water	1 cup steel-cut oats

Instructions:

1. Pour the water into the Instant Pot.
2. Stir in the oats and lock the lid. Select the Manual mode and cook for 3 minutes at High Pressure.
3. Once cooking is complete, do a natural pressure release for 10 minutes. Carefully open the lid.
4. Pour the oatmeal into a serving bowl. Top with the strawberries and flaxseed, then serve.

Nutritional info:

Calories 320, Fat 5g, Carbs 54g, Protein 12g

Eggs En Cocotte

Prep Time: 10 mins, Cook Time: 20 mins, Servings: 4

Ingredients:

1 cup water	4 eggs
1 tbsp. butter	1 tbsp. chives
4 tbsps. heavy whipping cream	Salt and pepper, to taste

Instructions:

1. Arrange a steamer rack in the Instant Pot, then pour in the water.
2. Grease four ramekins with butter.
3. Divide the heavy whipping cream in the ramekins, then break each egg in each ramekin.
4. Sprinkle them with chives, salt, and pepper.
5. Arrange the ramekins on the steamer rack.
6. Lock the lid. Set to the Manual mode, then set the timer for 20 minutes at High Pressure.
7. Once the timer goes off, perform a natural pressure release for 10 minutes, then release any remaining pressure. Carefully open the lid.
8. Transfer them on a plate and serve immediately.

Nutritional info:

Calories 166, Carbs 3.1g, Protein 9.7g, Fat 12.7g

Cauliflower Breakfast Hash

Prep Time: 6 mins, Cook Time: 7 mins, Servings: 4

Ingredients:

4 eggs	1 grated cauliflower head, liquid squeezed out
4 chopped jalapeño peppers	
1 tbsp. olive oil	Salt and pepper, to taste
3 minced garlic cloves	½ cup water

Instructions:

1. Press the Sauté button on the Instant Pot and heat the oil.
2. Stir in the garlic and sauté for 1 minute until fragrant.
3. Stir in the grated cauliflower, pepper and salt.
4. Pour in ½ cup water and spread the cauliflower mixture evenly in the bottom of the Instant Pot.
5. Make four wells in the cauliflower and gently crack an egg into each well.
6. Sprinkle with jalapeño peppers.
7. Lock the lid. Select the Manual mode and set the cooking time for 6 minutes at High Pressure.
8. Once cooking is complete, do a quick pressure release. Carefully open the lid.
9. Cool for a few minutes and serve on plates.

Nutritional info:

Calories 113, Carbs 6.2g, Protein, 4.6g, Fat 9.5g

Pumpkin and Apple Butter

Prep Time: 12 mins, Cook Time: 10 mins, Servings: 6

Ingredients:

30 oz. pumpkin purée	1 cup sugar
4 apples, cored, peeled, and cubed	1 tbsp. pumpkin pie spice
12 oz. apple cider	

Instructions:

1. In the Instant Pot, stir together the pumpkin purée with apples, apple cider, sugar, and pumpkin pie spice.
2. Lock the lid. Select the Manual mode and cook for 10 minutes at High Pressure.
3. Once cooking is complete, do a quick pressure release. Carefully open the lid.
4. Remove from the pot and serve in bowls.

Nutritional info:

Calories 182, Fat 6g, Carbs 8g, Protein 2g

Creamy Tomatoes and Quinoa

Prep Time: 12 mins, Cook Time: 12 mins, Servings: 6
Ingredients:

1 tbsp. grated ginger
1 (28 oz) can tomatoes, chopped
¼ cup quinoa

14 oz. coconut milk
1 small yellow onion, chopped

Instructions:
1. In the Instant Pot, mix the onion with quinoa, tomatoes, milk and ginger, and stir well.
2. Lock the lid. Select the Manual mode and cook for 12 minutes at High Pressure.
3. Once cooking is complete, do a natural pressure release for 5 minutes, then release any remaining pressure. Carefully open the lid.
4. Stir the mixture one more time and divide into bowls to serve.

Nutritional info:
Calories 260, Fat 9g, Carbs 30g, Protein 7g

Blackberry Egg Cake

Prep Time: 12 mins, Cook Time: 8 mins, Servings: 3
Ingredients:

Zest from ½ an orange
½ cup fresh blackberries
1 tbsp. coconut oil

3 tbsps. coconut flour
5 eggs, whisked
1 cup water
Pinch salt

Instructions:
1. Place a steamer basket in the Instant Pot and pour in a cup of water.
2. In a mixing bowl, combine the eggs, coconut oil, and coconut flour until well combined. Season with a pinch of salt.
3. Add the blackberries and orange zest.
4. Pour into muffin cups.
5. Place the muffin cups in the steamer basket.
6. Lock the lid. Press the Steam button and set the cooking time for 8 minutes at High Pressure.
7. Once cooking is complete, do a quick pressure release. Carefully open the lid.
8. Allow to cool for 5 minutes before serving.

Nutritional info:
Calories 172, Carbs 11.4g, Protein 5.6g, Fat 16.9g

Turkey Breast and Avocado Breakfast

Prep Time: 12 mins, Cook Time: 7 mins, Servings: 4
Ingredients:

4 whisked eggs
4 avocado slices
2 tbsps. olive oil
2 tbsps. vegetable

stock
4 cooked turkey breast slices

Instructions:
1. Set the Instant Pot to Sauté and heat the olive oil.
2. Add the turkey and brown for 2 minutes, then transfer to a plate.
3. Add the eggs and vegetable stock to the pot and whisk well.
4. Lock the lid. Select the Manual mode and cook for 5 minutes at High Pressure.
5. Once cooking is complete, do a quick pressure release. Carefully open the lid.
6. Divide the eggs and avocado slices next to turkey breast slices and serve.

Nutritional info:
Calories 185, Fat 2g, Carbs 16g, Protein 6g

French Eggs

Prep Time: 12 mins, Cook Time: 8 mins, Servings: 4
Ingredients:

¼ tsp. salt
4 bacon slices
1 tbsp. olive oil
4 tbsps. chopped

chives
4 eggs
1½ cups water

Instructions:
1. Grease 4 ramekins with a drizzle of oil and crack an egg into each ramekin.
2. Add a bacon slice on top and season with salt. Sprinkle the chives on top.
3. Add 1½ cups water and steamer basket to your Instant Pot. Transfer the ramekins to the basket.
4. Lock the lid. Select the Manual mode and set the cooking time for 8 minutes at High Pressure.
5. Once cooking is complete, do a quick pressure release. Carefully open the lid.
6. Serve your baked eggs immediately.

Nutritional info:
Calories 182, Fat 5, Carbs 10, Protein 5

Cream and Cinnamon Puddings

Prep Time: 20 mins, Cook Time: 15 mins, Servings: 6

Ingredients:

2 cups fresh cream	5 tbsps. sugar
1 tsp. cinnamon powder	6 egg yolks
	2 cups water
Zest of 1 orange	

Instructions:

1. Set the pot on Sauté mode and heat it up.
2. Add cream, cinnamon and orange zest and sauté for a few minutes and leave aside for 20 minutes.
3. Using a bowl, combine the sugar and egg yolks. Pour the egg yolk mixture in the cream mixture, whisk well, strain the mixture, divide it into ramekins and cover them with tin foil.
4. Clean the pot, add the water, add steamer basket, add ramekins.
5. Lock the lid. Set the Instant Pot to Manual mode, then set the timer for 10 minutes at High Pressure.
6. When the timer goes off, perform a natural release for 5 minutes, then release any remaining pressure. Carefully open the lid.
7. Refrigerate the puddings for several hours, then serve chilled.

Nutritional info:

Calories 211, Fat 8g, Carbs 20g, Protein 10g

Zucchini Toast

Prep Time: 12 mins, Cook Time: 8 mins, Servings: 2

Ingredients:

½ zucchini, sliced	½ tsp. salt
¼ tsp. black pepper	4 whole-grain bread slices, toasted
1 tbsp. olive oil	

Instructions:

1. In a bowl, toss the zucchini slices with salt. Set aside.
2. Select the Sauté mode on the Instant Pot and heat the olive oil.
3. Add the zucchini slices and sauté for about 6 minutes until softened, stirring occasionally. Season with black pepper.
4. Divide the zucchini slices evenly among bread slices and serve warm.

Nutritional info:

Calories 248, Fat 9g, Carbs 32g, Protein 8g

Eggs and Bacon Breakfast Risotto

Prep Time: 12 mins, Cook Time: 12 mins, Servings: 2

Ingredients:

1½ cups chicken stock	Parmesan cheese
2 poached eggs	3 chopped bacon slices
2 tbsps. grated	¾ cup Arborio rice

Instructions:

1. Set your Instant Pot to Sauté and add the bacon and cook for 5 minutes until crispy, stirring occasionally.
2. Carefully stir in the rice and let cook for an additional 1 minute.
3. Add the chicken stock and stir well.
4. Lock the lid. Select the Manual mode and set the cooking time for 6 minutes at Low Pressure.
5. Once cooking is complete, do a quick pressure release. Carefully open the lid.
6. Add the Parmesan cheese and keep stirring until melted. Divide the risotto between two plates. Add the eggs on the side and serve immediately.

Nutritional info:

Calories 214, Fat 5g, Carbs 12g, Protein 5g

Tofu and Sweet Potato Mix

Prep Time: 12 mins, Cook Time: 10 mins, Servings: 4

Ingredients:

2 tbsps. red pepper sauce	⅓ cup vegetable stock
1 lb. cubed extra-firm tofu	1 cup chopped sweet potato
2 tsps. sesame oil	

Instructions:

1. Select the Sauté mode and heat the sesame oil.
2. Add the sweet potato, stir, and cook for 2 minutes.
3. Add the tofu and stock, stir, and cook for 2 minutes more.
4. Lock the lid. Select the Manual mode and cook for 3 minutes at High Pressure.
5. Once cooking is complete, do a quick pressure release. Carefully open the lid.
6. Pour in the red pepper sauce and stir to incorporate. Serve immediately.

Nutritional info:

Calories 172, Fat 7g, Carbs 20g, Protein 6g

Broccoli and Egg Casserole

Prep Time: 5 mins, Cook Time: 15 mins, Servings: 6

Ingredients:

6 eggs, beaten
⅓ cup all-purpose flour
3 cups cottage cheese
¼ cup butter, melted

Salt and pepper, to taste
2 tbsps. chopped onions
3 cups broccoli florets

Instructions:

1. Combine the eggs, flour, cheese, butter, salt, and pepper in a large bowl. Stir to mix well.
2. Put the onions and broccoli in the Instant Pot. Pour the egg mixture over. Stir to combine well.
3. Lock the lid. Set to Manual mode, then set the timer to 15 minutes at High pressure.
4. Once the timer goes off, perform a natural pressure release for 10 minutes, then release any remaining pressure. Carefully open the lid.
5. Transfer them on a plate and serve immediately.

Nutritional info:

Calories407, Carbs 15.8g, Protein 27.8g, Fat 25.7g

Pumpkin Spice Oatmeal

Prep Time: 6 mins, Cook Time: 10 mins, Servings: 2

Ingredients:

¼ tsp. ground cinnamon
⅛ tsp. ground pumpkin spice

1 cup steel-cut oats
1 tbsp. sugar
1 cup almond milk
1½ cups water

Instructions:

1. Place all ingredients into your Instant Pot and mix well.
2. Lock the lid. Select the Manual mode and set the cooking time for 6 minutes at High Pressure.
3. Once cooking is complete, do a natural pressure release for 5 minutes. Carefully open the lid.
4. Ladle into two serving bowls and serve.

Nutritional info:

Calories 377, Fat 6.6g, Carbs 69.4g, Protein: 10.7g

Millet and Oats Porridge

Prep Time: 12 mins, Cook Time: 13 mins, Servings: 8

Ingredients:

2 cored and chopped apples
½ cup rolled oats

3 cups water
½ tsp. ginger powder
1 cup millet

Instructions:

1. Set the Instant Pot to Sauté and add the millet. Stir and toast for 3 minutes.
2. Add the oats, water, ginger and apples to the Instant Pot, and whisk to combine.
3. Lock the lid. Select the Manual mode and cook for 10 minutes at High Pressure.
4. Once cooking is complete, do a natural pressure release for 7 minutes, then release any remaining pressure. Carefully open the lid.
5. Stir the porridge again and ladle into bowls to serve.

Nutritional info:

Calories 200, Fat 2g, Carbs 4g, Protein 5g

Breakfast Cobbler

Prep Time: 12 mins, Cook Time: 15 mins, Servings: 2

Ingredients:

2 tbsps. honey
¼ cup shredded coconut
1 plum, pitted and chopped

3 tbsps. coconut oil, divided
1 apple, cored and chopped

Instructions:

1. In the Instant Pot, combine the plum with apple, half of the coconut oil, and honey, and blend well.
2. Lock the lid. Select the Manual mode and cook for 10 minutes at High Pressure.
3. Once cooking is complete, do a quick pressure release. Carefully open the lid.
4. Transfer the mixture to bowls and clean your Instant Pot.
5. Set your Instant Pot to Sauté and heat the remaining coconut oil. Add the coconut, stir, and toast for 5 minutes.
6. Sprinkle the coconut over fruit mixture and serve.

Nutritional info:

Calories 172, Fat 7g, Carbs 6g, Protein 2g

Breakfast Coconut Yogurt

Prep Time: 20 mins, Cook Time: 8 hours, Servings: 4

Ingredients:

2 cans coconut cream starter
1 package yogurt 1 tbsp. gelatin

Instructions:

1. Pour the coconut cream into the Instant Pot.
2. Lock the lid. Select the Yogurt mode, then bring to a boil at High Pressure.
3. When the coconut cream boils, perform a natural pressure release. Carefully open the lid.
4. Add the yogurt starter and stir to mix well.
5. Lock the lid. Set the timer for 8 hours to ferment at High Pressure.
6. When the timer goes off, perform a normal release for 10 minutes, then release any remaining pressure. Carefully open the lid.
7. Stir in the gelatin and keep stirring until smooth.
8. Pour the yogurt in a jar or a glass and put in the refrigerator for at least 6 hours before serving.

Nutritional info:

Calories 352, Fat 21.9g, Carbs 15.2g, Protein 6.3g

Peaches Oatmeal

Prep Time: 12 mins, Cook Time: 15 mins, Servings: 8

Ingredients:

3½ cups water 4 peaches, pitted and
4 cups rolled oats chopped
3½ cups milk ⅓ cup sugar

Instructions:

1. In the Instant Pot, combine the water, milk, oats, sugar, and peaches, and stir to mix.
2. Lock the lid. Press the Manual mode on the Instant Pot and cook for 15 minutes at High Pressure.
3. Once cooking is complete, do a natural pressure release for 10 minutes. Carefully open the lid.
4. Give it a good stir and ladle into bowls, then serve.

Nutritional info:

Calories 152, Fat 4g, Carbs 8g, Protein 4g

Brown Rice and Chickpeas Medley

Prep Time: 12 mins, Cook Time: 25 mins, Servings: 4

Ingredients:

1½ cups brown rice 14 oz. tomatoes,
1 tbsp. olive oil chopped
1 cup chickpeas 1 red onion, chopped

Instructions:

1. Set your Instant Pot to Sauté and heat the olive oil.
2. Add the onions, stir, and cook for 3 minutes until translucent.
3. Add the tomatoes, chickpeas, and rice, and stir well.
4. Lock the lid. Select the Manual mode and cook for 20 minutes at Low Pressure.
5. Once cooking is complete, do a natural pressure release for 10 minutes, then release any remaining pressure. Carefully open the lid.
6. Let the mixture cool for 5 minutes before serving.

Nutritional info:

Calories 253, Fat 4g, Carbs 9g, Protein 7g

Potato and Spinach Hash

Prep Time: 12 mins, Cook Time: 10 mins, Servings: 4

Ingredients:

¼ tsp. salt cubed
1 small yellow onion, 11 oz. baby spinach
chopped 12 oz. chopped
3 baked sweet chorizo
potatoes, peeled and

Instructions:

1. Set the Instant Pot to Sauté and add the chorizo and onion. Cook for 2 to 3 minutes.
2. Add the potato cubes, baby spinach and salt, and stir to combine.
3. Lock the lid. Select the Manual mode and cook for 7 minutes at High Pressure.
4. Once cooking is complete, do a quick pressure release. Carefully open the lid.
5. Divide the mixture between plates and serve.

Nutritional info:

Calories 192, Fat 4g, Carbs 6g, Protein 2g

Western Omelet

Prep Time: 12 mins, Cook Time: 30 mins, Servings: 4

Ingredients:

½ cup half-and-half   ¼ tsp. salt
4 chopped spring   8 oz. bacon, chopped
onions   1½ cups water
6 whisked eggs

Instructions:

1. Place the steamer basket in the Instant Pot and pour in 1½ cups water.
2. In a bowl, combine the eggs with half-and-half, bacon, spring onions and salt, and whisk well. Pour the egg mixture into a soufflé dish and transfer to the steamer basket.
3. Lock the lid. Select the Steam mode and cook for 30 minutes at High Pressure.
4. Once cooking is complete, do a quick pressure release. Carefully open the lid.
5. Allow to cool for 5 minutes before serving.

Nutritional info:

Calories 200, Fat 6g, Carbs 12g, Protein 6g

Blueberry Breakfast Bowl

Prep Time: 1 hour 10 mins, Cook Time: 2 mins, Servings: 4

Ingredients:

1 cup apple juice   1 tbsp. honey
3 tbsps. blueberries   1½ cups quinoa
1½ cups water

Instructions:

1. In the Instant Pot, stir together the water with quinoa.
2. Lock the lid. Select the Manual mode and set the cooking time for 2 minutes at High Pressure.
3. Once cooking is complete, do a natural pressure release for 10 minutes, then release any remaining pressure. Carefully open the lid.
4. Divide the quinoa into four bowls. Drizzle each bowl evenly with honey and apple juice. Sprinkle the blueberries on top and serve.

Nutritional info:

Calories 172, Fat 5g, Carbs 5g, Protein 6g

Cheesy Cauliflower Bowls

Prep Time: 12 mins, Cook Time: 4 mins, Servings: 6

Ingredients:

1 tbsps. chopped   1 head cauliflower,
parsley   cut into florets
½ cup vegetable   ⅓ cup grated
stock   Parmesan cheese
3 tbsps. olive oil

Instructions:

1. In a bowl, combine the olive oil with cauliflower florets, and toss well.
2. Transfer to the Instant Pot and add stock.
3. Lock the lid. Select the Manual mode and set the cooking time for 4 minutes at High Pressure.
4. Once cooking is complete, do a quick pressure release. Carefully open the lid.
5. Add the parsley and Parmesan cheese, and stir to combine. Serve immediately.

Nutritional info:

Calories 120, Fat 2g, Carbs 5g, Protein 3g

Breakfast Banana Bread

Prep Time: 12 mins, Cook Time: 45 mins, Servings: 8

Ingredients:

⅓ cup honey   1½ cups steel-cut
½ tsp. baking soda   oats
2 bananas, peeled   4 whisked eggs
and chopped   1½ cups water

Instructions:

1. In a blender, add the oats, bananas, eggs, honey, and baking soda, and pulse until completely mixed. Pour the mixture into a loaf pan.
2. Add 1½ cups water and trivet to the Instant Pot. Place the loaf pan on the trivet.
3. Lock the lid. Select the Manual mode and set the cooking time for 45 minutes at High Pressure.
4. Once cooking is complete, do a quick pressure release. Carefully open the lid.
5. Let cool for 5 minutes and serve.

Nutritional info:

Calories 192, Fat 5g, Carbs 6g, Protein 2g

Pearl Barley Porridge

Prep Time: 12 mins, Cook Time: 12 mins, Servings: 6
Ingredients:

3 tbsps. lemon juice
1 red bell pepper, chopped
1 onion, sliced
1 cup pearl barley
3 cups vegetable stock

Instructions:
1. Add the barley and stock to the Instant Pot and stir well.
2. Press the Manual button and set the cooking time for 12 minutes at High Pressure.
3. Once cooking is complete, do a natural pressure release for 6 minutes. Carefully open the lid.
4. Transfer to a bowl and stir in the remaining ingredients, then serve.

Nutritional info:
Calories 62, Fat 1g, Carbs 9g, Protein 1g

Banana and Raisin Porridge

Prep Time: 12 mins, Cook Time: 6 mins, Servings: 4
Ingredients:

3 cups rice milk
1 cup buckwheat
¼ cup raisins
1 tsp. cinnamon
powder
1 banana, peeled and sliced

Instructions:
1. In the Instant Pot, mix the buckwheat with banana, milk, cinnamon and raisins, and stir to incorporate.
2. Lock the lid. Select the Manual mode and set the cooking time for 6 minutes at High Pressure.
3. Once cooking is complete, do a natural pressure release for 5 minutes, then release any remaining pressure. Carefully open the lid.
4. Give the porridge a good stir and divide into bowls to serve.

Nutritional info:
Calories 182, Fat 4g, Carbs 6g, Protein 7g

Pomegranate Porridge

Prep Time: 6 mins, Cook Time: 3 mins, Servings: 4
Ingredients:

2 pomegranates seeds
2 tbsps. sugar
2 cups shredded
coconut
1 cup pomegranate juice
2 cup water

Instructions:
1. In the Instant Pot, combine the coconut with water and pomegranate juice, and whisk well.
2. Lock the lid. Select the Manual mode and cook for 3 minutes at High Pressure.
3. Once cooking is complete, do a natural pressure release for 5 minutes, then release any remaining pressure. Carefully open the lid.
4. Add the pomegranate seeds and sugar and give a good stir. Ladle into bowls and serve warm.

Nutritional info:
Calories 153, Fat 3g, Carbs 10g, Protein 4g

Squash Porridge with Apples

Prep Time: 12 mins, Cook Time: 8 mins, Servings: 4
Ingredients:

2 tbsps. maple syrup
4 small apples, cored and chopped
½ cup water
2 tbsps. cinnamon powder
1 squash, peeled and chopped

Instructions:
1. In the Instant Pot, mix the apples with squash, cinnamon, maple syrup and water, and whisk to combine.
2. Lock the lid. Select the Porridge mode and set the cooking time for 8 minutes at High Pressure.
3. Once cooking is complete, do a natural pressure release for 5 minutes, then release any remaining pressure. Carefully open the lid.
4. Stir the porridge one more time, then divide into bowls and serve.

Nutritional info:
Calories 162, Fat 5g, Carbs 8g, Protein 2g

Ham and Spinach Frittata

Prep Time: 3 mins, Cook Time: 10 mins, Servings: 8

Ingredients:

1 cup diced ham	½ cup coconut milk
2 cups chopped spinach	1 onion, chopped
8 eggs, beaten	1 tsp. salt

Instructions:

1. Put all the ingredients into the Instant Pot. Stir to mix well.
2. Lock the lid. Set to Manual mode, then set the timer for 10 minutes at High Pressure.
3. Once the timer goes off, perform a natural pressure release for 5 minutes. Carefully open the lid.
4. Transfer the frittata on a plate and serve immediately.

Nutritional info:

Calories 63, Carbs 5.0g, Protein 8.0g, Fat 3.0g

Mini Frittata

Prep Time: 12 mins, Cook Time: 5 mins, Servings: 6

Ingredients:

1 chopped red bell pepper	2 tbsps. grated Cheddar cheese
1 tbsp. almond milk	5 whisked eggs
¼ tsp. salt	1½ cups water

Instructions:

1. In a bowl, combine the salt, eggs, cheese, almond milk, and red bell pepper, and whisk well. Pour the egg mixture into 6 baking molds.
2. Add 1½ cups water and steamer basket to your Instant Pot. Transfer the baking molds to the basket.
3. Lock the lid. Select the Manual mode and cook for 5minutes at High Pressure.
4. Once cooking is complete, do a quick pressure release. Carefully open the lid. Serve hot.

Nutritional info:

Calories 200, Fat 4g, Carbs 7g, Protein 6g

Veggie Quiche

Prep Time: 12 mins, Cook Time: 20 mins, Servings: 6

Ingredients:

½ cup milk	chopped
1 red bell pepper, chopped	Salt, to taste
2 green onions,	8 whisked eggs
	1 cup water

Instructions:

1. In a bowl, combine the whisked eggs with milk, bell pepper, onions and salt, and stir well. Pour the egg mixture into a pan.
2. In your Instant Pot, add the water and trivet. Place the pan on the trivet and cover with tin foil.
3. Lock the lid. Select the Manual mode and cook for 20 minutes at High Pressure.
4. Once cooking is complete, do a quick pressure release. Carefully open the lid.
5. Slice the quiche and divide between plates to serve.

Nutritional info:

Calories 200, Fat 3g, Carbs 7g, Protein 6g

Breakfast Rice Pudding

Prep Time: 12 mins, Cook Time: 12 mins, Servings: 6

Ingredients:

1 cup coconut cream	1 cup basmati rice
¼ cup maple syrup	2 cups almond milk
1¼ cups water	

Instructions:

1. In the Instant Pot, mix together the milk with water, rice, cream and maple syrup.
2. Lock the lid. Select the Manual mode and cook for 12 minutes at Low Pressure.
3. Once cooking is complete, do a natural pressure release for 5 minutes, then release any remaining pressure. Carefully open the lid.
4. Stir the pudding again and divide into bowls to serve.

Nutritional info:

Calories 251, Fat 5g, Carbs 6g, Protein 5g

Strawberry and Orange Juice Compote

Prep Time: 10 mins, Cook Time: 15 mins, Servings: 4
Ingredients:

2 lbs. fresh strawberries, rinsed, trimmed, and cut in half
2 oz. fresh orange juice
1 vanilla bean, chopped
½ tsp. ground ginger
¼ cup sugar
Toast, for serving

Instructions:

1. Put all the ingredients into the Instant Pot. Stir to mix well.
2. Lock the lid. Set to the Manual Mode, then set the timer for 15 minutes at High Pressure.
3. When the timer goes off, perform a natural pressure release for 10 minutes. Carefully open the lid.
4. Allow to cool and thicken before serving with the toast.

Nutritional info:
Calories 152, Fat 1.6g, Carbs 35.5g, Protein 2.4g

Cheesy Egg and Bacon Muffins

Prep Time: 12 mins, Cook Time: 8 mins, Servings: 4
Ingredients:

4 cooked bacon slices, crumbled
4 tbsps. shredded Cheddar cheese
¼ tsp. salt
1 green onion, chopped
4 eggs, beaten
1½ cups water

Instructions:

1. In a bowl, mix the eggs with cheese, bacon, onion and salt, and whisk well. Pour the egg mixture evenly into four muffin cups.
2. Add 1½ cups water and steamer basket to the Instant Pot. Place the muffin cups in the basket.
3. Lock the lid. Select the Manual mode and set the cooking time for 8 minutes at High Pressure.
4. Once cooking is complete, do a quick pressure release. Carefully open the lid.
5. Divide the muffins between plates and serve warm.

Nutritional info:
Calories 182, Fat 7g, Carbs 8g, Protein 12g

Banana Quinoa

Prep Time: 5 mins, Cook Time: 12 mins, Servings: 2
Ingredients:

½ cup peeled and sliced banana
¾ cup quinoa, soaked in water for at least 1 hour
1 (8 oz.) can almond milk
2 tbsps. honey
1 tsp. vanilla extract
Pinch of salt
¾ cup water

Instructions:

1. Combine all the ingredients in the Instant Pot. Stir to mix well.
2. Lock the lid. Set to Rice mode, then set the timer for 12 minutes at Low Pressure.
3. Once the timer goes off, perform a quick pressure release. Carefully open the lid.
4. Serve immediately.

Nutritional info:
Calories 371, Carbs 41.4g, Protein 7.3g, Fat 20.4g

Pineapple and Peas Breakfast Curry

Prep Time: 12 mins, Cook Time: 20 mins, Servings: 4
Ingredients:

4 cups water
1 cup peas, soaked and drained
1 tsp. curry powder
1 cup canned pineapple, sliced
¼ cup cashew butter

Instructions:

1. In the Instant Pot, stir together the peas and water.
2. Lock the lid. Select the Manual mode and cook for 16 minutes at High Pressure.
3. Once cooking is complete, do a quick pressure release. Carefully open the lid.
4. Drain the peas and transfer to a bowl.
5. Clean the pot and set it to Sauté. Add the peas, curry powder, pineapple and cashew butter, and stir for 1 minute.
6. Lock the lid. Select the Manual mode and cook for 2 minutes at High Pressure.
7. Once cooking is complete, do a quick pressure release. Carefully open the lid.
8. Serve warm.

Nutritional info:
Calories 181, Fat 6g, Carbs 15g, Protein 8g

Strawberry Quinoa

Prep Time: 12 mins, Cook Time: 2 minute, Servings: 4
Ingredients:

2¼ cups water	¼ tsp. pumpkin pie spice
2 tbsps. honey	1 ½ cups quinoa
2 cups chopped strawberries	

Instructions:
1. In the Instant Pot, mix the quinoa with honey, water, spice, and strawberries. Stir to combine.
2. Lock the lid. Select the Manual mode and set the cooking time for 2 minutes at High Pressure.
3. Once cooking is complete, do a natural pressure release for 10 minutes, then release any remaining pressure. Carefully open the lid.
4. Let the quinoa rest for 10 minutes. Give a good stir and serve immediately.

Nutritional info:
Calories 162, Fat 3g, Carbs 6g, Protein 3g

Cranberry Beans Salad

Prep Time: 12 mins, Cook Time: 15 mins, Servings: 4
Ingredients:

3 tbsps. olive oil	½ red onion, chopped
1 ½ cups fresh green beans	1 cup cranberry beans, soaked and drained
5 tbsps. apple cider vinegar	1 cup water

Instructions:
1. Add 1 cup water and steamer basket to your Instant Pot.
2. Place the cranberry beans and green beans in the basket.
3. Lock the lid. Select the Manual mode and cook for 15 minutes at High Pressure.
4. Once cooking is complete, do a quick pressure release. Carefully open the lid.
5. Drain all beans and transfer them to a salad bowl. Add the onions, vinegar, and olive oil, and gently toss to combine. Serve immediately.

Nutritional info:
Calories 170, Fat 4g, Carbs 15g, Protein 6g

Special Pancake

Prep Time: 12 mins, Cook Time: 30 mins, Servings: 4
Ingredients:

2½ tsps. baking powder	2 tbsps. sugar
2 eggs, beaten	1½ cups milk
	2 cups white flour

Instructions:
1. In a bowl, mix the flour with eggs, milk, sugar, and baking powder. Stir to incorporate.
2. Spread out the mixture onto the bottom of the Instant Pot.
3. Lock the lid. Select the Manual mode and cook for 30 minutes at High Pressure.
4. Once cooking is complete, do a quick pressure release. Carefully open the lid.
5. Let the pancake cool for a few minutes before slicing to serve.

Nutritional info:
Calories 251, Fat 5g, Carbs 6g, Protein 3g

Breakfast Arugula Salad

Prep Time: 12 mins, Cook Time: 15 mins, Servings: 6
Ingredients:

2 blood oranges, peeled and sliced	1 tsp. sunflower oil
2 cups water	1 cup kamut grains, soaked
4 oz. arugula	

Instructions:
1. In the Instant Pot, combine the kamut grains with sunflower oil and water, and whisk well.
2. Lock the lid. Select the Manual mode and set the cooking time for 15 minutes at High Pressure.
3. Once cooking is complete, do a natural pressure release for 10 minutes, then release any remaining pressure. Carefully open the lid.
4. Drain the kamut grains and transfer to a large bowl. Add the arugula and oranges, and toss well. Serve immediately.

Nutritional info:
Calories 163, Fat 6g, Carbs 7g, Protein 3g

Swiss Chard Salad

Prep Time: 12 mins, Cook Time:5 mins, Servings: 4
Ingredients:

¼ tsp. red pepper flakes
1 bunch Swiss chard, sliced
¼ cup toasted pine

nuts
1 tbsp. balsamic vinegar
2 tbsps. olive oil

Instructions:

1. Set your Instant Pot to Sauté and heat the olive oil.
2. Add the chard, stir, and cook for 2 minutes until tender.
3. Add pepper flakes and vinegar and stir well.
4. Lock the lid. Select the Steam mode and cook for 3 minutes at High Pressure.
5. Sprinkle with the pine nuts and divide into bowls to serve.

Nutritional info:

Calories 110, Fat 2g, Carbs 6g, Protein 4g

Garlic Eggplants with Tomato Sauce

Prep Time: 12 mins, Cook Time: 9 mins, Servings: 3
Ingredients:

3 minced garlic cloves
1 cup tomato sauce
1 tbsp. olive oil

1 tbsp. garlic powder
4 cups cubed eggplant

Instructions:

1. Press the Sauté button on the Instant Pot and heat the olive oil.
2. Add the garlic, stir, and cook for 2 minutes until tender.
3. Add the eggplant, garlic powder, and tomato sauce, and stir well.
4. Lock the lid. Select the Manual mode and cook for 7 minutes at High Pressure.
5. Once cooking is complete, do a quick pressure release. Carefully open the lid.
6. Transfer to three bowls and serve warm.

Nutritional info:

Calories 172, Fat 4g, Carbs 7g, Protein 4g

Celeriac and Bacon Mix

Prep Time: 12 mins, Cook Time: 10 mins, Servings: 6
Ingredients:

2 tbsps. chicken stock
2 tsps. dried parsley
4 oz. shredded

Cheddar cheese
3 bacon strips
2 lbs. peeled and cubed celeriac

Instructions:

1. Set the Instant Pot to Sauté and cook the bacon for 2 minutes.
2. Add the parsley, celeriac and stock, and stir.
3. Lock the lid. Select the Manual mode and cook for 6 minutes at High Pressure.
4. Once cooking is complete, do a quick pressure release. Carefully open the lid.
5. Add the cheese and keep stirring until melted. Serve warm.

Nutritional info:

Calories 164, Fat 3g, Carbs 6g, Protein 7g

Fruit Yogurt

Prep Time: 30 mins, Cook Time: 8 hours, Servings: 4
Ingredients:

3 cups milk
1 tbsp. vanilla bean paste
1 cup Greek yogurt

1 cup puréed fruit of your choice
¼ cup sugar

Instructions:

1. Pour the milk into the Instant Pot.
2. Lock the lid. Set to the Adjust mode, then pasteurize the milk for 45 minutes.
3. Once the pasteurizing is complete, perform a natural pressure release. Carefully open the lid.
4. Pour in the vanilla bean paste and Greek yogurt.
5. Lock the lid. Set to Yogurt mode, then set the timer for 8 hours at High pressure.
6. Once the timer goes off, perform a natural pressure release for 10 minutes, then release any remaining pressure. Carefully open the lid.
7. Pour the yogurt in a jar or a glass, then put in the refrigerator to chill for at least 1 hour.
8. Remove the yogurt from the refrigerator and mix in the puréed fruits and sugar before serving.

Nutritional info:

Calories 172, Carbs 24.6g, Protein 3.8g, Fat 2.3g

Super Thick Cashew and Almond Milk Yogurt

Prep Time: 10 mins, Cook Time: 8 hours, Servings: 4

Ingredients:

⅓ cup raw cashews
2 tbsps. arrowroot powder
4 cups almond milk
¼ cup yogurt with live culture
1 tbsp. maple syrup

Instructions:

1. Combine the cashews, arrowroot powder, and almond milk in a food processor. Process until the mixture in creamy and smooth.
2. Pour the mixture in a saucepan and simmer for 5 minutes over medium heat. Keep stirring.
3. Turn off the heat and allow to cool.
4. Pour the mixture into the Instant Pot, then mix in the yogurt.
5. Lock the lid. Set to the Yogurt mode, then set the timer for 8 hours at High Pressure.
6. When the timer goes off, perform a natural pressure release for 10 minutes, then release any remaining pressure. Carefully open the lid.
7. Pour the yogurt in four mason jars, then put them in the refrigerator to chill for at least an hour.
8. Remove the jars from the refrigerator. Drizzle the yogurt with maple syrup and serve chilled.

Nutritional info:

Calories 285, Carbs 36.5g, Protein 4.6g, Fat 14.7g

Tapioca Pudding

Prep Time: 12 mins, Cook Time: 15 mins, Servings: 4

Ingredients:

1 cup water
1¼ cups almond milk
¼ cup rinsed and drained seed tapioca
pearls
½ cup sugar
½ tsp. lemon zest

Instructions:

1. Pour the water into the Instant Pot.
2. Add the steamer basket inside the pot.
3. In a heat-proof bowl, mix all the ingredients until the sugar has dissolved.
4. Cover with foil and put the bowl on top of the basket.
5. Lock the lid. Set the Instant Pot to Manual mode, then set the timer for 10 minutes at High Pressure.
6. When the timer goes off, perform a natural release for 5 minutes, then release any remaining pressure. Carefully open the lid.
7. Serve immediately or refrigerate for several hours and serve chilled.

Nutritional info:

Calories 187, Fat 2.5g, Carbs 28.9g, Protein: 2.5g

Ketogenic Vanilla Jell-O

Prep Time: 2 hours, Cook Time: 6 mins, Servings: 6

Ingredients:

1 cup boiling water
2 tbsps. unsweetened gelatin powder
1 tsp. vanilla extract
1 cup heavy cream
3 tbsps. erythritol

Instructions:

1. Place the boiling water in the Instant Pot.
2. Press the Sauté button on the Instant Pot. Bring the water to a simmer.
3. Add the gelatin powder and allow to dissolve.
4. Add the remaining ingredients.
5. Pour the mixture into Jell-O molds.
6. Place in the refrigerator to set for 2 hours.

Nutritional info:

Calories 105, Carbs 5.2g, Protein 3.3g, Fat 7.9g

Chocolate Chia Pudding

Prep Time: 6 mins, Cook Time: 3 hours, Servings: 4

Ingredients:

2 tbsps. cacao powder
¼ tsp. salt
¼ cup chia seeds
½ tsp. liquid stevia
1 cup freshly squeezed coconut milk

Instructions:

1. Pour all the ingredients in the Instant Pot and stir to mix well.
2. Lock the lid. Set the Instant Pot to Slow Cook mode, then set the timer for 3 hours at High Pressure.
3. When the timer goes off, perform a natural release for 10 minutes, then release any remaining pressure. Carefully open the lid.
4. Serve immediately or refrigerate for several hours and serve chilled.

Nutritional info:

Calories 346, Carbs 21.2g, Protein 8.4g, Fat 27.5g

Coconut Cream and Cinnamon Pudding

Prep Time: 12 mins, Cook Time: 10 mins, Servings: 6

Ingredients:

Zest of 1 grated lemon
2 cups coconut cream
5 tbsps. sugar
6 tbsps. flour
1 tsp. cinnamon powder
1 cup water

Instructions:

1. Set the Instant Pot on Sauté mode and add coconut cream, cinnamon and orange zest, then stir.
2. Simmer for 3 minutes then transfer to a bowl and leave aside.
3. Add flour and sugar, stir well and divide this into ramekins.
4. Add the water to the Instant Pot, add steamer basket, add ramekins.
5. Lock the lid. Set the Instant Pot to Manual mode, then set the timer for 10 minutes at Low Pressure.
6. When the timer goes off, perform a natural release for 5 minutes, then release any remaining pressure. Carefully open the lid.
7. Serve cold.

Nutritional info:

Calories 170, Fat 5g, Carbs 8g, Protein 10g

Coconut Pudding

Prep Time: 6 mins, Cook Time: 3 hours, Servings: 2

Ingredients:

1 tsp. erythritol
½ cup coconut milk
A dash of vanilla extract
½ tsp. cinnamon
powder
¼ cup dried coconut flakes
Salt, to taste
½ cup water

Instructions:

1. Put all ingredients in the Instant Pot.
2. Mix until well combined.
3. Lock the lid. Set the Instant Pot to Slow Cook mode, then set the timer for 3 hours at High Pressure.
4. When the timer goes off, perform a natural release for 10 minutes, then release any remaining pressure. Carefully open the lid.
5. Serve immediately or refrigerate for several hours and serve chilled.

Nutritional info:

Calories 188, Carbs 9.3g, Protein 1.7g, Fat 17.3g

Cocoa and Milk Pudding

Prep Time: 50 mins, Cook Time: 3 mins, Servings: 4

Ingredients:

2 cups hot coconut milk
4 tbsps. sugar
½ tsp. cinnamon powder
4 tbsps. cocoa powder
2 tbsps. gelatin
1 cup plus 2 tbsps. water

Instructions:

1. In a bowl, mix the milk with sugar, cinnamon and cocoa powder and stir well.
2. In a bowl, mix gelatin with 2 tablespoons of water, stir well, add to cocoa mix, stir and divide into ramekins.
3. Add 1 cup of water to the Instant Pot, add the steamer basket and ramekins inside.
4. Lock the lid. Set the Instant Pot to Manual mode, then set the timer for 4 minutes at High Pressure.
5. When the timer goes off, perform a natural release. Carefully open the lid.
6. Serve puddings cold.

Nutritional info:

Calories 120, Fat 2g, Carbs 4g, Protein 3g

Lemon and Maple Syrup Pudding

Prep Time: 12 mins, Cook Time: 5 mins, Servings: 7

Ingredients:

½ cup maple syrup
3 cups milk
Lemon zest from 2 grated lemons
2 tbsps. gelatin
Juice of 2 lemons
1 cup water

Instructions:

1. In the blender, mix milk with lemon juice, lemon zest, maple syrup and gelatin, pulse really well and divide into ramekins.
2. In the Instant Pot, set in the water, add steamer basket, add ramekins inside.
3. Lock the lid. Set the Instant Pot to Manual mode, then set the timer for 5 minutes on High Pressure.
4. When the timer goes off, perform a natural release. Carefully open the lid.
5. Refrigerate and serve the puddings chilled.

Nutritional info:

Calories 151, Fat 3g, Carbs 18g, Protein 3g

Chocolate Mug Cake

Prep Time: 12 mins, Cook Time: 10 mins, Servings: 1

Ingredients:

1 cup water
6 drops liquid stevia
1½ tbsps. cocoa powder
1 egg, beaten
¼ tsp. baking powder
¼ cup almond powder
Salt, to taste

Instructions:

1. Place a steam rack in the Instant Pot and pour in the water.
2. In a bowl, add all the remaining ingredients.
3. Mix until well combined.
4. Pour into a heat-proof mug.
5. Place the mug on the steam rack.
6. Lock the lid. Set the Instant Pot to Steam mode, then set the timer for 10 minutes at High Pressure.
7. When the timer goes off, perform a quick release. Carefully open the lid.
8. Serve the cake immediately.

Nutritional info:

Calories 149, Carbs 5.8g, Protein 6.8g, Fat 10.5g

Apple Bread

Prep Time: 12 mins, Cook Time: 1 hour, Servings: 4

Ingredients:

1 tbsp. baking powder
3 eggs
1½ cups sweetened condensed milk
2½ cups white flour
3 apples, peeled, cored and chopped
1 tbsp. melted coconut oil
1 cup water

Instructions:

1. In a bowl, mix the baking powder with eggs and whisk well.
2. Add the milk, flour and apple pieces, whisk well and pour into a loaf pan greased with coconut oil.
3. In the Instant Pot, add the water. Arrange a trivet in the pot, then place the loaf pan on the trivet.
4. Lock the lid. Set the Instant Pot to Slow Cook mode, then set the timer for 1 hour at High Pressure.
5. When the timer goes off, perform a natural release for 10 minutes, then release any remaining pressure. Carefully open the lid.
6. Leave apple bread to cool down, slice and serve.

Nutritional info:

Calories 211, Fat 2g, Carbs 14g, Protein 4g

Coconut Boosters

Prep Time: 2 hours, Cook Time: 5 mins, Servings: 5

Ingredients:

1 cup coconut oil
½ cup chia seeds
1 tsp. vanilla extract
1 tsp. erythritol
¼ cup unsweetened dried coconut flakes

Instructions:

1. Press the Sauté button on the Instant Pot.
2. Heat the coconut oil and add the chia seeds, vanilla extract, erythritol, and coconut flakes and sauté for 5 minutes.
3. Allow to cool and remove the mixture from the pot. Form the mixture into balls and set on a baking sheet.
4. Allow to set in the refrigerator for 2 hours before serving.

Nutritional info:

Calories 480, Carbs 9.4g, Protein 2.9g, Fat 50g

Pineapple Pudding

Prep Time: 12 mins, Cook Time: 5 mins, Servings: 8
Ingredients:

1 cup rice	Sugar, to taste
1 tbsp. avocado oil	8 oz. chopped canned
14 oz. milk	pineapple

Instructions:
1. In the Instant Pot, mix oil, milk and rice, stir.
2. Lock the lid. Set the Instant Pot to Manual mode, then set the timer for 3 minutes at Low Pressure.
3. When the timer goes off, perform a natural release. Carefully open the lid.
4. Add sugar and pineapple, stir.
5. Lock the lid, then set the timer for 2 minutes at Low Pressure.
6. When the timer goes off, perform a natural release. Carefully open the lid.
7. Divide into dessert bowls and serve.

Nutritional info:
Calories 154, Fat 4g, Carbs 14g, Protein 4g

Coconut and Avocado Pudding

Prep Time: 2 hours, Cook Time: 2 mins, Servings: 3
Ingredients:

14 oz. canned coconut milk	peeled and chopped
1 tbsp. cocoa powder	4 tbsps. sugar
1 avocado, pitted,	½ cup avocado oil

Instructions:
1. In a bowl, mix oil with cocoa powder and half of the sugar, stir well, transfer to a lined container, keep in the fridge for 1 hour and chop into small pieces.
2. In the Instant Pot, mix coconut milk with avocado and the rest of the sugar, blend using an immersion blender.
3. Lock the lid. Set the Instant Pot to Manual mode, then set the timer for 2 minutes at High Pressure.
4. When the timer goes off, perform a natural release. Carefully open the lid.
5. Add chocolate chips, stir, divide pudding into bowls and keep in the fridge until you serve it.

Nutritional info:
Calories 140, Fat 3g, Carbs 3g, Protein 4g

Cream Cheese Pudding

Prep Time: 12 mins, Cook Time: 20 mins, Servings: 2 minutes
Ingredients:

¼ tsp. vanilla extract	2 oz. cream cheese
1½ tsps. caramel extract	1½ tbsps. sugar
2 eggs	1 cup water

Instructions:
1. Mix cream cheese with eggs, caramel extract, vanilla extract and sugar in a blender and pulse well to divide into greased ramekins.
2. In the Instant Pot, set in the water, add steamer basket and ramekins inside.
3. Lock the lid. Set the Instant Pot to Manual mode, then set the timer for 20 minutes at High Pressure.
4. When the timer goes off, perform a natural release for 10 minutes, then release any remaining pressure. Carefully open the lid.
5. Serve the puddings cold.

Nutritional info:
Calories 174, Fat 7g, Carbs 2g, Protein 4g

Cinnamon Butter Bites

Prep Time: 6 mins, Cook Time: 5 hours, Servings: 12
Ingredients:

5 eggs, beaten	1 tbsp. cinnamon
1 cup all-purpose flour	¼ cup liquid stevia
1 grass-fed unsalted butter stick	¼ cup olive oil
	Salt, to taste

Instructions:
1. Mix all ingredients in a mixing bowl, except for the olive oil.
2. Grease the Instant Pot with olive oil.
3. Pour in the batter.
4. Lock the lid. Set the Instant Pot to Slow Cook mode, then set the timer for 5 hours at High Pressure.
5. When the timer goes off, perform a natural release for 10 minutes, then release any remaining pressure. Carefully open the lid.
6. Serve immediately.

Nutritional info:
Calories 161, Carbs 1.2g, Protein 4.5g, Fat 15.5g

Keto Almond Bread

Prep Time: 12 mins, Cook Time: 5 hours, Servings: 10

Ingredients:

1½ tsps. baking powder

1½ cups erythritol

3 eggs, beaten

2½ cups all-purpose flour

¼ cup olive oil

Salt, to taste

Instructions:

1. Mix all ingredients in a mixing bowl.
2. Once properly mixed, pour the batter in the greased Instant Pot.
3. Lock the lid. Set the Instant Pot to Slow Cook mode, then set the timer for 5 hours at High Pressure.
4. When the timer goes off, perform a natural release for 10 minutes, then release any remaining pressure. Carefully open the lid.
5. Serve immediately.

Nutritional info:

Calories 67, Carbs 0.6g, Protein 0.9g, Fat 6.9g

Bulletproof Hot Choco

Prep Time: 6 mins, Cook Time: 5 mins, Servings: 1

Ingredients:

2 tbsps. coconut oil, divided

½ cup coconut milk

½ cup water

2 tbsps. unsweetened cocoa powder

Dash of cinnamon

1 tsp. erythritol

Instructions:

1. Place 1 tablespoon of coconut oil and milk in the Instant Pot and pour in the water.
2. Lock the lid. Set the Instant Pot to Manual mode, then set the timer for 5 minutes at High Pressure.
3. When the timer goes off, perform a quick release.
4. Open the lid and press the Sauté button.
5. Add 1 tablespoon of coconut oil, cocoa powder, cinnamon and erythritol. Stir to combine well and the mixture has a thick consistency.
6. Transfer the mixture on a baking sheet, then put the sheet in the refrigerator for several hours. Serve chilled.

Nutritional info:

Calories 534, Carbs 12.9g, Protein 4.7g, Fat 57.2g

Keto Brownies

Prep Time: 12 mins, Cook Time: 5 hours, Servings: 9

Ingredients:

2 tsps. erythritol

¼ cup all-purpose flour

½ cup coconut oil

⅓ cup dark chocolate

chips

5 beaten eggs

Salt, to taste

2 tbsps. olive oil

Instructions:

1. Place all the ingredients in a mixing bowl, except for the olive oil.
2. Make sure they are well combined.
3. Grese the Instant Pot with olive oil. Pour the mixture into the greased Instant Pot.
4. Lock the lid. Set the Instant Pot to Slow Cook mode, then set the timer for 5 hours at High Pressure.
5. When the timer goes off, perform a natural release for 10 minutes, then release any remaining pressure. Carefully open the lid.
6. Transfer the brownies on a platter and slice to serve.

Nutritional info:

Calories 214, Carbs 3.4g, Protein 5.4g, Fat 20.7g

Coconut Pancake

Prep Time: 12 mins, Cook Time: 40 mins, Servings: 4

Ingredients:

1½ cups coconut milk

2 cups self-raising flour

2 eggs

1 tbsp. olive oil

2 tbsps. sugar

Instructions:

1. In a bowl, mix eggs with sugar, milk and flour and whisk until you obtain a batter.
2. Grease the Instant Pot with oil, add the batter, spread into the pot.
3. Lock the lid. Set the Instant Pot to Manual mode, then set the timer for 40 minutes at Low Pressure.
4. When the timer goes off, perform a natural release for 10 minutes, then release any remaining pressure. Carefully open the lid.
5. Slice pancake, divide between plates and serve cold.

Nutritional info:

Calories 162, Fat 3, Carbs 7g, Protein 3g

Simple Banana Cake

Prep Time: 12 mins, Cook Time: 1 hour, Servings: 4

Ingredients:

1 tsp. nutmeg powder
2 cups flour
1 tsp. cinnamon powder
¼ cup sugar
4 bananas, peeled and mashed
1 cup water

Instructions:

1. In a bowl, mix sugar with flour, bananas, cinnamon and nutmeg, stir, pour into a greased cake pan and cover with tin foil.
2. In the Instant Pot, set in the water, add steamer basket, add cake pan.
3. Lock the lid. Set the Instant Pot to Manual mode, then set the timer for 1 hour at High Pressure.
4. When the timer goes off, perform a natural release for 10 minutes, then release any remaining pressure. Carefully open the lid.
5. Slice and divide between plates to serve cold.

Nutritional info:

Calories 300, Fat 10g, Carbs 45g, Protein 4g

Chocolate Cake

Prep Time: 12 mins, Cook Time: 6 mins, Servings: 3

Ingredients:

4 tbsps. self-raising flour
1 egg
4 tbsps. sugar
4 tbsps. milk
1 tbsp. cocoa powder
1 tbsp. melted coconut oil
1 cup water

Instructions:

1. In a bowl, combine the flour, egg, sugar, milk and cocoa powder, stir well and set the mixture to a cake pan greased with coconut oil.
2. Add the water to the Instant Pot, add steamer basket, add cake inside.
3. Lock the lid. Set the Instant Pot to Manual mode, then set the timer for 6 minutes at High Pressure.
4. When the timer goes off, perform a natural release for 5 minutes, then release any remaining pressure. Carefully open the lid.
5. Serve the cake warm.

Nutritional info:

Calories 261, Fat 5g, Carbs 20g, Protein 4g

Easy Sweet Soufflé

Prep Time: 12 mins, Cook Time: 30 mins, Servings: 6

Ingredients:

8 oz. chocolate, melted
1 tsp. vanilla extract
¼ cup sugar
3 egg yolks, beaten
¼ tsp. cream of tartar
1 cup water

Instructions:

1. In a bowl, mix melted chocolate with vanilla, sugar, egg yolks and cream of tartar, whisk well and divide into greased ramekins.
2. Set up the Instant Pot. Add the water, add steamer basket, add ramekins.
3. Lock the lid. Set the Instant Pot to Manual mode, then set the timer for 30 minutes at High Pressure.
4. When the timer goes off, perform a natural release for 10 minutes, then release any remaining pressure. Carefully open the lid.
5. Leave soufflé to cool down and serve.

Nutritional info:

Calories 190, Fat 2g, Carbs 7g, Protein 3g

Peanut Butter Cups

Prep Time: 12 mins, Cook Time: 4 mins, Servings: 12

Ingredients:

8 oz. chocolate pudding mix
4 cups milk
12 oz. heavy whipping cream
10 oz. prepared and cubed cake
16 oz. mini peanut butter cups
1½ cups water

Instructions:

1. In a bowl, mix the chocolate pudding mix with milk and whipped cream and whisk.
2. Divide cake cubes in small ramekins, add chocolate mixture and top with peanut butter cups.
3. Add the water to the Instant Pot, add trivet inside, add ramekins.
4. Lock the lid. Set the Instant Pot to Manual mode, then set the timer for 4 minutes at High Pressure.
5. When the timer goes off, perform a quick release. Carefully open the lid.
6. Leave cups to cool down a bit and serve.

Nutritional info:

Calories 177, Fat 2g, Carbs 6g, Protein 7g

Tasty Blackberry Pie

Prep Time: 12 mins, Cook Time: 35 mins, Servings: 6

Ingredients:

⅓ cup tapioca pearls
2 tbsps. sugar
4 cups blackberries
2 tbsps. soft butter
1 graham cracker pie crust
1½ cups water

Instructions:

1. In a bowl, mix tapioca with sugar, blackberries and butter and whisk until sugar melts and pour the mixture into pie crust.
2. Add the water to the Instant Pot, arrange the steamer basket in the pot, then add the pie.
3. Lock the lid. Set the Instant Pot to Manual mode, then set the timer for 35 minutes at High Pressure.
4. When the timer goes off, perform a natural release for 10 minutes, then release any remaining pressure. Carefully open the lid.
5. Let the pie cool down, slice, divide between plates and serve.

Nutritional info:

Calories 251, Fat 3g, Carbs 7g, Protein 8g

Nut-Free Keto Fudge

Prep Time: 6 mins, Cook Time: 4 hours, Servings: 15

Ingredients:

4 tbsps. erythritol
½ tsp. baking powder
6 eggs, beaten
¼ cup cocoa powder
1 butter stick, melted
¼ tsp. salt

Instructions:

1. Mix all ingredients in a bowl. Stir to combine well.
2. Pour the mixture into the Instant Pot.
3. Lock the lid. Set the Instant Pot to Slow Cook mode, then set the timer for 4 hours at High Pressure.
4. When the timer goes off, perform a natural release for 10 minutes, then release any remaining pressure. Carefully open the lid.
5. Divide the fudges and serve immediately.

Nutritional info:

Calories 131, Carbs 1.3g, Protein 4.3g, Fat 12.2g

Dates and Ricotta Cake

Prep Time: 30 mins, Cook Time: 20 mins, Servings: 6

Ingredients:

1 lb. softened ricotta cheese
4 eggs
4 oz. honey
6 oz. dates, soaked and drained
Juice of 2 oranges
1 cup water

Instructions:

1. In a bowl, mix soft ricotta with eggs and whisk well.
2. Add honey, dates, and orange juice, whisk, pour into a cake pan and cover with tin foil.
3. Add the water to the Instant Pot, add steamer basket, add cake pan.
4. Lock the lid. Set the Instant Pot to Manual mode, then set the timer for 20 minutes at High Pressure.
5. When the timer goes off, perform a natural release for 10 minutes, then release any remaining pressure. Carefully open the lid.
6. Allow cake to cool down, slice and serve.

Nutritional info:

Calories 212, Fat 7g, Carbs 20g, Protein 9g

White Chocolate Mousse

Prep Time: 12 mins, Cook Time: 3 mins, Servings: 6

Ingredients:

12 oz. chopped white chocolate
12 oz. chopped black chocolate
2 cups heavy cream
1 tbsp. sugar
1 tsp. vanilla extract

Instructions:

1. In the Instant Pot, mix white and black chocolate with cream. Stir to combine well.
2. Lock the lid. Set the Instant Pot to Manual mode, then set the timer for 3 minutes at High Pressure.
3. When the timer goes off, perform a quick release. Carefully open the lid.
4. Add the sugar and vanilla, stir until the sugar melts, divide into bowls and serve cold.

Nutritional info:

Calories 176, Fat 4g, Carbs 12g, Protein 3g

Simple Pumpkin and Yogurt Cake

Prep Time: 12 mins, Cook Time: 45 mins, Servings: 12

Ingredients:

½ cup Greek yogurt
1½ cups all-purpose flour
¾ cup sugar
½ tsp. baking powder
8 oz. canned pumpkin purée
3 tbsps. butter
1½ cups water

Instructions:

1. In a bowl, combine the yogurt, flour, sugar, baking powder and pumpkin purée, whisk well and pour into a cake pan coat with butter.
2. Add the water to the Instant Pot, add trivet inside, add cake pan.
3. Lock the lid. Set the Instant Pot to Manual mode, then set the timer for 45 minutes at High Pressure.
4. When the timer goes off, perform a natural release for 10 minutes, then release any remaining pressure. Carefully open the lid.
5. Leave cake to cool down, slice and serve.

Nutritional info:

Calories 201, Fat 3g, Carbs 15g, protein 4g

Ginger Cookies Cheesecake

Prep Time: 15 mins, Cook Time: 15 mins, Servings: 6

Ingredients:

16 oz. soft cream cheese
½ cup crumbled ginger cookies
½ cup sugar
2 eggs
2 cups water
2 tsps. melted butter

Instructions:

1. Grease a cake pan with the butter, add cookie crumbs and spread them evenly.
2. In a bowl, beat cream cheese with a mixer.
3. Add eggs and sugar and stir very well.
4. Add the water to the Instant Pot, add steamer basket, add cake pan inside.
5. Lock the lid. Set the Instant Pot to Manual mode, then set the timer for 15 minutes at High Pressure.
6. When the timer goes off, perform a natural release for 10 minutes. Carefully open the lid.
7. Keep cheesecake in the fridge for a few hours before serving it.

Nutritional info:

Calories 394, Fat 12g, Carbs 20g, Protein 6g

Simple Cake Bars

Prep Time: 12 mins, Cook Time: 20 mins, Servings: 12

Ingredients:

1 yellow cake mix
½ cup milk
1 egg, whisked
⅓ cup canola oil
1 cup baking chips
1½ cups water

Instructions:

1. In a bowl, mix cake mix with milk, eggs, oil and baking chips, stir well, pour into a baking pan and spread well.
2. Add the water to the Instant Pot, add trivet, add baking pan inside.
3. Lock the lid. Set the Instant Pot to Manual mode, then set the timer for 20 minutes at High Pressure.
4. When the timer goes off, perform a natural release for 8 to 10 minutes. Carefully open the lid.
5. Leave cake to cool down, cut into medium bars and serve.

Nutritional info:

Calories 276, Fat 6g, Carbs 8g, Protein 3g

Special Cookies

Prep Time: 12 mins, Cook Time: 10 mins, Servings: 20

Ingredients:

17 oz. chocolate cookie mix
¼ cup canola oil
1 egg
1½ cups chopped
chocolate covered coffee beans
1 cup chopped macadamia nuts
1 cup water

Instructions:

1. In a bowl, mix chocolate cookie mix with oil, egg, coffee beans and nuts, whisk well and make the mixture into 20 small cookies.
2. Add the water to the Instant Pot, add steamer basket, add cookies inside.
3. Lock the lid. Set the Instant Pot to Manual mode, then set the timer for 10 minutes at High Pressure.
4. When the timer goes off, perform a quick release. Carefully open the lid.
5. Set the cookies aside to cool down and serve them.

Nutritional info:

Calories 200, Fat 3g, Carbs 6g, Protein 4g

Easy Lemon Pie

Prep Time: 12 mins, Cook Time: 10 mins, Servings: 8

Ingredients:

8 oz. cream cheese
15 oz. canned lemon pie filling
½ cup sugar
1 graham cracker pie

crust
8 oz. heavy whipping cream
1½ cups water

Instructions:

1. In a bowl, mix cream cheese with lemon pie filling and sugar, whisk well, spread into pie crust.
2. Put the pie crust in a baking pan, then top with cream.
3. Add the water to the Instant Pot. Arrange the trivet in the pot, then place the baking pan on the trivet.
4. Lock the lid. Set the Instant Pot to Manual mode, then set the timer for 10 minutes at High Pressure.
5. When the timer goes off, perform a natural release for 5 minutes. Carefully open the lid.
6. Leave the pie aside to cool down, slice and serve.

Nutritional info:

Calories 233, Fat 4g, Carbs 6g, Protein 3g

Cherry Pie

Prep Time: 12 mins, Cook Time: 30 mins, Servings: 16

Ingredients:

1 yellow cake mix
½ cup butter
20 oz. canned cherries

2 tbsps. blueberries
½ cup chopped walnuts
1½ cups water

Instructions:

1. In a bowl, combine cake mix with butter, stir until you obtain a crumbly mixture and use a pie pan to press it down.
2. In a separate bowl, mix cherries with blueberries and walnuts, stir and spread over the crust.
3. Add the water to the Instant Pot, add steamer basket, add pie inside.
4. Lock the lid. Set the Instant Pot to Manual mode, then set the timer for 30 minutes at High Pressure.
5. When the timer goes off, perform a natural release for 10 minutes, then release any remaining pressure. Carefully open the lid.
6. Set the pie aside to cool down, slice and divide between plates. Serve.

Nutritional info:

Calories 261, Fat 3g, Carbs 12g, Protein 3g

Simple Ricotta Mousse

Prep Time: 12 mins, Cook Time: 8 mins, Servings: 4

Ingredients:

⅔ cup maple syrup
¼ cup chopped pecans
1¼ cups ricotta

cheese
½ cup heavy cream
½ cup mascarpone cheese

Instructions:

1. In the Instant Pot, mix the maple syrup with pecans and ricotta, stir.
2. Lock the lid. Set the Instant Pot to Manual mode, then set the timer for 3 minutes at High Pressure.
3. When the timer goes off, perform a quick release. Carefully open the lid.
4. Add the heavy cream and mascarpone, stir to mix well. Divide into bowls, let stand to cool down and serve.

Nutritional info:

Calories 182, Fat 3g, Carbs 10g, Protein 4g

Glazed Fruits

Prep Time: 12 mins, Cook Time: 12 mins, Servings: 6

Ingredients:

½ cup honey
½ cup balsamic vinegar
¼ tsp. salt

6 peaches, pitted and halved
Vanilla ice cream

Instructions:

1. Set the Instant Pot on Sauté mode, add honey and balsamic vinegar, sauté for 2 minutes.
2. Add the salt and peaches, stir.
3. Lock the lid. Set the Instant Pot to Manual mode, then set the timer for 10 minutes at High Pressure.
4. When the timer goes off, perform a quick release. Carefully open the lid.
5. Divide into bowls, leave aside to cool down, add vanilla ice cream on top and serve.

Nutritional info:

Calories 169, Fat 2g, Carbs 7g, Protein 3g

Lemon Cookies

Prep Time: 12 mins, Cook Time: 15 mins, Servings: 30
Ingredients:

1 egg, whisked
18 oz. lemon cake mix
1 cup crisp rice cereal
½ cup butter
1 tsp. lemon zest
1 cup water

Instructions:

1. In a bowl, mix the egg with cake mix, rice cereal, butter and lemon zest, whisk well, shape cookies out of this mix and arrange on a baking sheet.
2. Set up the Instant Pot. Add the water, arrange the trivet in the pot, place the baking sheet on the trivet.
3. Lock the lid. Set the Instant Pot to Manual mode, then set the timer for 15 minutes at Low Pressure.
4. When the timer goes off, perform a natural release for 10 minutes, then release any remaining pressure. Carefully open the lid.
5. Leave cookies to cool down and serve them.

Nutritional info:
Calories 221, Fat 3g, Carbs 6g, Protein 3g

Delicious Berry Cobbler

Prep Time: 12 mins, Cook Time: 35 mins, Servings: 12
Ingredients:

1 package cake mix
1¼ cups milk
½ cup canola oil
40 oz. canned
raspberry filling
1½ cups water
Vanilla ice cream

Instructions:

1. In a bowl, combine the cake mix with milk and oil and whisk well.
2. In a pie pan, spread the raspberry filling on top of the cake mix mixture.
3. Add the water to the Instant Pot, add steamer basket, add cake pan.
4. Lock the lid. Set the Instant Pot to Manual mode, then set the timer for 35 minutes at High Pressure.
5. When the timer goes off, perform a quick release. Carefully open the lid.
6. Set the cobbler aside to cool down, add vanilla ice cream on top and serve.

Nutritional info:
Calories 227, Fat 4g, Carbs 8g, Protein 3g

Baked Custard

Prep Time: 12 mins, Cook Time: 15 mins, Servings: 6
Ingredients:

2 egg yolks
3 eggs
¾ cup sugar
2 cups heated heavy
cream
¼ cup heated Irish cream liqueur
1½ cups water

Instructions:

1. In a bowl, mix egg yolks with eggs and sugar and whisk until sugar melts.
2. Add cream and liqueur, whisk well and divide into ramekins.
3. Add the water to the Instant Pot. Arrange the steamer basket in the pot, put in the custard.
4. Lock the lid. Set the Instant Pot to Manual mode, then set the timer for 15 minutes at High Pressure.
5. When the timer goes off, perform a natural release for 10 minutes, then release any remaining pressure. Carefully open the lid.
6. Leave custards to cool down and serve.

Nutritional info:
Calories 191, Fat 3g, Carbs 9g, Protein 4g

Winter Cherry Mix

Prep Time: 12 mins, Cook Time: 5 mins, Servings: 6
Ingredients:

Sugar, to taste
2 tbsps. water
2 tbsps. cornstarch
16 oz. cherries, pitted
2 tbsps. lemon juice

Instructions:

1. In the Instant Pot, mix cherries with sugar and lemon juice, stir.
2. Lock the lid. Set the Instant Pot to Manual mode, then set the timer for 3 minutes at High Pressure.
3. When the timer goes off, perform a natural release. Carefully open the lid.
4. In a bowl, mix water with cornstarch, stir well, add to the pot, set the pot on Sauté mode, add the rest of the cherries, stir, cook for 2 minutes, divide into bowls and serve cold.

Nutritional info:
Calories 161, Fat 4g, Carbs 8g, Protein 6g

Stuffed Strawberries

Prep Time: 12 mins, Cook Time: 2 mins, Servings: 24

Ingredients:

11 oz. soft cream cheese
¼ tsp. almond extract
½ cup sugar
24 strawberries
1 cup water
1 tbsp. grated chocolate

Instructions:

1. In a bowl, mix the cream cheese with almond extract and sugar, stir until sugar melts and stuff strawberries with this mix.
2. Add the water to the Instant Pot, add steamer basket, arrange strawberries inside.
3. Lock the lid. Set the Instant Pot to Manual mode, then set the timer for 2 minutes at High Pressure.
4. When the timer goes off, perform a quick release. Carefully open the lid.
5. Divide strawberries on dessert plates. Spread with chocolate on top and serve them cold.

Nutritional info:

Calories 200, Fat 4g, Carbs 6g, Protein 3g

Rhubarb and Strawberries Mix

Prep Time: 12 mins, Cook Time: 6 mins, Servings: 6

Ingredients:

3 cups sliced rhubarb
⅓ cup sugar
¼ cup orange juice
2 cups halved
strawberries
1 cup whipping cream

Instructions:

1. In the Instant Pot, mix the rhubarb with sugar and orange juice, stir.
2. Lock the lid. Set the Instant Pot to Manual mode, then set the timer for 6 minutes at High Pressure.
3. When the timer goes off, perform a quick release. Carefully open the lid.
4. Pulse the mixture with an immersion blender, cool down a bit, add strawberries and whipping cream, divide into bowls and serve cold.

Nutritional info:

Calories 222, Fat 5g, Carbs 10g, Protein 3g

Apples and Wine Sauce

Prep Time: 12 mins, Cook Time: 10 mins, Servings: 6

Ingredients:

6 apples, peeled and cored
1 cup red wine
1 tsp. cinnamon
powder
¼ cup raisins
½ cup sugar

Instructions:

1. In the Instant Pot, add apples, wine, cinnamon, raisins and sugar.
2. Lock the lid. Set the Instant Pot to Manual mode, then set the timer for 10 minutes at High Pressure.
3. When the timer goes off, perform a natural release for 5 minutes, then release any remaining pressure. Carefully open the lid.
4. Divide apples on dessert plates and serve warm.

Nutritional info:

Calories 200, Fat 3g, Carbs 34g, Protein 3g

Blueberry and Coconut Sweet Bowls

Prep Time: 12 mins, Cook Time: 6 mins, Servings: 1

Ingredients:

1 cup vanilla yogurt
1 cup coconut milk
1 cup blueberries
2 tsps. sugar
1 cup unsweetened and flaked coconut
1½ cups water

Instructions:

1. Combine milk with coconut, yogurt, blueberries and sugar in a heat-proof dish and stir well then cover with tin foil.
2. Add the water to the Instant Pot, add trivet, add dish.
3. Lock the lid. Set the Instant Pot to Manual mode, then set the timer for 6 minutes at High Pressure.
4. When the timer goes off, perform a natural release for 5 minutes, then release any remaining pressure. Carefully open the lid.
5. Divide into bowls and serve cold.

Nutritional info:

Calories 142, Fat 2g, Carbs 4g, Protein 6g

Poached Pears

Prep Time: 12 mins, Cook Time: 10 mins, Servings: 6

Ingredients:

1 cup red wine	¼ tsp. cinnamon
½ cup sugar	6 green pears
2 tsps. vanilla extract	

Instructions:

1. In the Instant Pot, mix the wine with sugar, vanilla, cinnamon and pears.
2. Lock the lid. Set the Instant Pot to Manual mode, then set the timer for 10 minutes at High Pressure.
3. When the timer goes off, perform a quick release. Carefully open the lid.
4. Let the pears cool and transfer them to bowls. Reserve the wine sauce remains in the Instant Pot.
5. Drizzle wine sauce all over and serve.

Nutritional info:

Calories 172, Fat 5g, Carbs 20g, Protein 4g

Flavored Pears

Prep Time: 12 mins, Cook Time: 10 mins, Servings: 4

Ingredients:

11 oz. currant jelly	lemon
26 oz. grape juice	4 pears
Juice and zest of 1	2 rosemary springs

Instructions:

1. Transfer the currant jelly and grape juice to the Instant Pot and add lemon zest and juice before stirring.
2. Add pears and rosemary springs.
3. Lock the lid. Set the Instant Pot to Manual mode, then set the timer for 10 minutes at High Pressure.
4. When the timer goes off, perform a quick release. Carefully open the lid.
5. Arrange pears on plates and serve them cold with the cooking juice on top.

Nutritional info:

Calories 172, Fat 4g, Carbs 17g, Protein 12g

Lemon and Orange Jam

Prep Time: 12 mins, Cook Time: 30 mins, Servings: 8

Ingredients:

Juice and zest of 2 lemons	1 tsp. vanilla extract
	2 cups water
1 lb. oranges, halved, peeled and grated	½ cup sugar

Instructions:

1. In the Instant Pot, mix the lemon juice and zest with orange, vanilla extract, water.
2. Lock the lid. Set the Instant Pot to Manual mode, then set the timer for 15 minutes at High Pressure.
3. When the timer goes off, perform a natural release for 10 minutes, then release any remaining pressure. Carefully open the lid.
4. Add the sugar, set the pot on Sauté mode, cook until sugar dissolves, divide into jars and serve cold.

Nutritional info:

Calories 87, Fat 1g, Carbs 13g, Protein 2g

Easy Plum Jam

Prep Time: 20 mins, Cook Time: 8 mins, Servings: 12

Ingredients:

1 tsp. vanilla extract	2 tbsps. lemon juice
3 lbs. plums, pitted and roughly chopped	1 cup water
	1 cup sugar

Instructions:

1. In the Instant Pot, combine plums with sugar and vanilla extract, stir and leave aside for 20 minutes
2. Add lemon juice and water, stir.
3. Lock the lid. Set the Instant Pot to Manual mode, then set the timer for 8 minutes at High Pressure.
4. When the timer goes off, perform a natural release for 5 minutes, then release any remaining pressure. Carefully open the lid.
5. Divide into bowls and serve cold.

Nutritional info:

Calories 191, Fat 3g, Carbs 12g, Protein 4g

Ginger and Peach Marmalade

Prep Time: 12 mins, Cook Time: 5 mins, Servings: 6
Ingredients:

3 tbsps. grated ginger	cubed peaches
½ cup sugar	1 box fruit pectin
4½ cups peeled and	½ tsp. vanilla extract

Instructions:
1. Set the Instant Pot on Sauté mode, add peaches, ginger, vanilla extract and pectin, stir, bring to a boil, add sugar, stir.
2. Lock the lid. Set the Instant Pot to Manual mode, then set the timer for 5 minutes at High Pressure.
3. When the timer goes off, perform a natural release. Carefully open the lid.
4. Divide jam into jars and serve.

Nutritional info:
Calories 87, Fat 4g, Carbs 9g, Protein 2g

Peach and Cinnamon Compote

Prep Time: 12 mins, Cook Time: 5 mins, Servings: 6
Ingredients:

2 tbsps. grape nuts cereal	cinnamon
8 peaches, chopped	6 tbsps. sugar
1 tsp. ground	1 tsp. vanilla extract

Instructions:
1. Put peaches in the Instant Pot, add sugar, cinnamon and vanilla extract, stir well.
2. Lock the lid. Set the Instant Pot to Manual mode, then set the timer for 5 minutes at High Pressure.
3. When the timer goes off, perform a natural release. Carefully open the lid.
4. Add grape nuts, stir, divide into bowls and serve cold.

Nutritional info:
Calories 121, Fat 4g, Carbs 17g, Protein 4g

Strawberry and Chia Marmalade

Prep Time: 12 mins, Cook Time: 4 mins, Servings: 6
Ingredients:

4 tbsps. sugar	Zest of 1 grated lemon
2 tbsps. chia seeds	½ tsp. vanilla extract
2 lbs. halved strawberries	

1. **Instructions:**
2. In the Instant Pot, mix sugar with strawberries, vanilla extract, lemon zest and chia seeds, stir.
3. Lock the lid. Set the Instant Pot to Manual mode, then set the timer for 4 minutes at High Pressure.
4. When the timer goes off, perform a natural release. Carefully open the lid.
5. Stir again, divide into cups and serve cold

Nutritional info:
Calories 110, Fat 2g, Carbs 2g, Protein 3g

Cocoa and Walnuts Sweet Cream

Prep Time: 12 mins, Cook Time: 2 mins, Servings: 6
Ingredients:

2 oz. avocado oil	1 cup chopped walnuts
4 tbsps. cocoa powder	4 tbsps. sugar
1 tsp. vanilla extract	

Instructions:
1. Put the avocado oil with cocoa, vanilla, walnuts and sugar in a large bowl.
2. Blend with an immersion blender.
3. Pour the mixture in the Instant Pot.
4. Lock the lid. Set the Instant Pot to Manual mode, then set the timer for 2 minutes at High Pressure.
5. When the timer goes off, perform a natural release. Carefully open the lid.
6. Divide into small bowls and keep in the fridge until you serve it.

Nutritional info:
Calories 120, Fat 4g, Carbs 9g, Protein 2g

Chapter 4 Fish and Seafood Recipe

Lemony Salmon

Prep Time: 6 mins, Cook Time: 3 mins, Servings: 2

Ingredients:

¼ cup lemon juice
Cooking spray
Salt and pepper, to taste

2 salmon fillets, frozen
1 cup water

Instructions:

1. Add the water and steamer rack to the Instant Pot. Spray the rack with cooking spray.
2. Place the salmon fillets in the steamer rack. Season with salt and pepper.
3. Drizzle with lemon juice.
4. Lock the lid. Select the Steam mode and cook for 3 minutes at Low Pressure.
5. Once cooking is complete, do a quick pressure release. Carefully open the lid.
6. Remove from the pot and serve on a plate.

Nutritional info:

Calories 172, Fat 6.7g, Carbs 2.6g, Protein 24.6g

Chili-Garlic Salmon

Prep Time: 3 mins, Cook time: 7 mins, Servings: 4

Ingredients:

¼ cup soy sauce
4 salmon fillets
5 tbsps. organic sugar-free chili sauce
Salt and pepper, to

taste
¼ cup water
3 tbsps. chopped green onions

Instructions:

1. In the Instant Pot, add all the ingredients except for the green onions.
2. Lock the lid. Select the Manual mode and cook for 7 minutes at Low Pressure.
3. Once cooking is complete, do a quick pressure release. Carefully open the lid.
4. Garnish with green onions and serve.

Nutritional info:

Calories 409, Fat 14.4g, Carbs 0.9g, Protein 65.4g

Salmon Tandoori

Prep Time: 2 hours, Cook Time: 6 mins, Servings: 4

Ingredients:

1½ lbs. salmon fillets
3 tbsps. coconut oil
Salt and pepper, to

taste
1 tbsp. tandoori spice mix

Instructions:

1. In a bowl, add all the ingredients. Toss well until the fish is fully coated. Allow the fish to marinate for 2 hours in the fridge.
2. Place the marinated salmon in the Instant Pot.
3. Lock the lid. Select the Manual mode and cook for 6 minutes at Low Pressure. Flip the fish halfway through the cooking time.
4. Once cooking is complete, do a quick pressure release. Carefully open the lid.
5. Remove from the pot and serve on a plate.

Nutritional info:

Calories 354, Carbs 1.4g, Protein 22.4g, Fat 35.2g

Savory Salmon with Dill

Prep Time: 12 mins, Cook Time: 10 mins, Servings: 2

Ingredients:

2 tbsps. dill
⅓ cup olive oil
1 tbsp. fresh lemon juice
2 tbsps. butter

2 salmon fillets
1 cup water
Salt and pepper, to taste

Instructions:

1. Add the water and steam rack to the Instant Pot.
2. Put the remaining ingredients in a heatproof dish and stir well.
3. Place the dish on the steam rack.
4. Lock the lid. Select the Steam mode and cook for 10 minutes at Low Pressure.
5. Once cooking is complete, do a quick pressure release. Carefully open the lid.
6. Divide the salmon fillets among two serving plates and serve.

Nutritional info:

Calories 914, Carbs 4.1g, Protein 63.2g, Fat, 80.9g

Salmon with Basil Pesto

Prep Time: 6 mins, Cook Time: 6 mins, Servings: 6

Ingredients:

3 garlic cloves, minced
1½ lbs. salmon fillets
2 cups basil leaves
2 tbsps. freshly
squeezed lemon juice
½ cup olive oil
Salt and pepper, to taste

Instructions:

1. Make the pesto sauce: Put the basil leaves, olive oil, lemon juice, and garlic in a food processor, and pulse until smooth.
2. Season with salt and pepper.
3. Place the salmon fillets in the Instant Pot and add the pesto sauce.
4. Lock the lid. Select the Manual mode and set the cooking time for 6 minutes at Low Pressure.
5. Once cooking is complete, do a quick pressure release. Carefully open the lid.
6. Divide the salmon among six plates and serve.

Nutritional info:

Calories 336, Carbs 0.9g, Protein 20.5g, Fat 28.1g

Simple Steamed Salmon Fillets

Prep Time: 6 mins, Cook time: 10 mins, Servings: 3

Ingredients:

1 cup water
2 tbsps. freshly squeezed lemon juice
2 tbsps. soy sauce
10 oz. salmon fillets
Salt and pepper, to taste
1 tsp. toasted sesame seeds

Instructions:

1. Set a trivet in the Instant Pot and pour the water into the pot.
2. Using a heat-proof dish, combine all ingredients.
3. Place the heat-proof dish on the trivet.
4. Lock the lid. Select the Manual mode and cook for 10 minutes at Low Pressure.
5. Once cooking is complete, do a quick pressure release. Carefully open the lid.
6. Garnish with toasted sesame seeds and serve.

Nutritional info:

Calories 160, Fat 7.4g, Carbs 2.6g, Protein 20.1g

Instant Pot Curried Salmon

Prep Time: 6 mins, Cook Time: 8 mins, Servings: 4

Ingredients:

2 cups coconut milk
2 tbsps. coconut oil
1 onion, chopped
1 lb. raw salmon,
diced
1½ tbsps. minced garlic

Instructions:

1. Press the Sauté button on the Instant Pot and heat the oil.
2. Sauté the garlic and onions until fragrant, about 2 minutes.
3. Add the diced salmon and stir for 1 minute.
4. Pour in the coconut milk.
5. Lock the lid. Select the Manual mode and cook for 4 minutes at Low Pressure.
6. Once cooking is complete, do a quick pressure release. Carefully open the lid.
7. Let the salmon cool for 5 minutes before serving.

Nutritional info:

Calories 524, Carbs 10.3g, Protein 26.7g, Fat 43.6g

Steamed Chili-Rubbed Tilapia

Prep Time: 6 mins, Cook time: 10 mins, Servings: 4

Ingredients:

1 cup water
½ tsp. garlic powder
1 lb. skinless tilapia fillet
2 tbsps. extra virgin
olive oil
Salt and pepper, to taste
2 tbsps. chili powder

Instructions:

1. Set a trivet in the Instant Pot and pour the water into the pot.
2. Season the tilapia fillets with salt, pepper, chili powder, and garlic powder. Drizzle with olive oil on top.
3. Place in the steamer basket.
4. Lock the lid. Select the Steam mode and cook for 10 minutes at Low Pressure.
5. Once cooking is complete, do a quick pressure release. Carefully open the lid.
6. Serve warm.

Nutritional info:

Calories 211, Fat 10g, Carbs 2g, Protein 26g

Tuna Salad with Lettuce

Prep Time: 12 mins, Cook Time: 10 mins, Servings: 4
Ingredients:

2 tbsps. olive oil	1 head lettuce
½ lb. tuna, sliced	Salt and pepper, to
1 tbsp. fresh lemon	taste
juice	1 cup water
2 eggs	

Instructions:
1. In a large bowl, season the tuna with lemon juice, salt and pepper. Transfer the tuna to a baking dish.
2. Add the eggs, water, and steamer rack to the Instant Pot. Place the baking dish on the steamer rack.
3. Lock the lid. Select the Steam mode and set the cooking time for 10 minutes at Low Pressure.
4. Once cooking is complete, do a quick pressure release. Carefully open the lid.
5. Allow the eggs and tuna to cool. Peel the eggs and slice into wedges. Set aside.
6. Assemble the salad by shredding the lettuce in a salad bowl. Toss in the cooled tuna and eggs.
7. Sprinkle with olive oil, then serve.

Nutritional info:
Calories 260, Carbs 6.3g, Protein 17.2g, Fat 19.9g

Quick Salmon

Prep Time: 12 mins, Cook Time: 5 mins, Servings: 4
Ingredients:

1 cup water	4 boneless salmon
¼ cup lemon juice	fillets
1 tbsp. butter	1 bunch dill, chopped
¼ tsp. salt	

Instructions:
1. Place the water in the Instant Pot, add lemon juice, add steamer basket, add salmon inside, season with some salt, sprinkle dill and drizzle melted butter.
2. Lock the lid. Select the Manual mode and cook for 5 minutes at Low Pressure.
3. Once cooking is complete, do a quick pressure release. Carefully open the lid.
4. Divide salmon between plates and serve with a side dish.

Nutritional info:
Calories 412, Fat 12g, Carbs 27g, Protein 12g

Lemon Pepper Salmon

Prep Time: 15 mins, Cook time: 5 mins, Servings: 4
Ingredients:

1 cup water	2 tbsps. olive oil
1 tsp. ground dill	Salt, to taste
1 tsp. ground	4 lemon slices
tarragon	1 carrot, sliced
1 tsp. ground basil	1 zucchini, sliced
4 salmon fillets	

Instructions:
1. In the Instant Pot, add the water, dill, tarragon, and basil.
2. Place the steamer basket inside.
3. Set in the salmon. Drizzle with a tablespoon of olive oil, pepper and salt. Top with lemon slices.
4. Lock the lid. Select the Steam mode and cook for 3 minutes at Low Pressure.
5. Once cooking is complete, do a quick pressure release. Carefully open the lid.
6. Transfer the fish to a plate and discard the lemon slices.
7. Drizzle the Instant Pot with remaining olive oil. Add the carrot and zucchini to the Instant Pot. Set to Sauté mode, then sauté for 2minutes or until the vegetables are tender.
8. Serve the salmon with the veggies.
9. Garnish with fresh lemon wedges.

Nutritional info:
Calories 252, Fat 11.1g, Carbs 3.8g, Protein 35.3g

Red Curry Halibut

Prep Time: 3 mins, Cook time: 10 mins, Servings: 4
Ingredients:

2 tbsps. chopped	tomatoes
cilantro	1 tbsp. freshly
4 skinless halibut	squeezed lime juice
fillets	Salt and pepper, to
3 green curry leaves	taste
1 cup chopped	

Instructions:
1. Place all ingredients in the Instant Pot. Give a good stir to combine the ingredients.
2. Lock the lid. Select the Manual mode and cook for 10 minutes at Low Pressure.
3. Do a quick pressure release.

Nutritional info:
Calories 379, Fat 5.5g, Carbs 1.8g, Protein 76.1g

Thai Fish Curry

Prep Time: 6 mins, Cook Time: 6 mins, Servings: 6

Ingredients:

1½ lbs. salmon fillets
2 cups fresh coconut milk
¼ cup chopped cilantro
⅓ cup olive oil
2 tbsps. curry powder
Salt and pepper, to taste

Instructions:

1. In the Instant Pot, add all the ingredients. Give a good stir.
2. Lock the lid. Select the Manual mode and set the cooking time for 6 minutes at Low Pressure.
3. Once cooking is complete, do a quick pressure release. Carefully open the lid. Set warm.

Nutritional info:

Calories 470, Carbs 5.6g, Protein 25.5g, Fat 39.8g

Steamed Cod with Ginger and Scallions

Prep Time: 6 mins, Cook time: 12 mins, Servings: 4

Ingredients:

1 cup water
6 scallions, chopped
2 tbsps. grated ginger
4 skinless cod fillets
Salt and pepper, to taste
2 tbsps. soy sauce
3 tbsps. freshly squeezed lemon juice

Instructions:

1. Set a trivet in the Instant Pot and pour the water into the pot.
2. Place the cod fillets in a heat-proof dish that will fit inside the Instant Pot.
3. Pour the lemon juice, soy sauce, and ginger over the fish. Add salt and pepper for seasoning. Sprinkle with scallions last.
4. Place the dish on the trivet.
5. Lock the lid. Select the Steam mode and cook for 12 minutes at Low Pressure.
6. Once cooking is complete, do a quick pressure release. Carefully open the lid.
7. Serve warm.

Nutritional info:

Calories 94, Fat 0.6g, Carbs 3.2g, Protein 18.3g

Steamed Herbed Red Snapper

Prep Time: 3 mins, Cook time: 12 mins, Servings: 4

Ingredients:

1 cup water
4 red snapper fillets
1½ tsps. chopped fresh herbs
¼ tsp. paprika
3 tbsps. freshly squeezed lemon juice
Salt and pepper, to taste

Instructions:

1. Set a trivet in the Instant Pot and pour the water into the pot.
2. Mix all ingredients in a heat-proof dish that will fit in the Instant Pot. Combine to coat the fish with all ingredients.
3. Place the heat-proof dish on the trivet.
4. Lock the lid. Select the Manual mode and cook for 12 minutes at Low Pressure.
5. Once cooking is complete, do a quick pressure release. Carefully open the lid.
6. Serve warm.

Nutritional info:

Calories 226, Fat 3g, Carbs 2.1g, Protein 45.6g

Steamed Greek Snapper

Prep Time: 6 mins, Cook time: 10 mins, Servings: 4

Ingredients:

1 cup water
12 snapper fillets
3 tbsps. olive oil
2 tbsps. Greek yogurt
1 garlic clove, minced
Salt and pepper, to taste

Instructions:

1. Set a trivet in the Instant Pot and pour the water into the pot.
2. In a mixing bowl, combine the olive oil, garlic, and Greek yogurt. Sprinkle salt and pepper for seasoning.
3. Apply Greek yogurt mixture to the fish fillets. Place the fillets on the trivet.
4. Lock the lid. Select the Steam mode and cook for 10 minutes at Low Pressure.
5. Once cooking is complete, do a quick pressure release. Carefully open the lid.
6. Serve warm.

Nutritional info:

Calories 250, Fat 6.3g, Carbs 0.4g, Protein 44.8g

Cod with Orange Sauce

Prep Time: 12 mins, Cook Time: 7 mins, Servings: 4
Ingredients:

1 cup white wine	finely chopped
1 small ginger piece, grated	Juice of 1 orange
4 spring onions,	4 boneless cod fillets

Instructions:
1. In the Instant Pot, combine the wine with ginger, spring onions and orange juice, stir, add steamer basket, add cod fillets inside.
2. Lock the lid. Select the Manual mode, then set the timer for 7 minutes at Low Pressure.
3. Once the timer goes off, do a quick pressure release. Carefully open the lid.
4. Divide fish on plates, drizzle orange juice all over and serve.

Nutritional info:
Calories 172, Fat 5g, Carbs 7g, Protein 7g

Creamy Shrimp Pasta

Prep Time: 12 mins, Cook Time: 15 mins, Servings: 8
Ingredients:

12 oz. linguine pasta	peeled and deveined
1 small red onion, diced	1 tsp. butter
12 oz. shrimps,	⅓ cup heavy cream
	4 cups water

Instructions:
1. Add the water and pasta to the Instant Pot.
2. Lock the lid. Select the Manual mode and cook for 7 minutes at High Pressure.
3. Once cooking is complete, do a quick pressure release. Carefully open the lid.
4. Drain the pasta and transfer to a container.
5. Press the Sauté button and heat the butter until melted.
6. Add the shrimp and cook for 2 minutes per side. Add the mix with the pasta.
7. Add the onions; cook for 5 minutes until turn translucent and softened.
8. Stir in the cream; cook for 2 to 3 minutes more.
9. Serve the pasta with the cream sauce.

Nutritional info:
Calories 134, Fat 5g, Carbs 9g, Protein 14g

Steamed Lemon Mustard Salmon

Prep Time: 8 mins, Cook time: 10 mins, Servings: 4
Ingredients:

1 cup water	mustard
1 garlic clove, minced	Salt and pepper, to taste
4 skinless salmon fillets	2 tbsps. freshly squeezed lemon juice
2 tbsps. Dijon	

Instructions:
1. Set a trivet in the Instant Pot and pour the water into the pot.
2. In a bowl, mix lemon juice, mustard, and garlic. Sprinkle salt and pepper for seasoning.
3. Top the salmon fillets with the mustard mixture. Place the fish fillets on the trivet.
4. Lock the lid. Select the Steam mode and cook for 10 minutes at Low Pressure.
5. Once cooking is complete, do a quick pressure release. Carefully open the lid.
6. Serve warm.

Nutritional info:
Calories 402, Fat 14.8g, Carbs 2.2g, Protein 65.3g

Flounder with Dill and Capers

Prep Time: 3 mins, Cook time: 10 mins, Servings: 4
Ingredients:

1 cup water	capers
1 tbsp. chopped fresh dill	4 flounder fillets
4 lemon wedges	Salt and pepper, to taste
2 tbsps. chopped	

Instructions:
1. In the Instant Pot, set in a steamer basket and pour the water into the pot.
2. Sprinkle salt and pepper to the flounder fillets. Sprinkle with dill and chopped capers on top. Add lemon wedges on top for garnish.
3. Place the fillets on the trivet.
4. Lock the lid. Select the Steam mode and cook for 10 minutes at Low Pressure.
5. Once cooking is complete, do a quick pressure release. Carefully open the lid.
6. Serve warm.

Nutritional info:
Calories 135, Fat 3.6g, Carbs 5.5g, Protein 21.3g

Lemon Pepper Salmon

Prep Time: 12 mins, Cook Time: 10 mins, Servings: 4

Ingredients:

1 cup water
1 lemon, sliced
1 red bell pepper, julienned

1 lb. boneless salmon fillets
Black pepper, to taste
3 tsps. melted butter

Instructions:

1. Set the water in the Instant Pot, add steamer basket, add salmon fillets, season them with black pepper, drizzle melted butter all over, divide bell pepper and lemon slices on top.
2. Lock the lid. Select the Manual mode and cook for 7 minutes at Low Pressure.
3. Once cooking is complete, do a quick pressure release. Carefully open the lid.
4. Divide salmon and bell pepper on plates, top with lemon slices and serve.

Nutritional info:

Calories 281, Fat 8g, Carbs 16g, Protein 6g

Italian Salmon with Lemon Juice

Prep Time: 6 mins, Cook Time: 8 mins, Servings: 5

Ingredients:

1½ lbs. salmon fillets
2 tbsps. butter
3 tbsps. olive oil
1 tbsp. Italian herb seasoning mix

3 tbsps. freshly squeezed lemon juice
Salt and pepper, to taste
⅓ cup water

Instructions:

1. Place all ingredients in the Instant Pot and stir well.
2. Lock the lid. Select the Manual mode and set the cooking time for 8 minutes at Low Pressure. Flip the fish halfway through the cooking time.
3. Once cooking is complete, do a quick pressure release. Carefully open the lid.
4. Divide the salmon among plates and serve.

Nutritional info:

Calories 328, Carbs 1.6g, Protein 22.5g, Fat 28.3g

Steamed Tilapia

Prep Time: 12 mins, Cook Time: 10 mins, Servings: 4

Ingredients:

¼ cup chopped scallions
1 tbsp. Chinese black bean paste

1 tbsp. peanut oil
1 lb. tilapia fillets
3 tbsps. soy sauce
1 cup water

Instructions:

1. In a bowl, mix soy sauce with black bean paste and whisk well.
2. Add fish, toss and leave aside for 10 minutes.
3. Set the Instant Pot on Sauté mode, add oil, heat it up.
4. Add scallions, sauté for 2 minutes and transfer to a bowl.
5. Clean the pot, add the water, add steamer basket, add fish fillets inside, sprinkle scallions on top.
6. Lock the lid. Select the Manual mode and cook for 3 minutes at Low Pressure.
7. Once cooking is complete, do a quick pressure release. Carefully open the lid.
8. Divide everything between plates and serve with a side salad.

Nutritional info:

Calories 152, Fat 2g, Carbs 12g, Protein 5g

Halibut En Papillote

Prep Time: 12 mins, Cook time: 10 mins, Servings: 4

Ingredients:

1 cup water
1 cup chopped tomatoes
1 thinly sliced shallot

4 halibut fillets
½ tbsp. grated ginger
Salt and pepper, to taste

Instructions:

1. In the Instant Pot, set in a steamer basket and pour the water into the pot.
2. Get a large parchment paper and place the fillet in the middle. Season with salt and pepper. Add the grated ginger, tomatoes, and shallots. Fold the parchment paper to create a pouch and crimp the edges.
3. Place the parchment paper containing the fish.
4. Lock the lid. Select the Steam mode and cook for 10 minutes at Low Pressure.
5. Once cooking is complete, do a quick pressure release. Carefully open the lid.
6. Serve warm.

Nutritional info:

Calories 383, Fat 5.5g, Carbs 2.7g, Protein 76.3g

Coconut Curry Cod

Prep Time: 4 mins, Cook time: 8 mins, Servings: 4
Ingredients:

2 tsps. curry powder
2 tsps. grated ginger
4 cod fillets
1½ cups coconut milk

1 cilantro sprig, chopped
Salt and pepper, to taste

Instructions:
1. In the Instant Pot, set in all ingredients excluding the cilantro. Give a good stir to combine.
2. Lock the lid. Select the Steam mode and cook for 8 minutes at Low Pressure.
3. Once cooking is complete, do a quick pressure release. Carefully open the lid.
4. Garnish with chopped cilantro before serving.

Nutritional info:
Calories 291, Fat 22.1g, Carbs 5.7g, Protein 19.7g

Mussels with White Wine

Prep Time: 10 mins, Cook Time: 5 mins, Servings:4
Ingredients:

2 lbs. fresh mussels
1 tbsp. extra-virgin olive oil
3 large shallots, minced

2 garlic cloves, minced
½ cup water
½ cup dry white wine
Juice of ½ lemon

Instructions:
1. Scrub and de-beard the mussels. Place the mussels in a large bowl of cold water, discarding any shells that are not tightly closed. Set aside.
2. Set your Instant Pot to Sauté and heat the olive oil.
3. Add the shallots and garlic and cook for 2 minutes, stirring occasionally.
4. Put the mussels, water, and wine in the Instant Pot and give a good stir.
5. Lock the lid. Select the Manual mode and set the cooking time for 3 minutes at Low Pressure.
6. Once cooking is complete, do a quick pressure release. Carefully open the lid.
7. Remove the mussels from the pot to a platter. Pour the wine broth over the mussels and serve drizzled with the lemon juice.

Nutritional info:
Calories 260, Fat 2g, Carbs 10g, Protein 27g

Shrimp Scampi

Prep Time: 3 mins, Cook time: 6 mins, Servings: 4
Ingredients:

2 tsps. chopped garlic
Salt and pepper, to taste
1 lb. peeled and deveined raw shrimp

¼ cup low-sodium organic chicken broth
2 tsps. chopped parsley

Instructions:
1. Place all ingredients in the Instant Pot.
2. Lock the lid. Select the Manual mode and cook for 6 minutes at Low Pressure.
3. Once cooking is complete, do a quick pressure release. Carefully open the lid.
4. Serve warm.

Nutritional info:
Calories 123, Fat 1.7g, Carbs 1.8g, Protein 23.7g

Sea Scallops with Champagne Butter Sauce

Prep Time: 5 mins, Cook Time: 5 mins, Servings: 3
Ingredients:

1 lb. sea scallops
1 cup vegetable broth
½ cup Champagne
2 tbsps. butter
½ tsp. cayenne

pepper
¼ tsp. pink peppercorns, crushed
Sea salt and ground black pepper, to taste

Instructions:
1. Place all the ingredients in the Instant Pot.
2. Lock the lid. Select the Manual mode and set the cooking time for 3 minutes at Low Pressure.
3. Once cooking is complete, do a quick pressure release. Carefully open the lid.
4. Using a slotted spoon, transfer the scallops to a platter and set aside.
5. Set your Instant Pot to Sauté and cook the sauce, stirring constantly, or until the sauce is reduced by half.
6. Pour the sauce over the scallops and serve immediately.

Nutritional info:
Calories 166, Fat 8g, Carbs 5g, Protein 17g

Cheddar Creamy Haddock

Prep Time: 12 mins, Cook Time: 10 mins, Servings: 3

Ingredients:

12 oz. haddock fillets
3 tbsps. diced onions
1 tbsp. butter
Salt and pepper, to taste
½ cup heavy cream
5 oz. grated Cheddar cheese

Instructions:

1. Heat the Instant Pot on Sauté mode.
2. Add the butter and onions to the Instant Pot. Sauté until onions become translucent and softened, 3 minutes.
3. Season the fish with salt and pepper. Add the fish in the pot and cook for 2 minutes per side.
4. Add the cream and the cheese.
5. Lock the lid. Select the Manual mode and cook for 5 minutes at Low Pressure.
6. Once cooking is complete, do a quick pressure release. Carefully open the lid.
7. Serve immediately.

Nutritional info:

Calories 192, Carbs 5g, Fat 17.5g, Protein 18g

Cod Meal

Prep Time: 6 mins, Cook Time: 5 mins, Servings: 2

Ingredients:

1 cup water
2 tbsps. ghee
1 fresh large fillet cod
Salt and pepper, to taste

Instructions:

1. Cut fillet into 3 pieces. Coat with the ghee and season with salt and pepper.
2. Pour the water into the pot and place steamer basket/trivet inside.
3. Arrange the fish pieces over the basket/ trivet.
4. Lock the lid. Select the Manual mode and cook for 5 minutes at Low Pressure.
5. Once cooking is complete, do a quick pressure release. Carefully open the lid.
6. Serve warm.

Nutritional info:

Calories 197, Carbs 2g, Fat 12g, Protein 19.5g

Halibut and Broccoli Casserole

Prep Time: 6 mins, Cook Time: 6 mins, Servings: 6

Ingredients:

1 tbsp. Dijon mustard
1¼ cup full-fat coconut cream
2 tbsps. olive oil
1½ lbs. halibut fillets,
sliced
1 cup broccoli florets
Salt and pepper, to taste

Instructions:

1. In the Instant Pot, add all the ingredients. Give a good stir.
2. Lock the lid. Select the Manual mode and set the cooking time for 8 minutes at Low Pressure.
3. Once cooking is complete, do a quick pressure release. Carefully open the lid.
4. Let the fish and broccoli cool for 5 minutes before serving.

Nutritional info:

Calories 419, Carbs 3.7g, Protein 18.4g, Fat 37.7g

Halibut with Pesto

Prep Time: 12 mins, Cook time: 8 mins, Servings: 4

Ingredients:

2 tbsps. extra virgin olive oil
1 tbsp. freshly squeezed lemon juice
1 cup basil leaves
2 garlic cloves,
minced
4 halibut fillets
¼ cup water
Salt and pepper, to taste

Instructions:

1. Place the halibut fish in the Instant Pot. Set aside.
2. In a food processor, pulse the basil, olive oil, garlic, and lemon juice until coarse. Sprinkle salt and pepper for seasoning.
3. Spread pesto sauce over halibut fillets. Add the water.
4. Lock the lid. Select the Manual mode and cook for 8 minutes at Low Pressure.
5. Once cooking is complete, do a quick pressure release. Carefully open the lid.
6. Serve warm.

Nutritional info:

Calories 401, Fat 8.4g, Carbs 0.8g, Protein 75.8g

Delicious and Simple Octopus

Prep Time: 12 mins, Cook Time: 15 mins, Servings: 4

Ingredients:

¼ tsp. sweet paprika   pepper, to taste
2 lbs. octopus, rinsed ¼ tsp. chili powder
Salt and black

Instructions:

1. Season octopus with salt and pepper, add to the Instant Pot.
2. Add enough water to cover, then add chili powder and paprika, stir a bit.
3. Lock the lid. Select the Manual mode and cook for 15 minutes at Low Pressure.
4. Once cooking is complete, do a quick pressure release. Carefully open the lid.
5. Cut the octopus and serve.

Nutritional info:

Calories 112, Fat 6g, Carbs 7g, Protein 3g

Shrimp Green Curry

Prep Time: 12 mins, Cook Time: 60 mins, Servings: 5

Ingredients:

7 oz. cleaned and   2 tbsps. green curry
deveined shrimps   paste
4 tbsps. Thai basil   1 tsp. coconut oil
leaves   4 tsps. fish sauce

Instructions:

1. Press the Sauté bottom on the Instant Pot.
2. Add and heat the oil in the Instant Pot.
3. Add the chili and shrimp; sauté for 2 minutes.
4. Add the fish sauce, paste, and basil; cook for 1 minute more.
5. Lock the lid. Select the Manual mode and cook for 60 minutes at Low Pressure.
6. Once cooking is complete, do a quick pressure release. Carefully open the lid.
7. Transfer the cooked recipe on serving plates.
8. Serve the recipe warm.

Nutritional info:

Calories 62, Fat 1g, Carbs 2g, Protein 13g

Thyme-Sesame Crusted Halibut

Prep Time: 6 mins, Cook time: 8 mins, Servings: 4

Ingredients:

1 cup water   8 oz. halibut, sliced
1 tsp. dried thyme   Salt and pepper, to
leaves   taste
1 tbsp. toasted   1 tbsp. freshly
sesame seeds   squeezed lemon juice

Instructions:

1. Set a trivet in the Instant Pot and pour the water into the pot.
2. Season the halibut with lemon juice, salt, and pepper. Sprinkle with dried thyme leaves and sesame seeds.
3. Place the fish on the trivet.
4. Lock the lid. Select the Steam mode and cook for 8 minutes at Low Pressure.
5. Once cooking is complete, do a quick pressure release. Carefully open the lid.
6. Serve warm.

Nutritional info:

Calories 246, Fat 17.7g, Carbs 4.2g, Protein 17.5g

Yogurt Fish Patties

Prep Time: 12 mins, Cook Time: 8 mins, Servings: 4

Ingredients:

1 tsp. baking soda   1 lb. fish fillets,
¼ cup fat-free Greek   chopped
yogurt   3 tbsps. all-purpose
1 small onion,   flour
chopped   1 tbsp. olive oil

Instructions:

1. In a mixing bowl, thoroughly mix fish, yogurt, onion, flour, and baking soda.
2. Make 6 balls and press them to make patties.
3. Press Sauté. Grease the pot with olive oil.
4. Set in the patties and cook each side for 4 minutes. Serve warm.

Nutritional info:

Calories 288, Fat 14g, Carbs 30g, Protein 11g

Lemon White Fish

Prep Time: 3 mins, Cook Time: 6 mins, Servings: 4

Ingredients:

1 tbsp. olive oil	grated
4 white fish fillets	Salt and pepper, to
Juice and zest of 1	taste
lemon	4 spring onions,
1 cup fish stock	chopped
1 thumb-size ginger,	

Instructions:

1. Except for the spring onions, add all the ingredients to the Instant Pot.
2. Lock the lid. Select the Manual mode and set the cooking time for 6 minutes at Low Pressure.
3. Once cooking is complete, do a quick pressure release for 5 minutes. Carefully open the lid.
4. Sprinkle the spring onions on top for garnish before serving.

Nutritional info:

Calories 234, Fat 15g, Carbs 3g, Protein 22g

Wild Alaskan Cod with Cherry Tomatoes

Prep Time: 3 mins, Cook Time: 8 mins, Servings: 4

Ingredients:

1 large wild Alaskan	Salt and pepper, to
Cod fillet	taste
1 cup chopped cherry	2 tbsps. butter
tomatoes	

Instructions:

1. Except for the butter, add all the ingredients to the Instant Pot.
2. Lock the lid. Select the Manual mode and set the cooking time for 8 minutes at Low Pressure.
3. Once cooking is complete, do a quick pressure release. Carefully open the lid.
4. Stir in the butter and serve warm.

Nutritional info:

Calories 134, Fat 6g, Carbs 1g, Protein 17g

Buttery Smoked Cod with Scallions

Prep Time: 5 mins, Cook Time: 3 mins, Servings: 2

Ingredients:

½ lemon, sliced	scallions
½ cup water	2 tsps. butter
2 fillets smoked cod	Sea salt and ground
2 tbsps. chopped	black pepper, to taste

Instructions:

1. Add the lemon and water to the Instant Pot, then put the steamer rack on top.
2. Transfer the smoked cod fillets to the steamer basket.
3. Add the scallions, butter, salt, and black pepper to the fillets.
4. Lock the lid. Select the Steam mode and cook for 3 minutes at Low Pressure.
5. Once cooking is complete, do a quick pressure release. Carefully open the lid.
6. Remove from the pot to a plate and serve warm.

Nutritional info:

Calories 236, Fat 5g, Carbs 4g, Protein 41g

Easy Mahi Mahi with Enchilada Sauce

Prep Time: 3 mins, Cook Time: 8 mins, Servings: 2

Ingredients:

2 fresh Mahi Mahi	Salt and pepper, to
fillets	taste
¼ cup commercial	2 tbsps. butter
enchilada sauce	

Instructions:

1. Add all the ingredients, except for the butter, to the Instant Pot.
2. Lock the lid. Select the Manual mode and cook for 8 minutes at Low Pressure.
3. Once cooking is complete, do a quick pressure release. Carefully open the lid.
4. Stir in the butter and serve on plates.

Nutritional info:

Calories 369, Fat 27g, Carbs 11g, Protein 20g

Sardine and Plum Tomato Curry

Prep Time: 10 mins, Cook Time: 8 hours, Servings: 4

Ingredients:

1 tbsp. olive oil	2 plum tomatoes,
1 lb. fresh sardines,	chopped finely
cubed	1 garlic clove, minced
½ cup tomato puree	Salt and ground black
½ large onion, sliced	pepper, to taste

Instructions:

1. Select the Sauté button on your Instant Pot and heat the olive oil. Add the sardines and sauté for 2 minutes.
2. Add the remaining ingredients to the Instant Pot and stir to combine.
3. Lock the lid. Select the Slow Cook mode and cook for 8 hours at Low Pressure.
4. Once cooking is complete, do a quick pressure release. Carefully open the lid.
5. Give the cooked curry a good stir and serve.

Nutritional info:

Calories 297, Fat 16g, Carbs 6g, Protein 29g

Lemon-Butter Grouper

Prep Time: 10 mins, Cook Time: 4 mins, Servings: 4

Ingredients:

1½ cups water	smashed
4 grouper fillets	½ tsp. dried basil
2 tbsps. fresh lemon	½ tsp. sweet paprika
juice	Sea salt and ground
4 tbsps. butter	black pepper, to taste
2 garlic cloves,	

Instructions:

1. Add the water and steamer basket to the Instant Pot.
2. Arrange the grouper fillets in the steamer basket and add the remaining ingredients.
3. Lock the lid. Select the Manual mode and set the cooking time for 4 minutes at Low Pressure.
4. Once cooking is complete, do a quick pressure release. Carefully open the lid.
5. Transfer the fillets to four plates and serve warm.

Nutritional info:

Calories 345, Fat 15g, Carbs 1g, Protein 50g

Sole Fillets with Pickle-Mayo Sauce

Prep Time: 5 mins, Cook Time: 3 mins, Servings: 4

Ingredients:

1½ lbs. sole fillets	1 tbsp. pickle juice
1 tsp. paprika	½ cup mayonnaise
Sea salt and ground	2 cloves garlic,
black pepper, to taste	smashed
1½ cups water	

Instructions:

1. On a clean work surface, season the sole fillets with paprika, salt, and pepper.
2. Add the water and steamer basket to the Instant Pot. Arrange the sole fillets in the steamer basket.
3. Lock the lid. Select the Manual mode and set the cooking time for 3 minutes at Low Pressure.
4. Meanwhile, make the sauce: Mix together the pickle juice, mayo, and smashed garlic in a bowl until well combined.
5. Once cooking is complete, do a quick pressure release. Carefully open the lid.
6. Remove the fillets from the pot and serve alongside the sauce.

Nutritional info:

Calories 210, Fat 11g, Carbs 4g, Protein 24g

Chili-Lime Shrimps

Prep Time: 2 mins, Cook time: 4 mins, Servings: 4

Ingredients:

1½ lbs. peeled and	taste
deveined raw shrimp	1 tbsp. coconut oil
1 tbsp. chili powder	2 tbsps. freshly
Salt and pepper, to	squeezed lime juice

Instructions:

1. Place all ingredients in the Instant Pot.
2. Lock the lid. Select the Manual mode and cook for 4 minutes at Low Pressure.
3. Once cooking is complete, do a quick pressure release. Carefully open the lid.
4. Serve warm.

Nutritional info:

Calories 206, Fat 5.7g, Carbs 1.7g, Protein 34.9g

Sea Bass Risotto with Leeks

Prep Time: 5 mins, Cook Time: 7 mins, Servings:4

Ingredients:

2 tbsps. melted butter
½ cup leeks, sliced
2 cups basmati rice
1½ lbs. sea bass fillets, diced
2 garlic cloves, minced
2 cups vegetable broth
1 cup water
½ tsp. ground black pepper
Salt, to taste

Instructions:

1. Press the Sauté button on your Instant Pot and heat the butter.
2. Add the sliced leeks and cook for 2 to 3 minutes, stirring constantly.
3. Add the remaining ingredients to the pot and mix well.
4. Lock the lid. Select the Manual mode and set the cooking time for 4 minutes at Low Pressure.
5. Once cooking is complete, do a quick pressure release. Carefully open the lid.
6. Transfer the fish to a large plate and serve.

Nutritional info:

Calories 22, Fat 32g, Carbs 41g, Protein 1g

Szechuan Shrimps

Prep Time: 3 mins, Cook time: 6 mins, Servings: 4

Ingredients:

1 tbsp. julienned ginger
1½ lbs. unpeeled raw shrimps
3 tbsps. soy sauce
2 tbsps. crushed red pepper
Salt and pepper, to taste
3 tbsps. chopped green scallions

Instructions:

1. Place all ingredients in the Instant Pot.
2. Lock the lid. Select the Manual mode and cook for 6 minutes at Low Pressure.
3. Once cooking is complete, do a quick pressure release. Carefully open the lid.
4. Garnish with green scallions and serve.

Nutritional info:

Calories 179, Fat 2.3g, Carbs 2.1g, Protein 35.1g

Simple Shrimp

Prep Time: 12 mins, Cook Time: 3 mins, Servings: 3

Ingredients:

½ cup chicken stock
½ cup white wine
2 tbsps. olive oil
1 tbsp. minced garlic
2 lbs. shrimp, deveined and peeled

Instructions:

1. Set the Instant Pot on Sauté mode, add oil, heat it up.
2. Add garlic and sauté for 30 seconds.
3. Add shrimp, wine and stock, stir.
4. Lock the lid. Select the Manual mode and cook for 3 minutes at Low Pressure.
5. Once cooking is complete, do a quick pressure release. Carefully open the lid.
6. Divide into bowls and serve.

Nutritional info:

Calories 190, Fat 2g, Carbs 7g, Protein 2g

Shrimps with Mango Basil

Prep Time: 6 mins, Cook time: 5 mins, Servings: 4

Ingredients:

1 cup chopped basil
Salt and pepper, to taste
1 large ripe mange, peeled and cubed
¼ cup turmeric powder
1 lb. raw shrimp, peeled and deveined

Instructions:

1. Place the mango cubes in a blender or food processor and pulse until smooth.
2. Place the shrimps, basil, and turmeric powder in the Instant Pot. Sprinkle with salt and pepper. Mix until well combined.
3. Pour over the mango purée and mix.
4. Lock the lid. Select the Manual mode and cook for 5 minutes at Low Pressure.
5. Once cooking is complete, do a quick pressure release. Carefully open the lid.
6. Serve warm.

Nutritional info:

Calories 158, Fat 5g, Carbs 6g, Protein 16g

Simple Curried Shrimps

Prep Time: 6 mins, Cook time: 4 mins, Servings: 4
Ingredients:

1 tbsp. extra virgin olive oil
1½ lb. raw shrimp, peeled and deveined
2 oranges, peeled and separated
1 tbsp. curry powder
Salt and pepper, to taste

Instructions:
1. Press the Sauté button on the Instant Pot and heat the olive oil.
2. Toast the curry powder for a minute until fragrant. Add the shrimps and oranges. Sprinkle salt and pepper for seasoning.
3. Lock the lid. Select the Manual mode and cook for 4 minutes at Low Pressure.
4. Once cooking is complete, do a quick pressure release. Carefully open the lid.
5. Serve warm.

Nutritional info:
Calories 188, Fat 5g, Carbs 1g, Protein 24g

Instant Pot Lemon Shrimps

Prep Time: 8 mins, Cook time: 6 mins, Servings: 4
Ingredients:

¼ cup soy sauce
½ cup freshly squeezed lemon juice
Fresh rosemary sprig
1½ lbs. peeled and deveined shrimps
Salt and pepper, to taste
Parsley, for garnish

Instructions:
1. Combine all the ingredients in the Instant Pot.
2. Lock the lid. Select the Steam mode and cook for 6 minutes at Low Pressure.
3. Once cooking is complete, do a quick pressure release. Carefully open the lid.
4. Press the Sauté button and continue cooking until the sauce has reduced to half.
5. Garnish with parsley and serve.

Nutritional info:
Calories 184, Fat 2.4g, Carbs 3.7g, Protein 35.8g

Shrimp Boil

Prep Time: 12 mins, Cook Time: 35 mins, Servings: 4
Ingredients:

2 lbs. peeled and deveined shrimp
1 tsp. crushed red pepper
1 chopped sweet onion
1 cup chicken stock
1 tbsp. old bay seasoning

Instructions:
1. In the Instant Pot, mix stock with old bay seasoning, red pepper, onion and shrimp, stir.
2. Lock the lid. Select the Manual mode and cook for 30 minutes on Low Pressure.
3. Once cooking is complete, do a quick pressure release. Carefully open the lid.
4. Divide into bowls and serve.

Nutritional info:
Calories 162, Fat 2g, Carbs 6g, Protein 4g

Fast Shrimp Scampi

Prep Time: 12 mins, Cook Time: 4 mins, Servings: 4
Ingredients:

1 cup chicken stock
2 tbsps. butter
Juice of 1 lemon
1 lb. shrimp, peeled and deveined
2 shallots, chopped

Instructions:
1. Set the Instant Pot on Sauté mode, add butter, heat it up.
2. Add shallots and sauté for 1 to 2 minutes.
3. Add shrimp, lemon juice and stock, stir.
4. Lock the lid. Select the Manual mode and cook for 2 minutes at Low Pressure.
5. Once cooking is complete, do a quick pressure release. Carefully open the lid.
6. Divide into bowls and serve.

Nutritional info:
Calories 182, Fat 5g, Carbs 12g, Protein 5g

Teriyaki Scallops

Prep Time: 12 mins, Cook Time: 4 mins, Servings: 3

Ingredients:

½ cup soy sauce	chives
1 lb. sea scallops	1 tbsp. avocado oil
1 tbsp. chopped	3 tbsps. maple syrup

Instructions:

1. Set the Instant Pot on Sauté mode, add oil, heat it up.
2. Add scallops and sear for 1 minute on each side.
3. Add maple syrup, soy sauce and chives, toss to combine well.
4. Lock the lid. Select the Manual mode and cook for 2 minutes at Low Pressure.
5. Once cooking is complete, do a quick pressure release. Carefully open the lid.
6. Divide between plates and serve scallops immediately.

Nutritional info:

Calories 300, Fat 5g, Carbs 8g, Protein 12g

Steamed Crab Legs

Prep Time: 6 mins, Cook Time: 12 mins, Servings: 4

Ingredients:

¼ cup butter	1 tbsp. lemon juice
1½ cups water	2 lbs. king crab legs

Instructions:

1. Add the water and steamer basket to the Instant Pot. Arrange the crab legs in the basket.
2. Lock the lid. Select the Steam mode and cook for 12 minutes at Low Pressure.
3. Once cooking is complete, do a quick pressure release. Carefully open the lid.
4. Drizzle with lemon juice and let the butter melt on top of the legs before serving.

Nutritional info:

Calories 199, Fat 16g, Carbs 1.2g, Protein: 12.7g

Buttery Steamed Lobster Tails

Prep Time: 5 mins, Cook Time: 3 mins, Servings: 6

Ingredients:

1 cup water	Sea salt and freshly
¾ lb. lobster tails, halved	ground black pepper, to taste
½ tsp. red pepper flakes	¼ stick butter, at room temperature

Instructions:

1. Add the water and steamer basket to your Instant Pot. Arrange the lobster tails (shell-side down) in the steamer basket.
2. Lock the lid. Select the Steam mode and set the cooking time for 3 minutes at Low Pressure.
3. Once cooking is complete, do a quick pressure release. Carefully open the lid.
4. Remove the lobster tails from the pot to a large plate.
5. Sprinkle with the red pepper flakes, salt, and black pepper. Spread the butter over the lobster tails and serve.

Nutritional info:

Calories 234, Fat 13g, Carbs 0g, Protein 28g

Instant Pot Boiled Mussels

Prep Time: 8 mins, Cook time: 10 mins, Servings: 4

Ingredients:

1 tbsp. extra virgin olive oil	cleaned and soaked
	2 tbsps. lemon juice
1 onion, sliced	Salt and pepper, to
2 lbs. black mussels,	taste

Instructions:

1. Press the Sauté button on the Instant Pot and heat the oil.
2. Sauté the onion for 1 minute until fragrant.
3. Add the mussels and drizzle with lemon juice, sprinkle with salt and pepper. Stir until well combined.
4. Lock the lid. Select the Manual mode and cook for 10 minutes at Low Pressure.
5. Once cooking is complete, do a quick pressure release. Carefully open the lid.
6. Serve warm.

Nutritional info:

Calories 144, Fat 4.4g, Carbs 6.7g, Protein 19.2g

Tomato Mussels

Prep Time: 8 mins, Cook Time: 8 mins, Servings: 2

Ingredients:

1 cup diced tomatoes
2 lbs. cleaned and rinsed fresh mussels
½ cup white wine
Salt, to taste
½ tbsp. ground black pepper
½ tbsp. dried parsley

Instructions:

1. Put the tomatoes into the Instant Pot with the juices and add the wine, salt, pepper, and parsley.
2. Place the mussels in a steamer basket and lower it to the liquid.
3. Lock the lid. Select the Manual mode and cook for 3 minutes at Low Pressure.
4. Once cooking is complete, do a quick pressure release. Carefully open the lid.
5. Serve warm.

Nutritional info:

Calories 274, Carbs 5.5g, Fat 8.5g, Protein 32g

Spicy Prawns

Prep Time: 6 mins, Cook Time: 5 mins, Servings: 4

Ingredients:

1 tbsp. red pepper flakes
3 garlic cloves, minced
3 tbsps. olive oil
½ lb. prawns
1 tbsp. butter, melted
¼ cup water
Salt and pepper, to taste

Instructions:

1. Place all the ingredients in the Instant Pot.
2. Lock the lid. Select the Manual mode and cook for 5 minutes at Low Pressure.
3. Once cooking is complete, do a quick pressure release. Carefully open the lid.
4. Transfer to a large plate and serve.

Nutritional info:

Calories 174, Carbs 2.4g, Protein 8.9g, Fat 15.2g

Lemon Blue Crab with Herbs

Prep Time: 10 mins, Cook Time: 3 mins, Servings: 2

Ingredients:

1 lb. frozen blue crab
½ cup water
⅓ cup dry white wine
1 sprig thyme
1 sprig rosemary
Sea salt and ground black pepper, to taste
½ lemon, cut into wedges

Instructions:

1. Place all the ingredients except for the lemon wedges in the Instant Pot.
2. Lock the lid. Select the Manual mode and cook for 3 minutes at High Pressure.
3. Once cooking is complete, do a quick pressure release. Carefully open the lid.
4. Garnish with the lemon wedges on top and serve.

Nutritional info:

Calories 362, Fat 17g, Carbs 4g, Protein 2g

Boiled Garlic Clams

Prep Time: 7 mins, Cook time: 6 mins, Servings: 4

Ingredients:

1 cup water
½ cup freshly chopped parsley
2 tbsps. olive oil
6 garlic cloves
50 scrubbed small clams
Salt and pepper, to taste

Instructions:

1. Press the Sauté button on the Instant Pot and heat the olive oil. Sauté the garlic until fragrant and slightly browned.
2. Add the clams, water, and parsley. Sprinkle salt and pepper for seasoning.
3. Lock the lid. Select the Manual mode and cook for 6 minutes at Low Pressure.
4. Once cooking is complete, do a quick pressure release. Carefully open the lid.
5. Serve warm.

Nutritional info:

Calories 89, Fat 2.8g, Carbs 0.9g, Protein 11.3g

Orange-Butter Sea Bass

Prep Time: 3 mins, Cook Time: 18 mins, Servings: 2

Ingredients:

1 tbsp. safflower oil	½ orange, juiced
½ lb. sea bass	1 tbsp. tamari sauce
Sea salt, to taste	1 clove garlic, minced
¼ tsp. white pepper	1 tbsp. melted butter
1 cup water	½ tsp. dried dill weed

Instructions:

1. Press the Sauté button on the Instant Pot and heat the safflower oil.
2. Sear the sea bass for about 2 minutes on each side. Sprinkle the salt and white pepper to season.
3. Add the water and steamer rack to the Instant Pot, then transfer the sea bass to the steamer rack.
4. Lock the lid. Select the Steam mode and cook for 10 minutes at Low Pressure.
5. Once cooking is complete, do a quick pressure release. Carefully open the lid. Transfer the sea bass to a plate and set aside.
6. Add the orange juice, tamari sauce, garlic, butter, and dill weed to the cooking liquid in the Instant Pot, and stir to incorporate.
7. Press the Sauté button again and allow to simmer, or until the sauce is thickened.
8. Spoon the sauce over the sea bass and serve warm.

Nutritional info:

Calories 226, Fat 14g, Carbs 3g, Protein 22g

Chapter 5 Poultry Recipe

Salsa Chicken

Prep Time: 6 mins, Cook Time: 6 mins, Servings: 2

Ingredients:

½ cup chicken broth	fillets
½ cup salsa	1 oz. taco seasoning
1 lb. chicken breast	mix

Instructions:

1. On a clean work surface, rub the chicken with taco seasoning.
2. Add the chicken to the Instant Pot. Pour in the chicken broth and salsa.
3. Lock the lid. Select the Manual mode and cook for 6 minutes at High Pressure.
4. Once cooking is complete, do a natural pressure release for 5 minutes, then release any remaining pressure. Carefully open the lid.
5. Remove from the pot to a large plate. Shred the chicken and pour salsa on top before serving.

Nutritional info:

Calories 300, Fat 4.8g, Carbs 13.9g, Protein 45.9g

Garlicky Greek Chicken

Prep Time: 6 mins, Cook Time: 12 mins, Servings: 4

Ingredients:

1 tsp. dried oregano	3 minced garlic
1 sliced lemon	cloves
3 tbsps. extra-virgin olive oil	½ cup of water
1 lb. chicken thighs	Salt and pepper, to taste

Instructions:

1. Put all the ingredients in the Instant Pot and stir well.
2. Lock the lid. Select the Poultry mode and cook for 12 minutes at High Pressure.
3. Once cooking is complete, do a natural pressure release for 6 minutes, then release any remaining pressure. Carefully open the lid.
4. Let the chicken thighs cool for 5 minutes, then serve.

Nutritional info:

Calories 298, Carbs 2.1g, Protein 16.5g, Fat 23.3g

Cajun Chicken with Zucchini

Prep Time: 12 mins, Cook Time: 10 to 15 mins, Servings: 6
Ingredients:

1 lb. skinless chicken drumsticks
½ tsp. Cajun seasoning
1 small red bell pepper, sliced
1½ tsps. olive oil, divided
1 small zucchini, sliced

Instructions:
1. Select the Sauté mode and heat 1 teaspoon olive oil.
2. Add the chicken drumsticks and bell pepper and cook for 4 to 5 minutes per side until evenly browned. Transfer to a plate and set aside.
3. Heat the remaining olive oil in the Instant Pot.
4. Add the zucchini slices and Cajun and sauté for 2 to 3 minutes until crisp.
5. Remove from the pot and serve the chicken with zucchini on a plate.

Nutritional info:
Calories 154, Fat 8g, Carbs 3g, Protein 17g

Chicken Peas Rice

Prep Time: 12 mins, Cook Time: 15 mins, Servings: 4
Ingredients:

1 chopped small onion
4 oz. chicken breasts
2 cups white rice
1 tsp. olive oil
½ cup green peas
2 cups water

Instructions:
1. Press the Sauté button on the Instant Pot and heat the oil.
2. Add the chicken breasts and sauté for 6 to 7 minutes until lightly browned. Set aside on a plate.
3. Add the onions and cook 3 to 4 minutes until translucent.
4. Add the rice, 2 cups water, and green peas, and mix well.
5. Lock the lid. Select the Manual mode and cook for 4 minutes at Low Pressure.
6. Once cooking is complete, do a natural pressure release for 5 minutes, then release any remaining pressure. Carefully open the lid.
7. Serve the rice with the chicken breasts.

Nutritional info:
Calories 274, Fat 5g, Carbs 23g, Protein 34g

Chicken Coconut Curry

Prep Time: 12 mins, Cook Time: 30 mins, Servings: 6
Ingredients:

2 large onions, chopped
7 oz. chicken breasts
2 tbsps. green curry paste
1 tbsp. olive oil
¾ cup reduced-fat coconut milk
2 cups water

Instructions:
1. Press the Sauté button on the Instant Pot and heat the oil.
2. Add the chicken breast and sauté for 2 to 3 minutes per side.
3. Stir in the onions and cook for 3 to 4 minutes more until softened.
4. Pour in the milk and 2 cups water. Add the curry paste and stir well.
5. Lock the lid. Select the Manual mode and cook for 10 minutes at High Pressure.
6. Once cooking is complete, do a natural pressure release for 5 minutes, then release any remaining pressure. Carefully open the lid.
7. Remove from the pot and serve on plates.

Nutritional info:
Calories 232, Fat 7g, Carbs 1g, Protein 34g

Chicken Cacciatore

Prep Time: 6 mins, Cook time: 12 mins, Servings: 6
Ingredients:

1 bay leaf
½ cup pitted black olives
6 chicken drumsticks
2 cups tomato purée
Salt and pepper, to taste
1 cup water

Instructions:
1. Place all ingredients in the Instant Pot and stir well.
2. Lock the lid. Select the Manual mode and cook for 12 minutes at High Pressure.
3. Once cooking is complete, do a natural pressure release for 8 minutes, then release any remaining pressure. Carefully open the lid.
4. Allow to cool for a few minutes before serving.

Nutritional info:
Calories 256, Fat 13.2g, Carbs 9.5g, Protein 25.3g

Classic Lemon Chicken

Prep Time: 12 mins, Cook Time: 10 mins, Servings: 4

Ingredients:

4 chicken thighs
2 tbsps. fresh lemon juice
1 medium red onion, sliced

2 tsps. olive oil
1 garlic clove, crushed
1 cup water

Instructions:

1. Line a baking pan with parchment paper and set aside.
2. In a mixing bowl, thoroughly mix olive oil and lemon juice. Add the chicken thighs and toss to coat. Transfer to the baking pan and top with the garlic and onion slices.
3. Pour 1 cup water into the Instant Pot. Arrange a steamer basket inside it and place the baking pan on the basket.
4. Lock the lid. Select the Manual mode and cook for 6 minutes at High Pressure.
5. Once cooking is complete, do a quick pressure release. Carefully open the lid.
6. Allow to cool for 5 minutes before serving.

Nutritional info:

Calories 173, Fat 11g, Carbs 4g, Protein 14g

Garlicky Chicken

Prep Time: 12 mins, Cook time: 15 mins, Servings: 4

Ingredients:

5 garlic cloves, minced
4 chicken breasts, halved

3 tbsps. coconut oil
Salt and pepper, to taste
1 cup water

Instructions:

1. Press the Sauté button on the Instant Pot and heat the coconut oil. Sauté the garlic for 3 minutes until fragrant, then stir in the chicken breasts. Sprinkle pepper and salt for seasoning. Pour in the water.
2. Lock the lid. Select the Manual mode and cook for 6 minutes at High Pressure.
3. Once cooking is complete, do a natural pressure release for 5 minutes, then release any remaining pressure. Carefully open the lid.
4. Serve the chicken while warm.

Nutritional info:

Calories 591, Fat 37.5g, Carbs 1.1g, Protein 60.8g

Instant Pot Pesto Chicken

Prep Time: 12 mins, Cook time: 10 mins, Servings: 4

Ingredients:

4 chicken breasts
¼ cup extra virgin olive oil
Salt and pepper, to taste

2 cups basil leaves
5 sun-dried tomatoes
1 cup water, if needed

Instructions:

1. Put the basil leaves, olive oil, and tomatoes in the food processor until smooth. Season with salt and people to taste. Add a cup of water if needed.
2. Place the chicken in the Instant Pot. Pour the sauce over the chicken.
3. Lock the lid. Select the Manual mode and cook for 8 minutes at High Pressure.
4. Once cooking is complete, do a natural pressure release for 6 minutes, then release any remaining pressure. Carefully open the lid.
5. Transfer to a large plate and serve warm.

Nutritional info:

Calories 556, Fat 32.7g, Carbs 1.1g, Protein 60.8g

Chili Lime Chicken

Prep Time: 12 mins, Cook time: 6 mins, Servings:5

Ingredients:

6 garlic cloves, minced
1 tbsp. chili powder
1 tsp. cumin
1 lb. skinless and

boneless chicken breasts
1 ½ limes, juiced
1 cup water

Instructions:

1. In the Instant Pot, add the chicken breasts, garlic, chili powder, cumin, lime juice, salt, pepper, and water.
2. Lock the lid. Select the Manual mode and cook for 6 minutes at High Pressure.
3. Once cooking is complete, do a natural pressure release for 5 minutes, then release any remaining pressure. Carefully open the lid.
4. Cool for 5 minutes and serve warm.

Nutritional info:

Calories 166, Fat 8.5g, Carbs 1.5g, Protein 19.3g

Instant Pot Emergency Broccoli Chicken

Prep Time: 12 mins, Cook time: 10 mins, Servings: 4

Ingredients:

¼ cup soy sauce
1 head broccoli florets
1 tbsp. coconut oil

1½ lbs. chicken breasts, sliced
3 minced garlic cloves

Instructions:

1. Press the Sauté button on the Instant Pot and heat the oil. Sauté the garlic until fragrant, about 2 minutes.
2. Stir in the chicken breasts, broccoli florets, and soy sauce.
3. Lock the lid. Select the Manual mode and cook for 8 minutes at High Pressure.
4. Once cooking is complete, do a natural pressure release for 5 minutes, then release any remaining pressure. Carefully open the lid.
5. Serve the chicken with broccoli florets on a plate.

Nutritional info:

Calories 263, Fat 15.4g, Carbs 1.8g, Protein 28.6g

Spiced Chicken Drumsticks

Prep Time: 6 mins, Cook time: 15 mins, Servings: 10 to 12

Ingredients:

¼ tsp. dried thyme
1½ tbsps. paprika
Salt and pepper, to taste

½ tsp. onion powder
12 chicken drumsticks
2 cups water

Instructions:

1. On a clean work surface, rub the chicken drumsticks generously with the spices. Season with salt and pepper.
2. Transfer the chicken to the Instant Pot and add the water.
3. Lock the lid. Select the Poultry mode and cook for 15 minutes at High Pressure.
4. Once cooking is complete, do a natural pressure release for 8 minutes, then release any remaining pressure. Carefully open the lid.
5. Remove from the pot to a plate and serve.

Nutritional info:

Calories 218, Fat 12.1g, Carbs 2.5g, Protein 23.8g

Whole Roasted Chicken with Lemon and Rosemary

Prep Time: 2 hours, Cook time: 25 to 30 mins, Servings: 12

Ingredients:

1 (5 to 6 pounds) whole chicken
6 minced garlic cloves
Salt and pepper, to

taste
1 sliced lemon
1 rosemary sprig
1 cup water or chicken broth

Instructions:

1. On a clean work surface, rub the chicken with the minced garlic cloves, salt and pepper.
2. Stuff the lemon slices and rosemary sprig into the cavity of the chicken. Place the chicken into the Instant Pot and add the water or chicken broth.
3. Lock the lid. Select the Poultry mode and cook for 25 to 30 minutes at High Pressure.
4. Once cooking is complete, do a natural pressure release for 15 minutes, then release any remaining pressure. Carefully open the lid.
5. Remove the chicken from the pot and shred it. Serve immediately.

Nutritional info:

Calories 248, Fat 17.2g, Carbs 0.9g, Protein 21.3g

Easy Asian Chicken

Prep Time: 12 mins, Cook time: 10 mins, Servings: 5

Ingredients:

3 minced garlic cloves
¼ cup chicken broth
1½ lbs. boneless

chicken breasts
3 tbsps. soy sauce
1 tbsp. ginger slices

Instructions:

1. Place all ingredients in the Instant Pot. Give a good stir.
2. Lock the lid. Press the Poultry button and set the cooking time for 10 minutes.
3. Once cooking is complete, do a natural pressure release for 8 minutes, then release any remaining pressure. Carefully open the lid.
4. Garnish with chopped scallions and drizzle with sesame oil, if desired.

Nutritional info:

Calories 169, Fat 3.6g, Carbs 1.2g, Protein 30.9g

Chicken Curry

Prep Time: 6 mins, Cook time: 15 mins, Servings: 6

Ingredients:

2 cups freshly squeezed coconut milk
1½ lbs. boneless chicken breasts
2 cups chopped
tomatoes
2 tbsps. curry powder
1 ginger
Salt and pepper, to taste

Instructions:

1. Press the Sauté button on the Instant Pot. Add the chicken breasts and cook for 3 minutes until lightly golden. Season with salt and pepper.
2. Stir in the curry powder and continue cooking for 2 minutes more. Add the remaining ingredients and whisk well.
3. Press the Poultry button and set the cooking time for 10 minutes.
4. Once cooking is complete, do a natural pressure release for 6 minutes, then release any remaining pressure. Carefully open the lid.
5. Cool for 5 minutes and serve on plates.

Nutritional info:

Calories 336, Fat 22.4g, Carbs 7.4g, Protein 28.1g

Basil and Tomatoes Chicken Soup

Prep Time: 6 mins, Cook time: 20 mins, Servings: 4

Ingredients:

¼ cup fresh basil leaves
8 chopped plum tomatoes
4 skinless chicken
breasts, halved
Salt and pepper, to taste
5 cups water

Instructions:

1. Place all ingredients into the Instant Pot. Give a good stir to mix everything.
2. Lock the lid. Select the Manual mode and set the timer to 20 minutes at High Pressure.
3. Once cooking is complete, do a natural pressure release for 10 minutes, then release any remaining pressure. Carefully open the lid.
4. Let the soup cool for 10 minutes and serve warm.

Nutritional info:

Calories 431, Fat 7.2g, Carbs 22.4g, Protein 61.7g

Crispy Chicken Wings

Prep Time: 15 mins, Cook time: 15 mins, Servings: 8

Ingredients:

1 tbsp. paprika
1 tsp. rosemary leaves
Salt and pepper, to
taste
2 lbs. chicken wings
1 cup water

Instructions:

1. Put all the ingredients in the Instant Pot and stir well.
2. Lock the lid. Select the Manual mode and set the cooking time for 15 minutes at High Pressure.
3. Once cooking is complete, do a natural pressure release for 10 minutes, then release any remaining pressure. Carefully open the lid.
4. Transfer to a plate and serve.

Nutritional info:

Calories 148, Fat 4.1g, Carbs 1.1g, Protein 25.2g

Smoky Paprika Chicken

Prep Time: 5mins, Cook time: 15 mins, Servings: 6

Ingredients:

2 tbsps. smoked paprika
2 lbs. chicken breasts
Salt and pepper, to
taste
1 tbsp. olive oil
½ cup water

Instructions:

1. Press the Sauté button on the Instant Pot and heat the olive oil.
2. Stir in the chicken breasts and smoked paprika and cook for 3 minutes until lightly golden.
3. Season with salt and pepper and add ½ cup water.
4. Lock the lid. Select the Manual mode and cook for 12 minutes at High Pressure.
5. Once cooking is complete, do a natural pressure release for 8 minutes, then release any remaining pressure. Carefully open the lid.
6. Garnish with cilantro or scallions, if desired.

Nutritional info:

Calories 217, Fat 12.4g, Carbs 1.5g, Protein 34g

Lemony Fennel Chicken

Prep Time: 12 mins, Cook time: 12 mins, Servings: 8

Ingredients:

3 tbsps. freshly squeezed lemon juice
1 tsp. cinnamon
¼ cup fennel bulb
4 garlic cloves, minced

2 lbs. boneless and skinless chicken thighs
Salt and pepper, to taste
½ cup water

Instructions:

1. Place lemon juice, cinnamon, fennel bulb, garlic, and chicken thighs in the Instant Pot. Sprinkle pepper and salt for seasoning. Add ½ cup of water for moisture.
2. Lock the lid. Select the Manual mode and cook for 12 minutes at High Pressure.
3. Once cooking is complete, do a natural pressure release for 8 minutes, then release any remaining pressure. Carefully open the lid.
4. Remove the chicken from the pot and shred it, then serve.

Nutritional info:

Calories 257, Fat 18.8g, Carbs 1.9g, Protein 187g

Mexican Shredded Chicken

Prep Time: 12 mins, Cook time: 18 mins, Servings: 4

Ingredients:

½ tsp. paprika
3 lbs. chicken breasts
½ tsp. dried oregano
1 tbsp. chili powder

¼ tsp. cumin powder
Salt and pepper, to taste
2 cups water

Instructions:

1. Place all ingredients in the Instant Pot and whisk well.
2. Lock the lid. Select the Poultry mode and set the cooking time for 18 minutes at High Pressure.
3. Once cooking is complete, do a natural pressure release for 12 minutes, then release any remaining pressure. Carefully open the lid.
4. Remove the chicken breasts from the pot and shred them. Serve immediately.

Nutritional info:

Calories 196, Fat 10.5g, Carbs 0.1g, Protein 23.6g

Chinese Steamed Chicken

Prep Time: 6 mins, Coo time: 10 mins, Servings: 6

Ingredients:

1 tsp. grated ginger
1½ lbs. chicken thighs
1 tbsp. five-spice powder

¼ cup soy sauce
3 tbsps. sesame oil
1 cup water
Salt and pepper, to taste

Instructions:

1. In the Instant Pot, stir in all the ingredients.
2. Lock the lid. Select the Poultry mode and set the cooking time for 10 minutes at High Pressure.
3. Once cooking is complete, do a natural pressure release for 7 minutes, then release any remaining pressure. Carefully open the lid.
4. Serve the chicken thighs while warm.

Nutritional info:

Calories 236, Fat 11.3g, Carbs, 1.3g, Protein 31.3g

Broccoli Chicken with Black Beans

Prep Time: 10 mins, Cook Time: 25 mins, Servings: 4

Ingredients:

1 tbsp. olive oil
2 chicken breasts, skinless and boneless
1 cup broccoli florets
1½ cups chicken stock
2 tbsps. tomato

sauce
1 cup black beans, soaked overnight and drained
A pinch of salt and black pepper

Instructions:

1. Set your Instant Pot to Sauté and heat the olive oil. Add the chicken breasts and sauté for 5 minutes until lightly browned.
2. Add the remaining ingredients to the pot and stir well.
3. Lock the lid. Select the Poultry mode and cook for 20 minutes at High Pressure.
4. Once cooking is complete, do a natural pressure release for 10 minutes, then release any remaining pressure. Carefully open the lid.
5. Remove from the pot and serve on plates.

Nutritional info:

Calories 291, Fat 16g, Carbs 8g, Protein 16g

Sesame Chicken

Prep Time: 6 mins, Cook time: 25 mins, Servings: 12

Ingredients:

1½ cup soy sauce	or thighs
1 bay leaf	2 tbsps. toasted
2 packets dried star	sesame seeds
anise flowers	2 cups water
5 lbs. chicken breasts	

Instructions:

1. Place the chicken breasts, soy sauce, star anise flowers, and bay leaf into the Instant Pot.
2. Lock the lid. Select the Manual mode and set the cooking time for 25 minutes at High Pressure.
3. Once cooking is complete, do a natural pressure release for 15 minutes, then release any remaining pressure. Carefully open the lid.
4. Allow the chicken breasts cool for 5 minutes and serve.

Nutritional info:

Calories 159, Fat 3.5g, Carbs 5.4g, Protein 26.7g

Chicken Stew with Tomatoes

Prep Time: 13 mins, Cook time: 10 mins, Servings: 6

Ingredients:

1 ginger, sliced	tomatoes
3 garlic cloves,	1 lb. chicken breasts
minced	1 cup water
2 cups spinach leaves	Salt and pepper, to
1 cup chopped	taste

Instructions:

1. Press the Sauté button on the Instant Pot and add the chicken and garlic. Stir-fry for 3 minutes until the garlic becomes fragrant.
2. Add the ginger, tomatoes, spinach, and water. Season with salt and pepper.
3. Lock the lid. Select the Manual mode and set the cooking time for 6 minutes at High Pressure.
4. Once cooking is complete, do a natural pressure release for 5 minutes, then release any remaining pressure. Carefully open the lid.
5. Cool for a few minutes and serve warm.

Nutritional info:

Calories128, Fat 6.2g, Carbs 1.9g, Protein 15.6g

BBQ Chicken

Prep Time: 12 mins, Cook Time: 12 mins, Servings: 3

Ingredients:

½ cup barbecue	2½ tbsps. honey
sauce	½ cup chopped onion
2 lbs. chicken breasts	Salt and pepper, to
1 cup water	taste

Instructions:

1. In the Instant Pot, add all the ingredients and stir well.
2. Lock the lid. Select the Manual mode and set the timer to 12 minutes at High Pressure.
3. Once cooking is complete, do a natural pressure release for 5 minutes, then release any remaining pressure. Carefully open the lid.
4. Cook for a few minutes to thicken the sauce. Serve warm.

Nutritional info:

Calories 309, Carbs 47g, Fat 9g, Protein 11g

Creamy Chicken with Mushrooms

Prep Time: 12 mins, Cook time: 13 mins, Servings: 6

Ingredients:

4 garlic cloves,	6 boneless chicken
minced	breasts, halved
1 onion, chopped	½ cup coconut milk
1 cup mushrooms,	½ cup water
sliced	

Instructions:

1. Press the Sauté button on the Instant Pot and stir in the chicken breasts.
2. Fold in the onions and garlic and sauté for at least 3 minutes until tender. Season with salt and pepper. Add the remaining ingredients to the Instant Pot and whisk well.
3. Lock the lid. Select the Poultry mode and cook for 8 minutes at High Pressure.
4. Once cooking is complete, do a natural pressure release for 5 minutes, then release any remaining pressure. Carefully open the lid.
5. Allow to cool for 5 minutes before serving.

Nutritional info:

Calories 383, Fat 11.9g, Carbs 3.5g, Protein 62.2g

Eggplant and Chicken Sauté

Prep Time: 6 mins, Cook time: 10 mins, Servings: 6

Ingredients:

3 eggplants, sliced	1 lb. ground chicken
1 tbsp. coconut oil	Salt and pepper, to
1 tsp. red pepper flakes	taste

Instructions:

1. Press the Sauté button on the Instant Pot and heat the coconut oil.
2. Stir in the ground chicken and cook for 3 minutes until lightly golden.
3. Add the remaining ingredients and stir to combine.
4. Lock the lid. Select the Poultry mode and set the cooking time for 6 minutes at High Pressure.
5. Once cooking is complete, do a quick pressure release. Carefully open the lid.
6. Transfer to a large plate and serve warm.

Nutritional info:

Calories202, Fat 8.9g, Carbs 17.5g, Protein 16.7g

Simple Lime Turkey Wings

Prep Time: 10 mins, Cook Time: 30 mins, Servings:4

Ingredients:

1 tbsp. avocado oil	minced
1 yellow onion, chopped	1 cup chicken stock
2 turkey wings, halved	Lime juice and zest from 1 lime
4 garlic cloves,	A pinch of salt and black pepper

Instructions:

1. Set your Instant Pot to Sauté and heat the avocado oil. Sauté the onion for 2 minutes until translucent, stirring occasionally.
2. Add the remaining ingredients to the pot and mix well.
3. Lock the lid. Select the Poultry mode and set the cooking time for 28 minutes at High Pressure.
4. Once cooking is complete, do a natural pressure release for 10 minutes, then release any remaining pressure. Carefully open the lid.
5. Divide the turkey wings among plates and serve.

Nutritional info:

Calories 230, Fat 10g, Carbs 8g, Protein 17g

Broccoli Chicken with Parmesan

Prep Time: 8 mins, Cook Time: 5 mins, Servings: 2 to 3

Ingredients:

⅓ cup grated Parmesan cheese	3 cups cooked and shredded chicken
1 cup chicken broth	Salt and pepper, to
2 cups broccoli florets	taste
½ cup heavy cream	

Instructions:

1. In the Instant pot, add the broth, broccoli, chicken, salt, and pepper. Using a spatula, stir the ingredients.
2. Lock the lid. Select the Steam mode and cook for 3 minutes at High Pressure.
3. Once cooking is complete, do a quick pressure release. Carefully open the lid.
4. Set your Instant Pot to Sauté and stir in the cream.
5. Cook for 2 minutes. Transfer to a large plate and serve.

Nutritional info:

Calories 317, Carbs 6 g, Fat 23.5 g, Protein 34 g

Thyme Chicken with Brussels Sprouts

Prep Time: 10 mins, Cook Time: 25 mins, Servings: 4

Ingredients:

1 tbsp. olive oil	1 cup chicken stock
2 chicken breasts, skinless, boneless and halved	2 thyme springs, chopped
2 cups Brussels sprouts, halved	A pinch of salt and black pepper

Instructions:

1. Set your Instant Pot to Sauté and heat the olive oil. Add the chicken breasts and brown for 5 minutes.
2. Add the remaining ingredients to the pot and whisk to combine.
3. Lock the lid. Select the Poultry mode and set the cooking time for 20 minutes at High Pressure.
4. Once cooking is complete, do a natural pressure release for 10 minutes, then release any remaining pressure. Carefully open the lid.
5. Divide the chicken and Brussels sprouts among four plates and serve.

Nutritional info:

Calories 206, Fat 10g, Carbs 6g, Protein 17g

Ginger Chicken Congee

Prep Time: 12 mins, Cook Time: 25 mins, Servings: 4

Ingredients:

2 cups rice
8 medium chicken breasts
4 cups water
4-inch minced ginger

piece
1 chicken stock cube
Salt and pepper, to taste

Instructions:

1. Add the rice, water, chicken breasts, chicken stock, and ginger to the Instant Pot. Season with salt and pepper.
2. Lock the lid. Select the Poultry mode and set the cooking time for 25 minutes at High Pressure.
3. Once cooking is complete, do a natural pressure release for 10 minutes, then release any remaining pressure. Carefully open the lid. Serve warm.

Nutritional info:

Calories 218, Carbs 27.5 g, Fat 4 g, Protein 18 g

Fennel Chicken

Prep Time: 10 mins, Cook Time: 25 mins, Servings: 4

Ingredients:

2 tbsps. olive oil
2 tbsps. grated ginger
2 chicken breasts, skinless, boneless and halved

1 cup chicken stock
2 fennel bulbs, sliced
1 tbsp. basil, chopped
A pinch of salt and black pepper

Instructions:

1. Set your Instant Pot to Sauté and heat the olive oil. Cook the ginger and chicken breasts for 5 minutes until evenly browned.
2. Add the remaining ingredients to the pot and mix well.
3. Lock the lid. Select the Poultry mode and cook for 20 minutes at High Pressure.
4. Once cooking is complete, do a natural pressure release for 10 minutes, then release any remaining pressure. Carefully open the lid.
5. Allow the chicken cool for 5 minutes before serving.

Nutritional info:

Calories 220, Fat 12g, Carbs 7g, Protein 15g

Chicken Yogurt Salsa

Prep Time: 15 mins, Cook Time: 15 mins, Servings: 4

Ingredients:

1 medium jar salsa
½ cup water
1 cup plain Greek

yogurt
4 chicken breasts

Instructions:

1. Add all the ingredients to the Instant Pot. Using a spatula, gently stir to combine well.
2. Lock the lid. Select the Poultry mode and set the cooking time for 15 minutes at High Pressure.
3. Once cooking is complete, do a natural pressure release for 8 minutes, then release any remaining pressure. Carefully open the lid.
4. Transfer the cooked mixture to a salad bowl and serve warm.

Nutritional info:

Calories 314, Carbs 31 g, Fat 6.5 g, Protein 31 g

Chicken Wings and Scallions and Tomato Sauce

Prep Time: 10 mins, Cook Time: 25 mins, Servings:4

Ingredients:

1 tbsp. olive oil
6 scallions, chopped
A pinch of salt and black pepper

8 chicken wings
8 oz. tomato sauce
2 cups chicken stock
1 tomato, chopped

Instructions:

1. Set your Instant Pot to Sauté and heat the olive oil.
2. Add the scallions, salt, and pepper and sauté for 5 minutes, stirring occasionally.
3. Stir in the chicken wings and cook for 5 minutes until lightly browned. Add the remaining ingredients to the pot and stir well.
4. Lock the lid. Select the Manual mode and set the cooking time for 15 minutes at High Pressure.
5. Once cooking is complete, do a natural pressure release for 10 minutes, then release any remaining pressure. Carefully open the lid.
6. Remove from the pot to a plate and serve hot.

Nutritional info:

Calories 223, Fat 10g, Carbs 8g, Protein 10g

Filipino Chicken Adobo

Prep Time: 3 mins, Cook Time: 30 mins, Servings:4

Ingredients:

4 chicken legs	crushed
⅓ cup soy sauce	2 bay leaves
¼ cup white vinegar	1 onion, chopped
¼ cup sugar	Salt and pepper, to
5 cloves garlic,	taste

Instructions:

1. Add all the ingredients to your Instant Pot and stir to combine well.
2. Lock the lid. Select the Poultry mode and cook for 30 minutes at High Pressure.
3. Once cooking is complete, do a natural pressure release for 10 minutes, then release any remaining pressure. Carefully open the lid.
4. Divide the chicken legs among four plates and serve warm.

Nutritional info:

Calories 429, Fat 15g, Carbs 16g, Protein 53g

Paprika Chicken with Tomatoes

Prep Time: 10 mins, Cook Time: 20 mins, Servings:4

Ingredients:

1 tbsp. avocado oil	1 tbsp. smoked
1½ lbs. chicken	paprika
breast, skinless,	1 tsp. cayenne
boneless, and cubed	pepper
1 cup tomatoes,	A pinch of salt and
cubed	black pepper
1 cup chicken stock	

Instructions:

1. Set your Instant Pot to Sauté and heat the oil. Cook the cubed chicken in the hot oil for 2 to 3 minutes until lightly browned.
2. Add the remaining ingredients to the pot and stir well.
3. Lock the lid. Select the Poultry mode and set the cooking time for 18 minutes at High Pressure.
4. Once cooking is complete, do a natural pressure release for 10 minutes, then release any remaining pressure. Carefully open the lid.
5. Serve the chicken and tomatoes in bowls while warm.

Nutritional info:

Calories 228, Fat 9g, Carbs 7g, Protein 16g

Chicken with Artichokes and Bacon

Prep Time: 10 mins, Cook Time: 25 mins, Servings:4

Ingredients:

2 chicken breasts,	and crumbled
skinless, boneless,	1 cup water
and halved	2 tbsps. tomato paste
2 cups canned	1 tbsp. chives,
artichokes, drained,	chopped
and chopped	Salt, to taste
1 cup bacon, cooked	

Instructions:

1. Mix all the ingredients in your Instant Pot until well combined.
2. Lock the lid. Select the Poultry mode and set the cooking time for 25 minutes at High Pressure.
3. Once cooking is complete, do a natural pressure release for 10 minutes, then release any remaining pressure. Carefully open the lid.
4. Remove from the pot to a large plate and serve.

Nutritional info:

Calories 220, Fat 11g, Carbs 7g, Protein 10g

Lemon Garlic Chicken

Prep Time: 1 hour 20 mins, Cook time: 12 mins, Servings: 6

Ingredients:

3 tbsps. olive oil,	cloves
divided	1 tbsp. lemon juice
2 tsps. dried parsley	Salt and pepper, to
6 chicken breasts	taste
3 minced garlic	

Instructions:

1. Mix together 2 tablespoons olive oil, chicken breasts, parsley, garlic cloves, and lemon juice in a large bowl. Place in the refrigerator to marinate for 1 hour.
2. Press the Sauté button on the Instant Pot and heat the remaining olive oil.
3. Cook the chicken breasts for 5 to 6 minutes per side until cooked through.
4. Allow to cool for 5 minutes before serving.

Nutritional info:

Calories 341, Fat 17.9g, Carbs 0.7g, Protein 42.4g

Pomegranate-Glazed Turkey with Cranberries

Prep Time: 10 mins, Cook Time: 30 mins, Servings: 4

Ingredients:

2 tbsps. avocado oil	1 cup pomegranate
1 big turkey breast, skinless, boneless and sliced	juice
	1 bunch thyme, chopped
1 cup cranberries	A pinch of salt and
1 cup walnuts, chopped	black pepper

Instructions:

1. Press the Sauté button on the Instant Pot and heat the oil. Stir in the turkey slices and brown for 5 minutes.
2. Add the remaining ingredients to the pot and mix well.
3. Lock the lid. Select the Poultry mode and cook for 25 minutes at High Pressure.
4. Once cooking is complete, do a natural pressure release for 10 minutes, then release any remaining pressure. Carefully open the lid.
5. Remove from the pot and serve warm.

Nutritional info:

Calories 248, Fat 13g, Carbs 6g, Protein 16g

Classic Chicken Wings

Prep Time: 5 mins, Cook Time: 10 mins, Servings:4 to 5

Ingredients:

3 lbs. chicken wings	Kosher salt, to taste
1 cup water	2 cups wing sauce

Instructions:

1. Add the chicken wings and water to the Instant Pot. Sprinkle with the salt.
2. Pour the wing sauce into the pot and whisk to combine.
3. Lock the lid. Select the Manual mode and cook for 10 minutes at High Pressure.
4. Once cooking is complete, do a natural pressure release for 10 minutes, then release any remaining pressure. Carefully open the lid.
5. Allow the chicken wings cool for 5 minutes before serving.

Nutritional info:

Calories 444, Fat 12g, Carbs 8g, Protein 76g

Crispy Chicken with Herbs

Prep Time: 10 mins, Cook Time: 30 mins, Servings: 2 to 3

Ingredients:

2 tbsps. butter, softened	crushed
	½ tbsp. paprika
½ head of garlic, crushed	Salt and ground black pepper, to taste
1 thyme sprig, crushed	1½ lbs. whole chicken, patted dry
1 rosemary sprig,	2 cups water

Instructions:

1. Mix together the butter, garlic, thyme, rosemary, paprika, salt, and pepper in a shallow dish, and stir to incorporate.
2. Slather the butter mixture all over the chicken until well coated. Add the water and chicken to the Instant Pot.
3. Lock the lid. Select the Manual mode and cook for 20 minutes at High Pressure.
4. Once cooking is complete, do a natural pressure release for 10 minutes, then release any remaining pressure. Carefully open the lid.
5. Remove the chicken from the pot and place it under the broiler for 10 minutes, or until the skin is just lightly crisped. Serve warm.

Nutritional info:

Calories 492, Fat 2g, Carbs 70g, Protein 2g

Allspice Turkey Drumsticks

Prep Time: 5 mins, Cook Time: 20 mins, Servings: 2

Ingredients	¼ tsp. ground
1 lb. turkey drumsticks, boneless	allspice
	Sea salt and freshly
1 (6-oz) bottle beer	ground black pepper,
1 carrot, sliced	to taste
1 small leek, sliced	

Instructions:

1. Place all the ingredients in the Instant Pot and stir well.
2. Lock the lid. Select the Manual mode and cook for 20 minutes at High Pressure.
3. Once cooking is complete, do a natural pressure release for 10 minutes, then release any remaining pressure. Carefully open the lid.
4. Remove from the pot and serve on a plate.

Nutritional info:

Calories 17, Fat 4g, Carbs 50g, Protein 1g

Cheesy Chicken Tenders

Prep Time: 10 mins, Cook Time: 12 mins, Servings: 2

Ingredients:

1 tbsp. softened butter

1 lb. chicken tenders

½ cup vegetable broth

Sea salt and freshly ground black pepper, to taste

¼ tsp. smoked paprika

½ cup Cottage cheese, crumbled

1 heaping tbsp. fresh chives, roughly chopped

Instructions:

1. Press the Sauté button on your Instant Pot and melt the butter. Brown the chicken tenders for 2 to 3 minutes.
2. Add the broth, salt, black pepper, and paprika to the pot and whisk well.
3. Lock the lid. Select the Manual mode and set the cooking time for 8 minutes at High Pressure.
4. Once cooking is complete, do a natural pressure release for 5 minutes, then release any remaining pressure. Carefully open the lid.
5. Add the crumbled cheese to the pot, cover, and allow to sit for 5 minutes until melted.
6. Sprinkle the fresh chives on top for garnish before serving.

Nutritional info:

Calories 357, Fat 3g, Carbs 52g, Protein 2g

Cream Turkey Dinner

Prep Time: 12 mins, Cook Time: 15 mins, Servings: 3

Ingredients:

8 basil leaves, chopped

½ cup coconut cream

3 tbsps. olive oil, divided

5 garlic cloves,

minced

1lb. turkey breast, sliced

Salt and pepper, to taste

Instructions:

1. Season the meat with pepper and salt. Set aside for 10 minutes.
2. Press the Sauté button on the Instant Pot. Heat 2 tablespoons oil and add the meat. Cook for about 5 minutes until evenly browned, stirring occasionally.
3. Remove the meat from the pot to a plate.

4. Add the remaining olive oil and garlic to the pot.
5. Cook for 1 to 2 minutes until
6. Add the cream and let cook for 2 to 3 minutes.
7. Add the turkey and stir gently.
8. Lock the lid. Select the Manual mode and set the cooking time for 8 minutes at High Pressure.
9. Once cooking is complete, do a natural pressure release for 5 minutes, then release any remaining pressure. Carefully open the lid.
10. Top with the basil leaves before serving.

Nutritional info:

Calories 324, Carbs 11g, Fat 4g, Protein 35g

Thai Peanut Chicken

Prep Time: 6 mins, Cook time: 12 mins, Servings: 6

Ingredients:

2 tbsps. chopped scallions

Salt and pepper, to taste

1½ cups toasted peanuts, divided

2 garlic cloves, minced

1½ lbs. chicken breasts

1 cup water

Instructions:

1. Place 1 cup of toasted peanuts in a food processor and pulse until smooth. This will serve as your peanut butter.
2. On a flat work surface, chop the remaining toasted peanuts finely and set aside.
3. Press the Sauté button on the Instant Pot and add the chicken breasts and garlic. Keep on stirring for 3 minutes until the meat has turned lightly golden. Sprinkle pepper and salt for seasoning.
4. Pour in the prepared peanut butter and water. Give the mixture a good stir.
5. Lock the lid. Select the Poultry mode and set the cooking time for 8 minutes at High Pressure.
6. Once cooking is complete, do a natural pressure release for 5 minutes, then release any remaining pressure. Carefully open the lid.
7. Garnish with chopped peanuts and scallions before serving.

Nutritional info:

Calories 575, Fat 34.8g, Carbs 2.5g, Protein 42g

Balsamic Turkey and Onions

Prep Time: 10 mins, Cook Time: 30 mins, Servings: 4

Ingredients:

1 tbsp. olive oil	boneless and sliced
2 cups sliced red onions	1 cup chicken stock
2 tbsps. balsamic vinegar	2 tbsps. cilantro, chopped
2½ lbs. turkey breast, skinless,	A pinch of salt and black pepper

Instructions:

1. Set your Instant Pot to Sauté and heat the olive oil. Add the onions and balsamic vinegar and sauté for 5 minutes, stirring occasionally, or until the onions are translucent.
2. Stir in the turkey slices and brown for 5 minutes. Add the remaining ingredients to the pot and stir to incorporate.
3. Lock the lid. Select the Poultry mode and set the cooking time for 20 minutes at High Pressure.
4. Once cooking is complete, do a natural pressure release for 10 minutes, then release any remaining pressure. Carefully open the lid.
5. Transfer the turkey slices to plates and serve warm.

Nutritional info:
Calories 227, Fat 11g, Carbs 6g, Protein 18g

Sautéed Turkey with Cauliflower Purée

Prep Time: 12 mins, Cook Time: 10 mins, Servings: 4

Ingredients:

1 tsp. ground dried thyme	1 cup chopped cauliflower
½ tsp. garlic powder	1 tbsp. olive oil
1 tbsp. chopped fresh parsley	1 lb. turkey breasts
	1 cup water

Instructions:

1. Purée the cauliflower in a blender, then transfer the cauliflower purée to the Instant Pot.
2. Add the water, garlic powder, and thyme to the pot, and stir well.
3. Lock the lid. Select the Manual mode and cook for 3 minutes at High Pressure.
4. Once cooking is complete, do a quick pressure release. Carefully open the lid.

Drain and transfer the cauliflower purée to a bowl and set aside.

5. Set your Instant Pot to Sauté and heat the olive oil.
6. Add the turkey and cook for 3 to 4 on each side until evenly browned.
7. Remove from the pot and serve topped with cauliflower purée and parsley.

Nutritional info:
Calories 298, Fat 4g, Carbs 37g, Protein 31g

Turkey Rice Bowl

Prep Time: 12 mins, Cook Time: 25 mins, Servings: 6

Ingredients:

1 tbsp. olive oil	1½ cup brown rice
8 oz. turkey breasts	2 cups water
3 egg whites	¼ cup chopped spring onions
1 cubed carrot	

Instructions:

1. Press the Sauté button on the Instant Pot and heat the olive oil.
2. Add the turkey and cook for 4 to 5 minutes until evenly browned. Set aside on a plate.
3. Add the egg whites to the Instant Pot and cook for 2 minutes, then transfer to the plate of turkey.
4. Add 2 cups water, carrot cubes, and rice to the pot.
5. Lock the lid. Select the Rice mode and cook for 20 minutes at Low Pressure.
6. Once cooking is complete, do a natural pressure release for 10 minutes, then release any remaining pressure. Carefully open the lid.
7. Sprinkle with the spring onions and serve the turkey breasts over the rice.

Nutritional info:
Calories 167, Fat 3g, Carbs 16g, Protein 11g

Cashew Chicken with Sautéed Vegetables

Prep Time: 15 mins, Cook time: 20 mins, Servings: 6

Ingredients:

2 lbs. chicken breasts, thinly sliced	1 cup cubed red bell pepper
Salt and pepper, to taste	1 cup cashew nuts, toasted
1 head broccoli florets	½ cup water

Instructions:
1. Press the Sauté button on the Instant Pot. Stir in the chicken breasts and cook for 5 minutes. Sprinkle pepper and salt for seasoning. Pour in ½ cup water for additional moisture.
2. Press the Poultry button and set the cooking time for 10 minutes at High Pressure.
3. Once cooking is complete, do a quick pressure release. Carefully open the lid. Transfer the chicken breast to a large plate.
4. Press the Sauté button and stir in the broccoli and red bell pepper. Allow to simmer for 5 minutes. Scatter the toasted cashew nuts over the vegetables.
5. Serve the chicken breasts with sautéed vegetables on the side.

Nutritional info:
Calories 261, Fat 16.2g, Carbs 5.3g, Protein 23.7g

Thyme Duck and Chives

Prep Time: 10 mins, Cook Time: 20 mins, Servings: 4
Ingredients:

1 tbsp. avocado oil	chopped
2 duck breasts, boneless, skin scored and halved	2 tsps. thyme, dried
	A pinch of salt and black pepper
1 cup chicken stock	1 tbsp. chives,
1 yellow onion,	chopped

Instructions:
1. Press the Sauté button on the Instant Pot and heat the oil. Add the duck breasts (skin-side down) to the pot and sear for 2 minutes.
2. Add the chicken stock, onion, thyme, salt, and pepper to the pot. Stir well.
3. Lock the lid. Select the Poultry mode and cook for 18 minutes at High Pressure.
4. Once cooking is complete, do a natural pressure release for 10 minutes, then release any remaining pressure. Carefully open the lid.
5. Garnish with the chopped chives and serve.

Nutritional info:
Calories 294, Fat 16g, Carbs 5g, Protein 13g

Cilantro Turkey with Pomegranate Glaze

Prep Time: 10 mins, Cook Time: 30 mins, Servings: 4
Ingredients:

1 tbsp. olive oil	seeds
1 big turkey breast, skinless, boneless and sliced	1 tbsp. cilantro, chopped
	1 tbsp. sweet paprika
1 cup chicken stock	A pinch of salt and
1 cup pomegranate	black pepper

Instructions:
1. Set your Instant Pot to Sauté and heat the olive oil. Add the turkey slices and brown for 5 minutes, stirring occasionally.
2. Add the remaining ingredients to the Instant Pot and mix well.
3. Lock the lid. Select the Poultry mode and set the cooking time for 25 minutes at High Pressure.
4. Once cooking is complete, do a natural pressure release for 10 minutes, then release any remaining pressure. Carefully open the lid.
5. Remove from the pot to plates and serve.

Nutritional info:
Calories 262, Fat 7g, Carbs 8g, Protein 13g

Cheesy Jalapeño Chicken

Prep Time: 15 mins, Cook Time: 12 mins, Servings: 3
Ingredients:

1 lb. boneless chicken breast	8 oz. cream cheese
	Salt and pepper, to taste
3 jalapeños, sliced	
8 oz. Cheddar cheese	½ cup water
¾ cup sour cream	

Instructions:
1. Add ½ cup water, cream cheese, jalapeños, chicken breast, salt, and pepper to the pot. Stir to combine well.
2. Lock the lid. Select the Manual mode and set the cooking time for 12 minutes at High Pressure.
3. Once cooking is complete, do a natural pressure release for 8 minutes, then release any remaining pressure. Carefully open the lid.
4. Mix in the sour cream and Cheddar cheese, and serve warm!

Nutritional info:
Calories 528, Carbs 4.5 g, Fat 48.5 g, Protein 23 g

Chapter 6 Vegan and Vegetarian Recipe

Corn on Cob

Prep Time: 6 mins, Cook Time: 15 mins, Servings: 2

Ingredients:

2 cups water
2 ears corn
1 tbsp. vegan butter
Garlic salt, to taste

Instructions:

1. Add the water to the Instant Pot.
2. Put the steamer basket inside the pot.
3. Place the corn on top of the basket,
4. Lock the lid. Set the Instant Pot to Meat/Stew mode, then set the timer for 2 minutes at High Pressure.
5. Once cooking is complete, do a quick pressure release. Carefully open the lid.
6. Brush corn with vegan butter.
7. Sprinkle with a little garlic salt.
8. Serve as an appetizer or a side dish.

Nutritional info:

Calories 77, Fat 1.1g, Carbs 17.1g, Protein: 2.9g

Roasted Brussels Sprouts

Prep Time: 6 mins, Cook Time: 16 mins, Servings: 4

Ingredients:

2 tbsps. olive oil
1 onion, chopped
1 lb. Brussels sprouts
Salt and pepper, to
taste
½ cup vegetable broth

Instructions:

1. Set the Instant Pot to Sauté mode. Add the olive oil and sauté the onion for 2 minutes.
2. Sauté the Brussels sprouts for 1 minute.
3. Sprinkle salt and pepper on top.
4. Pour in the vegetable broth.
5. Lock the lid. Set the Instant Pot to Manual mode, then set the timer for 3 minutes at High Pressure.
6. Once cooking is complete, do a quick pressure release. Carefully open the lid.
7. Serve warm.

Nutritional info:

Calories 136, Fat 7.2g, Carbs 16.3g, Protein: 4.6g

Steamed Lemon Artichokes

Prep Time: 6 mins, Cook Time: 20 mins, Servings: 4

Ingredients:

1 cup water
2 garlic cloves, minced
Salt, to taste
1 bay leaf
4 artichokes, trimmed
2 tbsps. freshly squeezed lemon juice

Instructions:

1. Mix the water, garlic, salt and bay leaf inside the Instant Pot.
2. Place steamer basket in the pot.
3. Add the artichokes.
4. Drizzle each one with lemon juice.
5. Lock the lid. Set the Instant Pot to Steam mode, then set the timer for 10 minutes at High Pressure.
6. Once cooking is complete, do a quick pressure release. Carefully open the lid.
7. Remove outer petals and discard.
8. Discard the bay leaf, slice the artichokes into pieces and serve.

Nutritional info:

Calories 64, Fat 0.2g, Carbs 14.6g, Protein: 4.3g

Asparagus and Mushrooms

Prep Time: 4 mins, Cook time: 5 mins, Servings: 4

Ingredients:

1 lb. asparagus spears, trimmed
2 garlic cloves, minced
Salt and pepper, to
taste
¼ cup water
½ cup fresh mushrooms
1 tbsp. coconut oil

Instructions:

1. Press the Sauté button on the Instant Pot and heat the oil.
2. Add the garlic and sauté for 2 or 3 minutes until fragrant.
3. Add the asparagus spears and mushrooms.
4. Add salt and pepper and add the water.
5. Lock the lid. Set the Instant Pot to Manual mode, then set the timer for 5 minutes at High Pressure.
6. Once cooking is complete, do a quick pressure release. Carefully open the lid.
7. Serve warm.

Nutritional info:

Calories 61, Fat 3.6g, Carbs 6.5g, Protein 3.1g

Summer Beet Salad

Prep Time: 12 mins, Cook time: 6 mins, Servings: 6
Ingredients:

1 cup baby arugula	chopped
2 tbsps. extra virgin olive oil	4 medium-sized red beets, washed, peeled and cubed
Salt and pepper, to taste	1 cup water
1 large tomatoes,	

Instructions:
1. Place a trivet or the steamer rack in the Instant Pot and pour in the water.
2. Place the beets on the trivet.
3. Lock the lid. Set the Instant Pot to Steam mode, then set the timer for 6 minutes at High Pressure.
4. Once cooking is complete, do a quick pressure release. Carefully open the lid.
5. Take the beets out and allow to cool for a few minutes.
6. Assemble the salad by combining the steamed beets with the rest of the ingredients.
7. Serve chilled.

Nutritional info:
Calories 51, Fat 2.2g, Carbs 7.2g, Protein 1.4g

Coconut Cauliflower Rice

Prep Time: 6 mins, Cook time: 10 mins, Servings: 3
Ingredients:

1 onion, chopped	1 cauliflower head, grated
Salt and pepper, to taste	1 cup freshly squeezed coconut milk
3 garlic cloves, minced	

Instructions:
1. Put the cauliflower florets in a food processor and pulse to rice the cauliflower.
2. Place the riced cauliflower and remaining ingredients in the Instant Pot.
3. Lock the lid. Set the Instant Pot to Manual mode, then set the timer for 10 minutes at High Pressure.
4. Once cooking is complete, do a quick pressure release. Carefully open the lid.
5. Serve warm.

Nutritional info:
Calories 231, Fat 19.4g, Carbs 14.6g, Protein 4.4g

Chickpea and Lentil Salad

Prep Time: 50 mins, Cook Time: 3 hours, Servings: 4
Ingredients:

1 tbsp. olive oil	1 tsp. Herbes de Provence
12 oz. halved cherry tomatoes	2 cups vegetable broth
1 ½ cups chickpeas, soaked in water overnight, drained	1 cup green lentils
	1 cup water

Instructions:
1. In the Instant Pot, mix the olive oil, water and chickpeas.
2. Choose Manual mode and cook at High Pressure
3. Drain the chickpeas and set aside.
4. Add the lentils, vegetable broth and seasoning.
5. Lock the lid. Set the Instant Pot to Slow Cook mode, then set the timer for 3 hours at High Pressure.
6. Once cooking is complete, do a quick pressure release. Carefully open the lid.
7. Use a salad bowl to toss together chickpeas, tomatoes and lentils.

Nutritional info:
Calories 508, Fat 8.4g, Carbs 78.3g, Protein 31.9g

Instant Pot Veggie Stew

Prep Time: 6 mins, Cook time: 10 mins, Servings: 5
Ingredients:

½ cup chopped tomatoes	sliced
	1 onion, chopped
1 stalk celery, minced	Salt and pepper, to taste
2 zucchinis, chopped	
1 lb. mushrooms,	

Instructions:
1. Place all ingredients in the Instant Pot.
2. Pour in enough water until half of the vegetables are submerged.
3. Lock the lid. Set the Instant Pot to Manual mode, then set the timer for 10 minutes at High Pressure.
4. Once cooking is complete, do a quick pressure release. Carefully open the lid.
5. Serve warm.

Nutritional info:
Calories 281, Fat 0.9g, Carbs 71.2g, Protein 9.2g

Caramelized Onions

Prep Time: 6 mins, Cook time: 35 mins, Servings: 2

Ingredients:

1 tbsp. freshly squeezed lemon juice
3 tbsps. coconut oil
Salt and pepper, to taste
3 white onions, sliced
1 cup water

Instructions:

1. Press the Sauté button on the Instant Pot and heat the coconut oil.
2. Sauté the onions for 5 minutes and add the remaining ingredients.
3. Add the water and stir.
4. Lock the lid. Set the Instant Pot to Manual mode, then set the timer for 20 minutes at High Pressure.
5. Once cooking is complete, do a quick pressure release. Carefully open the lid.
6. Press the Sauté button and continue cooking for another 10 minutes.
7. Serve warm.

Nutritional info:

Calories 277, Fat 20.7g, Carbs 23.8g, Protein 2.8g

Onion Penne Pasta

Prep Time: 12 mins, Cook Time: 10 mins, Servings: 6

Ingredients:

3 cups water
12 oz. penne pasta
1 small onion, chopped
1 cup skim milk
1 tsp. olive oil

Instructions:

1. In the Instant Pot; add the water and pasta.
2. Lock the lid. Set the Instant Pot to Manual mode, then set the timer for 6 minutes at High Pressure.
3. Once cooking is complete, do a natural pressure release for 5 minutes. Carefully open the lid.
4. Drain water and transfer the cooked pasta in a container.
5. Press Sauté. Grease the pot with olive oil.
6. Add the onions and let cook for about 2 minutes until turn translucent and softened.
7. Add the milk and cook for 2 to 3 minutes.
8. Mix in the pasta and serve.

Nutritional info:

Calories 264, Fat 2g, Carbs 46g, Protein 11g

Instant Pot Steamed Asparagus

Prep Time: 5mins, Cook time: 5 mins, Servings: 1

Ingredients:

7 asparagus spears, washed and trimmed
¼ tsp. pepper
1 tbsp. extra virgin olive oil
Juice from freshly squeezed ¼ lemon
¼ tsp. salt
1 cup water

Instructions:

1. Place a trivet or the steamer rack in the Instant Pot and pour in the water.
2. In a mixing bowl, combine the asparagus spears, salt, pepper, and lemon juice.
3. Place on top of the trivet.
4. Lock the lid. Set the Instant Pot to Steam mode, then set the timer for 5 minutes at High Pressure.
5. Once cooking is complete, do a quick pressure release. Carefully open the lid.
6. Drizzle the asparagus with olive oil.

Nutritional info:

Calories 80, Fat 6.2g, Carbs 6.4g, Protein 1.5g

Instant Pot Mushrooms

Prep Time: 12 mins, Cook Time: 10 mins, Servings: 1

Ingredients:

½ cup water
4 oz. mushrooms, sliced
2 garlic cloves, minced
1 tbsp. olive oil
Salt and pepper, to taste

Instructions:

1. Pour water along with mushrooms in an Instant Pot.
2. Lock the lid. Set the Instant Pot to Manual mode, then set the timer for 5 minutes at High Pressure.
3. Once cooking is complete, do a quick pressure release. Carefully open the lid.
4. Drain the mushroom and then return back to the Instant Pot.
5. Now add olive oil to the pot and mix.
6. Press the Sauté function of the pot and let it cook for 3 minutes.
7. Sauté every 30 seconds.
8. Add the garlic and sauté for 2 minutes or until fragrant. Sprinkle with salt and pepper, then serve the dish.

Nutritional info:

Calories 153, Fat 14.4g, Carbs 5.7g, Protein 3.9g

Cauliflower Pasta

Prep Time: 12 mins, Cook Time: 20 mins, Servings: 6
Ingredients:

1 cup chopped cauliflower	pasta
2 tbsps. chopped green onions	1 tsp. olive oil
12 oz. vermicelli	1 small green chili pepper, chopped

Instructions:

1. In the Instant Pot; add the pasta and enough water to cover.
2. Lock the lid. Set the Instant Pot to Manual mode, then set the timer for 7 minutes at High Pressure.
3. Once cooking is complete, do a quick pressure release. Carefully open the lid.
4. Drain water and transfer the cooked pasta in a container.
5. Take the Instant Pot and place over dry kitchen surface; open its top lid and switch it on.
6. Press Sauté. Grease the pot with olive oil.
7. Add the cauliflower; cook for 7 to 8 minutes until turn softened.
8. Mix in the pasta and serve warm. Top with the green onions.

Nutritional info:
Calories 316, Fat 2g, Carbs 38g, Protein 4g

Chickpea Egg Bowl

Prep Time: 12 mins, Cook Time: 25 mins, Servings: 3
Ingredients:

2 tbsps. freshly chopped parsley	1 cup rinsed and drained chickpeas
2 boiled eggs, chopped	1 green onion, chopped
1 tbsp. lemon juice	

Instructions:

1. Add the chickpea and 1½ cups to the Instant Pot. Stir the ingredients to combine well.
2. Lock the lid. Set the Instant Pot to Manual mode, then set the timer for 12 minutes at High Pressure.
3. Once cooking is complete, do a quick pressure release. Carefully open the lid.
4. Mix in the remaining ingredients and serve.

Nutritional info:
Calories 267, Fat 6g, Carbs 34g, Protein 14g

Cauliflower Mushroom Risotto

Prep Time: 7 mins, Cook time: 10 mins, Servings: 3
Ingredients:

1 cup freshly squeezed coconut milk	1 onion, chopped
1 tbsp. coconut oil	1 lb. shiitake mushrooms, sliced
1 cauliflower head, cut into florets	Salt and pepper, to taste

Instructions:

1. Press the Sauté button and heat the coconut oil.
2. Sauté the onions for 3 minutes or until fragrant. Add the cauliflower and shiitake mushrooms.
3. Sprinkle salt and pepper for seasoning.
4. Add the coconut milk in three batches.
5. Allow to simmer for 10 minutes.
6. Garnish with chopped parsley if desired.

Nutritional info:
Calories 344, Fat 24.2g, Carbs 34g, Protein 6.3g

Chickpea Avocado Salad

Prep Time: 12 mins, Cook Time: 12 mins, Servings: 2
Ingredients:

1 cup soaked and rinsed chickpeas	2 tbsps. pomegranate seeds
1½ cup water	½ cup quinoa
¼ cup chopped avocado	1 tsp. rice vinegar

Instructions:

1. Add the chickpea and 1 cup of water to the Instant Pot. Stir to combine well.
2. Lock the lid. Set the Instant Pot to Manual mode, then set the timer for 10 minutes at High Pressure.
3. Once cooking is complete, do a quick pressure release. Carefully open the lid.
4. Drain water and set aside chickpea.
5. Add the quinoa and ½ cup of water to the Instant Pot. Stir to combine well.
6. Lock the lid, then set the timer for 1 minutes at High Pressure.
7. Once cooking is complete, do a natural pressure release. Carefully open the lid.
8. Drain and add quinoa with the chickpea.
9. Add the vinegar, pomegranate and avocado on top. Serve.

Nutritional info:
Calories 566, Fat 12g, Carbs 26g, Protein 25g

Mediterranean Couscous Salad

Prep Time: 50 mins, Cook time: 20 mins, Servings: 6

Ingredients:

2 tbsps. olive oil	1 tbsp. lemon juice
2 cups couscous	2 tomatoes, diced
4 cups water	1 cucumber, diced
Salt, to taste	

Instructions:

1. Select the Sauté function in the Instant Pot.
2. Add the olive oil.
3. Add the couscous.
4. Cook for 2 minutes.
5. Pour in the water.
6. Add the salt.
7. Lock the lid. Set the Instant Pot to Manual mode, then set the timer for 20 minutes at High Pressure.
8. Once cooking is complete, do a natural pressure release for 10 minutes, then release any remaining pressure. Carefully open the lid.
9. Fluff the couscous using a fork.
10. Toss in lemon juice, tomatoes and cucumber.

Nutritional info:

Calories 349, Fat 0.8g, Carbs 72.2g, Protein 12.1g

Coconut Cabbage

Prep Time: 6 mins, Cook time: 20 mins, Servings: 4

Ingredients:

2 cups freshly squeezed coconut milk	1 garlic bulb, crushed
1 halved onion	1 cabbage head, shredded
1 thumb-size ginger, sliced	Salt and pepper, to taste

Instructions:

1. In the Instant Pot, add all the ingredients. Stir to mix well.
2. Lock the lid. Set the Instant Pot to Manual mode, then set the timer for 20 minutes at High Pressure.
3. Once cooking is complete, do a quick pressure release. Carefully open the lid.
4. Serve warm.

Nutritional info:

Calories 331, Fat 28.9g, Carbs 19.7g, Protein 5.1g

Broccoli Cream Pasta

Prep Time: 12 mins, Cook Time: 15 mins, Servings: 7

Ingredients:

10 oz. rigatoni	chopped
½ cup heavy cream	1 cup grated Cheddar cheese
1 tsp. butter	
8 oz. broccoli,	

Instructions:

1. In the Instant Pot; add the pasta and enough water to cover.
2. Lock the lid. Set the Instant Pot to Manual mode, then set the timer for 7 minutes at High Pressure.
3. Once cooking is complete, do a quick pressure release. Carefully open the lid.
4. Drain water and transfer the cooked pasta in a container.
5. Take the Instant Pot and place over dry kitchen surface; open its top lid and switch it on.
6. Press Sauté.
7. Add and heat the butter in the Instant Pot.
8. Add the broccoli and cream; sauté for 3 to 4 minutes.
9. Add the cheese; cook for 7 minutes.
10. Mix in the pasta and serve.

Nutritional info:

Calories 263, Fat 17g, Carbs 23g, Protein 9g

Potato Mash

Prep Time: 15 mins, Cook Time: 8 mins, Servings: 4

Ingredients:

2 tbsps. coconut oil	1 tsp. ground nutmeg
4 medium potatoes	¼ cup coconut milk

Instructions:

1. Peel the potatoes and place them in the Instant Pot.
2. Add enough water to cover them.
3. Lock the lid. Set the Instant Pot to Manual mode, then set the timer for 8 minutes at High Pressure.
4. Once cooking is complete, do a quick pressure release. Carefully open the lid.
5. Drain any water present. Mash the potatoes.
6. Add the remaining ingredients.
7. Serve immediately!

Nutritional info:

Calories 210, Fat 7.2g, Carbs 34g, Protein 3.7g

Tangy Spinach Pasta

Prep Time: 12 mins, Cook Time: 16 mins, Servings: 5
Ingredients:

1 cup water	1 cup chopped
12 oz. fusilli pasta	spinach
1 tsp. olive oil	12 oz. diced
1 small onion,	tomatoes
chopped	

Instructions:

1. In the Instant Pot; add the water and pasta.
2. Lock the lid. Set the Instant Pot to Manual mode, then set the timer for 7 minutes at High Pressure.
3. Once cooking is complete, do a natural pressure release for 5 minutes. Carefully open the lid.
4. Drain water and transfer the cooked pasta in a container.
5. Press Sauté. Grease the pot with olive oil.
6. Add the onions and sauté for 4 minutes until turn translucent and softened.
7. Mix in the spinach and tomatoes; cook for 4 to 5 minutes.
8. Mix in the pasta and serve warm.

Nutritional info:
Calories 234, Fat 3g, Carbs 37g, Protein 9g

Steamed Paprika Broccoli

Prep Time: 6 mins, Cook time: 6 mins, Servings: 2
Ingredients:

¼ tsp. ground black	1 head broccoli, cut
pepper	into florets
1 tbsp. freshly	1 tbsp. paprika
squeezed lemon juice	1 cup water
¼ tsp. salt	

Instructions:

1. Place a trivet or the steamer rack in the Instant Pot and pour in the water.
2. Place the broccoli florets on the trivet and sprinkle salt, pepper, paprika, and lemon juice.
3. Lock the lid. Set the Instant Pot to Steam mode, then set the timer for 6 minutes at High Pressure.
4. Once cooking is complete, do a quick pressure release. Carefully open the lid.
5. Serve immediately.

Nutritional info:
Calories 22,Fat 0.5g, Carbs 4.7g, Protein1.3g

Pure Basmati Rice Meal

Prep Time: 12 mins, Cook Time: 10 mins, Servings: 4
Ingredients:

1 cup chopped	1 small onion, sliced
cauliflower	1 cup basmati rice
¼ cup chopped green	1 tsp. olive oil
onions	

Instructions:

1. Purée the cauliflower until smooth in a blender and set aside.
2. Press the Sauté bottom on the Instant Pot. Grease the pot with olive oil.
3. Add the onions and sauté for 3 minutes until translucent and softened.
4. Add the cauliflower purée, rice and green onions.
5. Lock the lid. Set the Instant Pot to Manual mode, then set the timer for 4 minutes at Low Pressure.
6. Once cooking is complete, do a natural pressure release. Carefully open the lid.
7. Transfer the cooked recipe on serving plates.
8. Serve warm.

Nutritional info:
Calories 183, Fat 4g, Carbs 34g, Protein 5g

Sesame Bok Choy

Prep Time: 6 mins, Cook Time: 4 mins, Servings: 4
Ingredients:

1 tsp. soy sauce	1 medium Bok choy
½ tsp. sesame oil	2 tsps. sesame seeds
1½ cups water	

Instructions:

1. Pour the water into the Instant Pot.
2. Place the Bok choy inside the steamer basket.
3. Lower the basket
4. Lock the lid. Set the Instant Pot to Manual mode, then set the timer for 4 minutes at High Pressure.
5. Once cooking is complete, do a quick pressure release. Carefully open the lid.
6. In a serving bowl, set in the Bok choy. Toss with the remaining ingredients to coat.
7. Serve immediately!

Nutritional info:
Calories 54, Fats 2g, Carbs 5g, Protein 3g

Mushroom Spinach Casserole

Prep Time: 12 mins, Cook Time: 20 mins, Servings: 3

Ingredients:

2 cups sliced button mushrooms
4 large eggs
1 small onion, chopped
1 cup water
7 oz. fresh spinach
¼ cup grated Parmesan cheese

Instructions:

1. In a mixing bowl, thoroughly mix the eggs and cheese.
2. Mix in the spinach, mushrooms, onion, and garlic.
3. Grease a baking pan and line with a parchment; add the mixture in the bowl.
4. Put the Instant Pot over dry kitchen surface; open its top lid and switch it on.
5. Pour the water in the Instant Pot. Arrange the trivet or steamer basket inside it; arrange the pan over the trivet/ basket.
6. Lock the lid. Set the Instant Pot to Manual mode, then set the timer for 20 minutes at High Pressure.
7. Once cooking is complete, do a quick pressure release. Carefully open the lid.
8. Transfer the cooked recipe on serving plates.
9. Serve warm.

Nutritional info:

Calories 563, Fat 24g, Carbs 8g, Protein 43g

Instant Pot Artichokes

Prep Time: 6 mins, Cook time: 30 mins, Servings: 8

Ingredients:

½ cup organic chicken broth
Salt and pepper, to taste
4 large artichokes,
trimmed and cleaned
1 onion, chopped
1 garlic clove, crushed

Instructions:

1. Place all ingredients in the Instant Pot.
2. Lock the lid. Set the Instant Pot to Manual mode, then set the timer for 30 minutes at High Pressure.
3. Once cooking is complete, do a quick pressure release. Carefully open the lid.
4. Serve the artichokes with lemon juice.

Nutritional info:

Calories 47, Fat 0.2g, Carbs 10.5g, Protein 3.1g

Coconut Milk Rice

Prep Time: 12 mins, Cook Time: 10 mins, Servings: 5

Ingredients:

1 cup jasmine rice
1 tsp. freshly grated ginger
1 tbsp. olive oil
1 cup water
1 onion, chopped
1 cup coconut milk

Instructions:

1. Take the Instant Pot and place over dry kitchen surface; open its top lid and switch it on.
2. Press Sauté and grease the pot with olive oil.
3. Add the onions and let cook for 2 to 3 minutes until turn translucent and softened.
4. Pour in the milk and stir the mix. Add the water and stir again; cook for 1 to 2 minutes.
5. Add the rice, ginger, and stir.
6. Lock the lid. Set the Instant Pot to Manual mode, then set the timer for 3 minutes at Low Pressure.
7. Once cooking is complete, do a natural pressure release. Carefully open the lid.
8. Transfer the cooked recipe on serving plates.
9. Serve the recipe warm.

Nutritional info:

Calories 134, Fat 8g, Carbs 9g, Protein 2g

Zucchini and Tomato

Prep Time: 12 mins, Cook Time: 10 Mins, Servings: 1

Ingredients:

¼ cup crumbled feta cheese
1 cup vegetable broth
Salt and pepper, to taste
½ cup fresh cherry tomatoes
1 fresh zucchini, chopped

Instructions:

1. Combine all the listed ingredients in the pot.
2. Lock the lid. Set the Instant Pot to Manual mode, then set the timer for 10 minutes at High Pressure.
3. Once cooking is complete, do a quick pressure release. Carefully open the lid.
4. Serve the chunky soup warm.

Nutritional info:

Calories 125, Fat 3.9g, Carbs 14.6g, Protein: 5g

Tomato Onion Rice

Prep Time: 12 mins, Cook Time: 12 mins, Servings: 4

Ingredients:

1 cup soaked and drained rice	1 tbsp. olive oil
2 tbsps. chopped parsley	1 red onion, chopped
	2 cups water
	1 tbsp. tomato paste

Instructions:

1. Take the Instant Pot and place over dry kitchen surface; open its top lid and switch it on.
2. Press Sauté. Grease the pot with olive oil.
3. Add the onions and sauté for 4 minutes until turn translucent and softened.
4. Add the rice and cook for another 3 to 4 minutes.
5. Add the water and tomato sauce.
6. Lock the lid. Set the Instant Pot to Manual mode, then set the timer for 4 minutes at Low Pressure.
7. Once cooking is complete, do a natural pressure release. Carefully open the lid.
8. Transfer the cooked recipe on serving plates.
9. Serve the recipe warm with some parsley on top.

Nutritional info:

Calories 146, Fat 4g, Carbs 14g, Protein 2g

Lemon Artichokes

Prep Time: 40 mins, Cook Time: 20 mins, Servings: 4

Ingredients:

1½ cups water	Juice of 1 lemon
2 artichokes, rinsed and trimmed	2 tbsps. Dijon mustard

Instructions:

1. Pour the water into the Instant Pot.
2. Place the artichokes inside the steamer basket, then drizzle the lemon juice over.
3. Arrange the basket in the Instant Pot.
4. Lock the lid. Set the Instant Pot to Manual mode, then set the timer for 20 minutes at High Pressure.
5. Once cooking is complete, do a quick pressure release. Carefully open the lid.
6. Serve immediately!

Nutritional info:

Calories 77, Fat 0.2g, Carbs 17g, Protein 5.3g

Broccoli and Mushrooms

Prep Time: 15 mins, Cook Time: 8 mins, Servings: 4

Ingredients:

2 tbsps. coconut oil	1 tbsp. soy sauce
1 cup sliced mushrooms	1 cup vegetable broth
2 cups broccoli florets	Salt and pepper, to taste

Instructions:

1. Set the Instant Pot to Sauté mode and add the coconut oil to melt.
2. Add the mushrooms and sauté for 4 to 5 minutes.
3. Add broccoli and soy sauce and sauté for 1 more minute.
4. Pour the broth over. Sprinkle with salt and pepper.
5. Lock the lid. Set the Instant Pot to Manual mode, then set the timer for 2 minutes at High Pressure.
6. Once cooking is complete, do a quick pressure release. Carefully open the lid.
7. Serve the veggies drizzled with the cooking liquid.
8. Serve immediately!

Nutritional info:

Calories 81, Fat 7g, Carbs 3.9g, Protein 2.1g

Graceful Vegetarian Recipe

Prep Time: 12 mins, Cook Time: 12 mins, Servings: 2

Ingredients:

2 tsps. olive oil	broth
1 cup shredded Cheddar cheese	Salt and pepper, to taste
2 cups broccoli florets	1 cup long grain uncooked white rice
1½ cups vegetable	

Instructions:

1. Grease an Instant Pot with olive oil and then add broth, rice, salt, and pepper.
2. Now add the broccoli.
3. Lock the lid. Set the Instant Pot to Manual mode, then set the timer for 12 minutes on High Pressure.
4. Once cooking is complete, do a quick pressure release. Carefully open the lid.
5. Add the cheese and stir twice.
6. Serve hot.

Nutritional info:

Calories 616, Fat 20.3g, Carbs 15g, Protein 3g

Sautéed Brussels Sprouts And Pecans

Prep Time: 4 mins, Cook time: 6 mins, Servings: 4
Ingredients:

¼ cup chopped pecans
2 garlic cloves, minced
Salt and pepper, to taste
2 tbsps. water
2 cups baby Brussels sprouts
1 tbsp. coconut oil

Instructions:
1. Press the Sauté button on the Instant Pot and heat the oil.
2. Sauté the garlic for 1 minute or until fragrant.
3. Add the Brussels sprouts. Sprinkle salt and pepper for seasoning.
4. Add the water.
5. Lock the lid. Set the Instant Pot to Manual mode, then set the timer for 3 minutes at High Pressure.
6. Once cooking is complete, do a quick pressure release. Carefully open the lid.
7. Add the pecans and set to the Sauté mode and sauté for 3 minutes or until the pecans are roasted.
8. Serve immediately.

Nutritional info:
Calories 98, Fat 8.1g, Carbs 6.3g, Protein 2.3g

Tomato and Tofu Bake

Prep Time: 12 mins, Cook Time: 4 mins, Servings: 4
Ingredients:

2 tbsps. jarred banana pepper rings
1 tofu block, crumbled
½ cup vegetable broth
1 tbsp. Italian seasoning
1 can undrained and diced tomatoes

Instructions:
1. In the Instant Pot, set in all ingredients.
2. Give the mixture a good stir to incorporate everything well.
3. Lock the lid. Set the Instant Pot to Manual mode, then set the timer for 4 minutes on High Pressure.
4. Once cooking is complete, do a quick pressure release. Carefully open the lid.
5. Serve immediately!

Nutritional info:
Calories 140, Fat 6g, Carbs 9g, Protein 11g

Cauliflower Mash

Prep Time: 12 mins, Cook time: 10 mins, Servings: 4
Ingredients:

1 cup water
1 cauliflower head, cut into florets
¼ tsp. salt
¼ tsp. ground black
pepper
¼ tsp. garlic powder
1 handful chopped chives

Instructions:
1. Set a trivet in the Instant Pot and pour in the water.
2. Place the cauliflower.
3. Lock the lid. Set the Instant Pot to Steam mode, then set the timer for 10 minutes at High Pressure.
4. Once cooking is complete, do a quick pressure release. Carefully open the lid.
5. Using a food processor, pulse the cauliflower.
6. Add the garlic powder, salt, and pepper.
7. Garnish with chives, then serve.

Nutritional info:
Calories 18, Fat 0.2g, Carbs 3.7g, Protein 1.3g

Vegetarian Smothered Cajun Greens

Prep Time: 6 mins, Cook time: 3 mins, Servings: 4
Ingredients:

2 tsps. crushed garlic
Salt and pepper, to taste
1 onion, chopped
6 cups raw greens
1 tbsp. coconut oil
1 cup water

Instructions:
1. Press the Sauté button on the Instant Pot and heat the coconut oil.
2. Sauté the onion and garlic for 2 minutes or until fragrant.
3. Add the greens and Sprinkle salt and pepper for seasoning.
4. Add the water.
5. Lock the lid. Set the Instant Pot to Manual mode, then set the timer for 3 minutes at High Pressure.
6. Once cooking is complete, do a quick pressure release. Carefully open the lid.
7. Sprinkle with red chili flakes, then serve.

Nutritional info:
Calories 70, Fat 3.8g, Carbs 8.2g, Protein 3.2g

Zucchini and Tomato Melange

Prep Time: 13 mins, Cook time: 10 mins, Servings: 4

Ingredients:

5 garlic cloves, minced
3 medium zucchinis, chopped
1 lb. puréed tomatoes
1 onion, chopped
1 tbsp. coconut oil
Salt and pepper, to taste
1 cup water

Instructions:

1. Place the tomatoes in a food processor and blend until smooth.
2. Press the Sauté button on the Instant Pot and heat the oil.
3. Sauté the garlic and onions for 2 minutes or until fragrant.
4. Add the zucchini and tomato purée.
5. Sprinkle salt and pepper for seasoning.
6. Add the water to add more moisture.
7. Lock the lid. Set the Instant Pot to Manual mode, then set the timer for 10 minutes at High Pressure.
8. Once cooking is complete, do a quick pressure release. Carefully open the lid.
9. Serve warm.

Nutritional info:

Calories 66, Fat 3.8g, Carbs 7.5g, Protein 2.1g

Puréed Chili Carrots

Prep Time: 25 mins, Cook time:5 mins, Servings: 4

Ingredients:

1½ cups water
1 tbsp. maple syrup
1 tbsp. coconut oil
1½ lbs. carrots, chopped
1 tsp. chili powder

Instructions:

1. Pour the water into the Instant Pot.
2. Place the chopped carrots inside the steamer basket.
3. Arrange the basket in the Instant Pot.
4. Lock the lid. Set the Instant Pot to Manual mode, then set the timer for 4 minutes on High Pressure.
5. Once cooking is complete, do a quick pressure release. Carefully open the lid.
6. Transfer the carrots along with the remaining ingredients to a food processor.
7. Process until puréed and smooth.
8. Serve immediately!

Nutritional info:

Calories 45, Fat 1g, Carbs 11g, Protein 1g

Zucchini and Bell Pepper Stir Fry

Prep Time: 6 mins, Cook time: 5 mins, Servings: 6

Ingredients:

2 large zucchinis, sliced
1 tbsp. coconut oil
4 garlic cloves, minced
2 red sweet bell
peppers, julienned
1 onion, chopped
Salt and pepper, to taste
¼ cup water

Instructions:

1. Press the Sauté button on the Instant Pot.
2. Heat the coconut oil and sauté the onion and garlic for 2 minutes or until fragrant.
3. Add the zucchini and red bell peppers.
4. Sprinkle salt and pepper for seasoning.
5. Pour in the water.
6. Lock the lid. Set the Instant Pot to Manual mode, then set the timer for 5 minutes at High Pressure.
7. Once cooking is complete, do a quick pressure release. Carefully open the lid.
8. Serve warm.

Nutritional info:

Calories 54, Fat 2.7g, Carbs 7.2g, Protein 1.8g

Eggplant, Zucchini, And Tomatoes

Prep Time: 6 mins, Cook time: 8 mins, Servings: 6

Ingredients:

3 zucchinis, sliced
1 eggplant, chopped
3 tbsps. olive oil
3 tomatoes, sliced
1 onion, diced
Salt and pepper, to taste
¼ cup water

Instructions:

1. Press the Sauté button on the Instant Pot and heat the olive oil.
2. Sauté the onions for 3 minutes or until translucent, then add the eggplants. Sauté for another 2 minutes.
3. Add the tomatoes and zucchini.
4. Sprinkle salt and pepper for seasoning.
5. Add the water.
6. Lock the lid. Set the Instant Pot to Manual mode, then set the timer for 6 minutes at High Pressure.
7. Once cooking is complete, do a quick pressure release. Carefully open the lid.
8. Serve warm.

Nutritional info:

Calories 92,Fat 6.8g, Carbs 7.9g, Protein1.3g

Instant Pot Baby Bok Choy

Prep Time: 9 mins, Cook time: 4 mins, Servings: 6

Ingredients:

1 tsp. peanut oil
1 lb. baby Bok choy, trimmed and washed
Salt and pepper, to taste
4 garlic cloves, minced
1 tsp. red pepper flakes
1 cup water

Instructions:

1. Press the Sauté button on the Instant Pot.
2. Heat the oil and sauté the garlic for 1 minute until fragrant.
3. Add the Bok choy and sprinkle salt and pepper for seasoning.
4. Pour in the water.
5. Lock the lid. Set the Instant Pot to Manual mode, then set the timer for 4 minutes at High Pressure.
6. Once cooking is complete, do a quick pressure release. Carefully open the lid.
7. Sprinkle with red pepper flakes, then serve.

Nutritional info:

Calories 273, Fat 4.7g, Carbs 53.2g, Protein 4.3g

Italian Vegetable Medley

Prep Time: 50 mins, Cook Time: 8 mins, Servings: 4

Ingredients:

1 cup water
1 tbsp. raisins
1 zucchini, sliced
1 eggplant, cubed
3 tbsps. olive oil
10 halved cherry tomatoes
2 potatoes, cubed
2 tbsps. raisins

Instructions:

1. In the Instant Pot, add the water. Add the potatoes and zucchini.
2. Lock the lid. Set the Instant Pot to Manual mode, then set the timer for 8 minutes on High Pressure.
3. Once cooking is complete, do a quick pressure release. Carefully open the lid.
4. Drain water and add olive oil.
5. Mix in the tomatoes and eggplant. Let cook for 2 minutes.
6. Top with the raisins before serving.

Nutritional info:

Calories 172, Fat 1g, Carbs 38.9g, Protein 6.3g

Vegetarian Mac and Cheese

Prep Time: 30 mins, Cook time: 4 mins, Servings: 10

Ingredients:

4 cups water
1 tsp. garlic powder
16 oz. elbow macaroni pasta
Salt and pepper, to taste
2 cups frozen mixed
vegetables
1 cup shredded Cheddar
1 cup milk
Fresh parsley, for garnish

Instructions:

1. To the Instant Pot, add the water, garlic powder and pasta. Sprinkle with salt and pepper.
2. Lock the lid. Set the Instant Pot to Manual mode, then set the timer for 4 minutes at High Pressure.
3. Once cooking is complete, do a quick pressure release. Carefully open the lid.
4. Add the vegetables, Cheddar and milk, then cover the pot and press Sauté.
5. Simmer until the vegetables have softened.
6. Garnish with fresh parsley and serve.

Nutritional info:

Calories 456, Fat 4.9g, Carbs 77.5g, Protein 22.1g

Quinoa and Veggies

Prep Time: 15 mins, Cook Time: 5 mins, Servings: 4

Ingredients:

1½ cups water
1 cup rinsed and drained uncooked quinoa
¼ cup crumbled feta cheese
Greek seasoning and olive oil mixture
¼ cup sliced cucumber
¼ cup diced black olives

Instructions:

1. Pour the water into the Instant Pot.
2. Add the quinoa.
3. Lock the lid. Set the Instant Pot to Manual mode, then set the timer for 1 minute at High Pressure.
4. Once cooking is complete, do a natural pressure release. Carefully open the lid.
5. In a bowl, mix cucumber and black olives.
6. Top with the quinoa and feta cheese.
7. Drizzle with the dressing, then serve.

Nutritional info:

Calories 233, Fat 10.9g, Carbs 28.1g, Protein 6.5g

Mango Tofu Curry

Prep Time: 15 mins, Cook Time: 35 mins, Servings: 2
Ingredients:

1 cup vegetable broth	tofu
1lb. vegetables, chopped	1 cup mango sauce
2 tbsps. curry paste	Salt and pepper, to taste
1lb. cubed extra firm	

Instructions:
1. Mix all the ingredients in the Instant Pot.
2. Lock the lid. Set the Instant Pot to Manual mode, then set the timer for 35 minutes at High Pressure.
3. Once cooking is complete, do a quick pressure release. Carefully open the lid.
4. Serve warm.

Nutritional info:
Calories 310, Carbs 20g, Fat 4g, Protein 37g

Stuffed Sweet Potatoes

Prep Time: 42 mins, Cook Time: 17 mins, Servings: 2
Ingredients:

1 cup cooked couscous	taste
2 sweet potatoes	1 cup cooked chickpeas
1 tbsp. olive oil	2 spring onions, chopped
1 tsp. paprika	
Salt and pepper, to	

Instructions:
1. Use a fork to pierce sweet potatoes.
2. To the Instant Pot, add enough water to cover.
3. Add the steamer rack inside and set the potatoes on top.
4. Lock the lid. Set the Instant Pot to Manual mode, then set the timer for 8 minutes on High Pressure.
5. Once cooking is complete, do a natural pressure release for 5 minutes. Carefully open the lid.
6. Set the sweet potato aside on a plate. Drain the pot.
7. While the Instant Pot is on Sauté mode, heat the olive oil. Set in chickpeas and paprika with salt and pepper.
8. Half the potatoes and mash the inside.
9. Add the chickpeas and couscous.
10. Top with the chopped spring onion and serve.

Nutritional info:
Calories 437, Fat 3.5g, Carbs 85.6g, Protein 16.5g

Garlic Baby Potatoes

Prep Time: 30 mins, Cook Time: 11 mins, Servings: 4
Ingredients:

1 tbsp. olive oil	1 cup vegetable stock
3 garlic cloves	Salt and pepper, to taste
2 lbs. baby potatoes	
1 sprig rosemary	

Instructions:
1. Hit the Sauté button in the Instant Pot.
2. Add the olive oil.
3. Add the garlic, baby potatoes and rosemary.
4. Brown the outside of the potatoes.
5. Pierce each potato with a fork.
6. Add the vegetable stock.
7. Lock the lid. Set the Instant Pot to Manual mode, then set the timer for 11 minutes at High Pressure.
8. Once cooking is complete, do a quick pressure release. Carefully open the lid.
9. Season with salt and pepper and serve.

Nutritional info:
Calories 135, Fat 0.2g, Carbs 29g, Protein 6g

Dump Cake

Prep Time: 12 mins, Cook Time: 25 mins, Servings: 2
Ingredients:

½ can apple pie filling	1 tbsp. butter
1 cup cake mix	1 cup water

Instructions:
1. Set butter in an oven to melt and then add to the cake mix.
2. Mix the ingredients well until lumpy.
3. Now pour the pie filling in it and mix well.
4. Now pour the water in the Instant Pot and adjust trivet on top.
5. Place the batter into a heatproof cake pan and adjust on top of the trivet.
6. Lock the lid. Set the Instant Pot to Manual mode, then set the timer for 25 minutes.
7. Once cooking is complete, do a natural pressure release for 10 minutes, then release any remaining pressure. Carefully open the lid.

Nutritional info:
Calories 635, Fat 18.7g, Carbs 114.5g, Protein 5.2g

Zucchini Bulgur Meal

Prep Time: 12 mins, Cook Time: 30 mins, Servings: 3

Ingredients:

1 cup bulgur	2 tsps. olive oil
1 tbsp. chopped fresh parsley	1 small onion, chopped
3 medium zucchinis, wedged	1½ cup water

Instructions:

1. Take the Instant Pot and place over dry kitchen surface; open its top lid and switch it on.
2. Add the bulgur and water to the Instant Pot.
3. Stir to combine well.
4. Lock the lid. Set the Instant Pot to Manual mode, then set the timer for 18 minutes at High Pressure.
5. Once cooking is complete, do a natural pressure release for 10 minutes, then release any remaining pressure. Carefully open the lid.
6. Drain water and set aside bulgur.
7. Press Sauté. Grease the pot with olive oil.
8. Add the onions; cook for 4 minutes until turn translucent and softened.
9. Add the zucchini and cook for 4 to 5 mins, stirring occasionally.
10. Add the bulgur to the pot and give it a good stir. Cook for 2 more minutes.
11. Serve warm with the parsley on top.

Nutritional info:

Calories 146, Fat 5g, Carbs 26g, Protein 4g

Couscous with Vegetables

Prep Time: 30 mins, Cook time: 10 mins, Servings: 3

Ingredients:

2 tsps. olive oil	2 cups couscous
1 onion, chopped	2 cups water
1 red bell pepper, chopped	Salt, to taste
1 cup grated carrot	½ tbsp. lemon juice

Instructions:

1. Grese the Instant Pot with olive oil. Add the onion.
2. Set to the Sauté mode and sauté the onion for 2 minutes.
3. Add the red bell pepper and carrot.
4. Cook for 3 minutes.
5. Add the couscous and water.
6. Season with salt.
7. Lock the lid. Set the Instant Pot to Manual mode, then set the timer for 2 minutes at High Pressure.
8. Once cooking is complete, do a natural pressure release. Carefully open the lid.
9. Fluff the couscous with a fork.
10. Drizzle with the lemon juice before serving.

Nutritional info:

Calories 477, Fat 0.9g, Carbs 99.4g, Protein 15.8g

Greek Style Beans

Prep Time: 10 hours, Cook time: 15 mins, Servings: 8

Ingredients:

8 cups water	crushed tomatoes
3 cups navy beans	1 garlic clove, peeled
Salt and pepper, to taste	¼ cup olive oil
28 oz. canned	1 onion, diced

Instructions:

1. In the Instant Pot, add the water and navy beans.
2. Season with a pinch of salt.
3. Soak for 10 hours.
4. Lock the lid. Set the Instant Pot to Bean/Chili mode, then set the timer for 3 minutes at High Pressure.
5. Once cooking is complete, do a natural pressure release. Carefully open the lid.
6. Set the beans in a bowl.
7. Set aside a cup of the cooking liquid. Drain the rest.
8. Select the Sauté mode and heat the olive oil. Add the tomatoes, garlic and onion to sauté for about 5 minutes.
9. Mix in the reserved cooking liquid.
10. Add the beans back.
11. Lock the lid. Set the Instant Pot to Bean/Chili mode, then set the timer for 5 minutes at High Pressure.
12. Once cooking is complete, do a natural pressure release. Carefully open the lid.
13. Add salt and pepper for seasoning.

Nutritional info:

Calories 352, Fat 7g, Carbs 55g, Protein 20.3g

Kale and Sweet Potatoes

Prep Time: 45 mins, Cook time: 6 mins, Servings: 4

Ingredients:

1 tbsp. tamari sauce
⅔ cup vegetable broth
1 sweet potato, cubed

2 cups chopped kale
8 oz. cubed tofu
Salt and pepper, to taste

Instructions:

1. Add tofu in the Instant Pot.
2. Drizzle with half of the tamari and the broth.
3. Cook for about 3 minutes on Sauté function.
4. Add the rest of the ingredients.
5. Lock the lid. Set the Instant Pot to Manual mode, then set the timer for about 3 minutes at High Pressure.
6. Once cooking is complete, do a quick pressure release. Carefully open the lid.
7. Serve immediately!

Nutritional info:

Calories 130, Fat 2.5g, Carbs 13g, Protein 11g

Stuffed Peppers

Prep Time: 20 mins, Cook Time: 8 mins, Servings: 4

Ingredients:

¼ cup tomato sauce
4 large bell peppers, trimmed
2 cup chopped tomatoes
Salt and pepper, to

taste
4 basil leaves, chopped
½ cup chopped olives
1 cup water

Instructions:

1. Using a bowl, mix basil leaves, olives and tomatoes.
2. Season with salt and pepper.
3. Stuff bell peppers with the mixture. Top with a drizzle of tomato sauce.
4. In the Instant Pot, add the water.
5. Add the steamer rack inside. Carefully lay the bell peppers.
6. Lock the lid. Set the Instant Pot to Manual mode, then set the timer for 8 minutes at High Pressure.
7. Once cooking is complete, do a quick pressure release. Carefully open the lid.
8. Serve warm.

Nutritional info:

Calories 77, Fat 2.3g, Carbs 14.4g, Protein 2.4g

Mushroom Rice Meal

Prep Time: 12 mins, Cook Time: 35 mins, Servings: 3

Ingredients:

2 tsps. olive oil
1 tbsp. white wine vinegar
1 small onion, chopped

1 cup wild rice
1 cup sliced button mushrooms
2 cups water

Instructions:

1. Take the Instant Pot and place over dry kitchen surface; open its top lid and switch it on.
2. Press Sauté. Grease the pot with olive oil.
3. Add the onions and let cook for 4 minutes until turn translucent and softened.
4. Add the mushrooms and cook for 8 to 10 minutes.
5. Pour in the vinegar; stir and cook for 1 minute more, then set aside the mixture in a bowl.
6. Add the water and rice.
7. Lock the lid. Set the Instant Pot to Manual mode, then set the timer for 20 minutes at Low Pressure.
8. Once cooking is complete, do a natural pressure release for 10 minutes, then release any remaining pressure. Carefully open the lid.
9. Transfer the cooked rice in a mushroom bowl.
10. Mix well and serve.

Nutritional info:

Calories 117, Fat 3g, Carbs 13g, Protein 3g

Instant Ratatouille

Prep Time: 20 mins, Cook Time: 10 mins, Servings: 4

Ingredients:

2 cups water	2 eggplants, sliced
2 medium zucchini, sliced	1 tbsp. olive oil
3 tomatoes, sliced	Salt and pepper, to taste

Instructions:

1. Pour the water into the Instant Pot.
2. In a baking dish, arrange a layer of the zucchini.
3. Top with a layer of the tomatoes.
4. Place a layer of eggplant slices on top.
5. Continue layering until you use all the ingredients.
6. Drizzle with olive oil.
7. Place the baking dish on the trivet and lower it.
8. Lock the lid. Set the Instant Pot to Manual mode, then set the timer for 10 minutes at High Pressure.
9. Once cooking is complete, do a quick pressure release. Carefully open the lid.
10. Sprinkle with salt and pepper and serve warm!

Nutritional info:

Calories 180, Fat 10g, Carbs 9.5g, Protein 2.5g

Chapter 7 Beef, Lamb and Pork Recipe

Beef and Cauliflower

Prep Time: 12 mins, Cook Time: 30 mins, Servings: 4

Ingredients:

1 tbsp. extra virgin olive oil	1 cup puréed tomato
1½ lbs. ground beef	6 cups cauliflower, cut into florets
1 tsp salt	1 cup water

Instructions:

1. Set the Instant Pot to Sauté setting, then add the olive oil and heat until shimmering.
2. Add the beef and sauté for 4 or 5 minutes or until browned.
3. Add the rest of the ingredients.
4. Lock the lid. Select the Manual setting and set the timer at 30 minutes on High Pressure.
5. When the timer beeps, press Cancel, then use a quick pressure release.
6. Carefully open the lid and allow to cool for a few minutes. Serve warm.

Nutritional info:

Calories 418, Carbs 13g, Fat 19g, Protein 47g

Sautéed Beef and Green Beans

Prep Time: 12 mins, Cook Time: 5 mins, Servings: 4

Ingredients:

1 tbsp. olive oil	7 oz. canned green beans
10 oz. fat removed beef sirloin	2 tbsps. soy sauce
2 spring onions, chopped	Salt and pepper, to taste

Instructions:

1. Press Sauté on the Instant Pot. Grease the pot with the olive oil.
2. Add the beef and sauté for 2 to 3 minutes to evenly brown.
3. Add the onions, green beans, and soy sauce, then sauté for another 2 to 3 minutes until the beans are soft. Sprinkle with salt and pepper.
4. Serve warm.

Nutritional info:

Calories 176, Fat 9g, Carbs 2g, Protein 14g

Beef and Corn Chili

Prep Time: 12 mins, Cook Time: 30 mins, Servings: 4
Ingredients:

1 tbsp. olive oil
2 small onions, chopped
2 small chili peppers, diced
¼ cup canned corn

10 oz. lean ground beef
3 cups water
Salt and pepper, to taste

Instructions:

1. Press Sauté on the Instant Pot. Heat the olive oil in the pot.
2. Add the onions, chili peppers, corn, and beef. Sauté for 2 to 3 minutes or until the onions are translucent and the peppers are softened.
3. Add the water to the Instant Pot, and sprinkle with salt and pepper. Mix to combine well.
4. Lock the lid. Press Meat/Stew. Set the timer to 20 minutes at High Pressure.
5. Once cooking is complete, press Cancel, then use a quick pressure release.
6. Open the lid, transfer them on 4 plates and serve.

Nutritional info:
Calories 94, Fat 5g, Carbs 2g, Protein 7g

Instant Pot Rib Roast

Prep Time: 6 mins, Cook Time: 2 hours 30 mins, Servings: 12
Ingredients:

5 lbs. beef rib roast
1 tsp. garlic powder
1 bay leaf
1 tbsp. olive oil

Salt and pepper, to taste
1 cup water

Instructions:

1. Put all the ingredients in the Instant Pot. Stir to mix well.
2. Lock the lid. Set the pot to Meat/Stew mode and set the timer to 2 hours 30 minutes at High Pressure.
3. Once cooking is complete, use a natural pressure release for 10 to 20 minutes, then release any remaining pressure.
4. Carefully open the lid. Allow to cool for a few minutes. Transfer them on a large plate and discard the bay leaf, then serve.

Nutritional info:
Calories 601, Fat 52.2g, Carbs 0.5g, Protein 32.3g

Italian Pork Cutlets

Prep Time: 6 mins, Cook Time: 20 mins, Servings: 6
Ingredients:

4 tbsps. olive oil
6 pork cutlets
Salt and pepper, to taste

1 tbsp. Italian herb mix
1½ cups water

Instructions:

1. In the Instant Pot, add all the ingredients. Stir to combine well.
2. Lock the lid. Press the Meat/Stew button and set the cooking time to 20 minutes at High Pressure.
3. Once cooking is complete, do a natural pressure release for 10 minutes, and then release any remaining pressure. Carefully open the lid.
4. Remove the meat and serve immediately.

Nutritional info:
Calories 322, Carbs 0.9g, Protein 19.4g, Fat 34.6g

Beef Meatballs with Tomato

Prep Time: 12 mins, Cook Time: 10 mins, Servings: 4
Ingredients:

1 lb. lean ground beef
2 large eggs
3 tbsps. all-purpose flour
Salt and pepper, to

taste
1 tbsp. olive oil
2 cups diced tomatoes
1 cup water

Instructions:

1. In a large bowl, thoroughly mix the beef, eggs, and flour, then sprinkle with salt and pepper. Mix well and make 6 meatballs of 1½ inch.
2. Grease a baking dish with olive oil and add the meatballs. Add the tomatoes and tightly wrap with a foil.
3. Pour the water in the Instant pot. Arrange the trivet or steamer basket inside, then place the dish on the trivet/basket.
4. Lock the lid. Press Manual. Set the timer to 10 minutes at High Pressure.
5. When the timer goes off, press Cancel, then use a quick pressure release.
6. Carefully open the lid. Allow to cool for a few minutes, then serve warm.

Nutritional info:
Calories 214, Fat 13g, Carbs 4g, Protein 18g

Lemon Beef Meal

Prep Time: 12 mins, Cook Time: 10 mins, Servings: 2

Ingredients:

1 tbsp. olive oil
2 beef steaks
½ tsp. garlic salt

1 garlic clove, crushed
2 tbsps. lemon juice

Instructions:

1. Press Sauté on the Instant Pot. Heat the olive oil in the pot until shimmering.
2. Add the beef and garlic salt and sauté for 4 to 5 minutes to evenly brown.
3. Add the garlic and sauté for 1 minute until fragrant.
4. Serve with lemon juice on top.

Nutritional info:

Calories 86, Fat 7g, Carbs 2g, Protein 2g

Cheesy Veal Steaks

Prep Time: 12 mins, Cook Time: 35 mins, Servings: 2

Ingredients:

1 tbsp. olive oil
2 fat removed veal steaks
1¼ cup water
2 cups cherry

tomatoes
3 tbsps. grated Cheddar cheese
¼ cup reduced fat coconut milk

Instructions:

1. Press Sauté on the Instant Pot. Grease the pot with the olive oil.
2. Add the steaks and sauté for 3 to 4 minutes to evenly brown.
3. Add 1 cup of water and mix well.
4. Lock the lid. Press Manual. Set the timer to 25 minutes at High Pressure.
5. When the timer beeps, press Cancel, then use a natural pressure release for 10 minutes, and then release any remaining pressure.
6. Open the lid, drain the liquid, transfer the steaks to a serving plate.
7. Clean the pot.
8. Press Sauté and add the tomatoes and ¼ cup of water and sauté for 3 to 4 minutes or until lightly wilted.
9. Stir in the cheese and milk, then cook until the cheese melts.
10. Pour them over the steaks and serve.

Nutritional info:

Calories 248, Fat 11g, Carbs 1g, Protein 27g

Beef Tenderloin with Cauliflower

Prep Time: 20 mins, Cook Time: 25 mins, Servings: 4

Ingredients:

1½ lbs. beef tenderloin
1 tsp. sea salt
1 tbsp. extra virgin olive oil

4 garlic cloves, finely chopped
4 cups cauliflower florets

Instructions:

1. On a clean work surface, slice the beef tenderloin into 1-inch thick slices and rub with salt.
2. Put the olive oil in the Instant Pot, set the Sauté setting.
3. Add and brown the beef for 4 to 5 minutes, then add the garlic and sauté for a minute.
4. Add the cauliflower.
5. Lock the lid. Set the Instant Pot to Manual mode and set the cooking time for 20 minutes at High Pressure.
6. Once cooking is complete, use a quick pressure release.
7. Carefully open the lid. Allow to cool for a few minutes. Transfer them on a large plate and serve immediately.

Nutritional info:

Calories 492, Carbs 13g, Fat 25g, Protein 52g

Black Bean Soup

Prep Time: 12 mins, Cook Time: 20 mins, Servings: 4

Ingredients:

2½ cups salsa
45 oz. canned black beans and juice
½ cup chopped

cilantro
1 garlic clove
2 cups water
2 tsps. ground cumin

Instructions:

1. In the Instant Pot, mix the salsa with black beans, cilantro, garlic, water, and cumin, stir to combine well.
2. Lock the lid. Select the Manual mode, then set the timer for 15 minutes at High Pressure.
3. Once the timer goes off, do a quick pressure release.
4. Carefully open the lid. Stir soup one more time, then ladle into bowls and serve.

Nutritional info:

Calories 184, Fat 8g, Carbs 20g, Protein 7g

Adobo Pork Chops

Prep Time: 6 mins, Cook Time: 15 mins, Servings: 5

Ingredients:

3 tbsps. olive oil	minced
1 lb. pork chops	½ cup soy sauce
¼ cup freshly	Salt and pepper, to
squeezed lemon juice	taste
3 garlic cloves,	¼ cup water

Instructions:

1. Coat the Instant pot with olive oil. Arrange the pork chops in the Instant Pot, then add the remaining ingredients.
2. Lock the lid. Press the Meat/Stew button and set the cooking time to 15 minutes at High Pressure.
3. Once cooking is complete, do a natural pressure release for 10 minutes, and then release any remaining pressure. Carefully open the lid.
4. Serve the pork chops on a large platter.

Nutritional info:

Calories 271, Carbs 2.3g, Protein, 18.2g, Fat 23.3g

Big Papa's Roast

Prep Time: 12 mins, Coo Time: 1 hour, Servings: 6

Ingredients:

3 lbs. beef chuck	crushed
roast	2 tbsps. extra virgin
2 tsps. salt	olive oil
6 peppercorns,	2 cups beef stock

Instructions:

1. On a clean work surface, rub the beef with salt and peppercorns.
2. Coat the Instant Pot with olive oil and set the Sauté setting. Heat the oil until shimmering.
3. Add and brown the beef roast for 4 to 5 minutes.
4. Pour in the beef stock.
5. Lock the lid. Set to Manual mode, set the cooking time for 60 minutes at High Pressure.
6. Once cooking is complete, use a natural pressure release for 10 minutes, then release any remaining pressure.
7. Carefully open the lid. Allow to cool for a few minutes. Transfer them on a large plate and serve immediately.

Nutritional info:

Calories 389,Carbs 11g, Fat 21g, Protein 34g

Sweet Apricot Beef

Prep Time: 12 mins, Cook Time: 30 mins, Servings: 4

Ingredients:

1½ lbs. beef	sliced thinly
tenderloin	½ cup chopped
1 tsp. sea salt	almonds
1 tbsp. coconut oil	1 cup water
4 apricots, pitted and	

Instructions:

1. On a clean work surface, sprinkle the beef with salt and cut into 1-inch thick slices.
2. Set the Instant Pot to Sauté setting, then add coconut oil and heat until melted.
3. Add the beef and sauté for 4 to 5 minutes or until browned.
4. Add the apricot and sauté for a minute. Add the chopped almonds. Pour in the water.
5. Lock the lid. Press the Manual setting and set the timer at 30 minutes at High Pressure.
6. When the timer beeps, press Cancel, then use a quick pressure release.
7. Carefully open the lid and allow to cool for a few minutes. Serve warm.

Nutritional info:

Calories 254, Carbs 7g, Fat 10g, Protein 33g

Mexican Pulled Pork

Prep Time: 6 mins, Cook Time: 1 hour, Servings: 12

Ingredients:

4 lbs. pork shoulder	1 tsp. cumin powder
1 tsp. cinnamon	1½ cups water
2 tsps. garlic powder	Salt and pepper, to
5 tbsps. coconut oil	taste

Instructions:

1. In the Instant Pot, add all the ingredients. Stir to combine well.
2. Lock the lid. Press the Meat/Stew button and set the cooking time to 1 hour at High Pressure.
3. Once cooking is complete, do a natural pressure release for 10 minutes, and then release any remaining pressure. Carefully open the lid.
4. Remove the meat and shred with two forks to serve.

Nutritional info:

Calories 364, Carbs 0.5g, Protein 20.4g, Fat 35.9g

Balsamic Pulled Pork Casserole

Prep Time: 6 mins, Cook Time: 8 hours, Servings: 4

Ingredients:

¼ tsp. balsamic vinegar
4 cups leftover pulled pork
¼ cup olive oil
Salt and pepper, to taste
4 eggs, beaten

Instructions:

1. In a mixing bowl, combine all ingredients until well incorporated.
2. Pour into the Instant Pot.
3. Lock the lid. Press the Slow Cook button and set the cooking time to 8 hours at High Pressure.
4. Once cooking is complete, perform a natural pressure release for 10 minutes, and then release any remaining pressure. Carefully open the lid.
5. Remove the pork from the pot and serve warm.

Nutritional info:

Calories 372, Carbs 2.1g, Protein 21.7g, Fat 32.2g

Corned Beef

Prep Time: 6 mins, Cook Time: 1 hour 30 mins, Servings: 4

Ingredients:

12 oz. beer
1 cup water
3 garlic cloves, minced
3 lbs. corned beef brisket
Salt and pepper, to taste

Instructions:

1. Pour the beer and water into the Instant Pot. Add the garlic and mix to combine well.
2. Put the steamer basket inside.
3. Add the beef to the basket and season with salt and pepper.
4. Cover the pot. Select the Meat/Stew mode and cook at High Pressure for 90 minutes.
5. Once cooking is complete, do a quick pressure release for 10 minutes, and then release any remaining pressure. Carefully open the lid.
6. Transfer the beef to a baking pan and cover it with foil.
7. Let it rest for 15 minutes before slicing to serve.

Nutritional info:

Calories 417, Fat 28.3g, Carbs 4.9g, Protein 27.7g

Sweet Potato Beef

Prep Time: 12 mins, Cook Time: 40 mins, Servings: 4

Ingredients:

1 tbsp. olive oil
1 lb. lean beef stew meat
4 cups low-sodium beef stock
1 small sweet potato,
diced
1 tomato, roughly chopped
2 bell peppers, sliced
Salt and pepper, to taste

Instructions:

1. Press Sauté on Instant Pot. Grease the pot with the olive oil.
2. Add the beef and sauté for 4 to 5 minutes to evenly brown.
3. Mix in the remaining ingredients.
4. Lock the lid. Press Manual. Set the timer to 35 minutes at High Pressure.
5. When the timer beeps, press Cancel, then use a quick pressure release.
6. Open the lid, transfer them in 4 plates and serve warm.

Nutritional info:

Calories 257, Fat 7g, Carbs 18g, Protein 29g

Blueberry Pork Yum

Prep Time: 12 mins, Cook time: 7 mins, Servings: 6

Ingredients:

1½ lbs. boneless pork chops
1 tbsp. sea salt
2 tbsps. extra virgin
olive oil
2 cups fresh blueberries
1 cup chicken stock

Instructions:

1. On a clean work surface, rub the chops with salt.
2. Set the Instant Pot to Sauté mode.
3. Add the olive oil to Instant Pot and heat until shimmering.
4. Add the pork and sear for 3 minutes until lightly browned.
5. Add the berries and chicken stock.
6. Lock the lid. Set the pot to Manual and set the timer for 7 minutes at High Pressure.
7. When the timer beeps, press Cancel, then use a quick pressure release.
8. Carefully open the lid. Allow to cool for a few minutes. Transfer them on a large plate and serve immediately.

Nutritional info:

Calories 364, Carbs 7g, Fat 15g, Protein 47g

Ginger Short Ribs

Prep Time: 12 mins, Cook Time: 25 mins, Servings: 6

Ingredients:

4 beef short ribs
1 tsp. salt
3 tbsps. extra virgin olive oil, plus 1 tbsp. for coating

1 large onion, diced
2-inch knob of ginger, grated
¾ cup water

Instructions:

1. On a clean work surface, rub the ribs with salt.
2. Lightly coat the Instant Pot with olive oil and set the setting to Sauté.
3. Add the onion and ginger, then sauté for a minute
4. Add the ribs and brown for 4 to 5 minutes. Pour in the water.
5. Lock the lid. Set to Manual mode and set the cooking time for 25 minutes at High Pressure.
6. Once cooking is complete, use a natural pressure release for 10 minutes, then release any remaining pressure.
7. Carefully open the lid. Allow to cool for a few minutes. Transfer them on a large plate and serve immediately.

Nutritional info:

Calories 454, Carbs 28g, Fat 18g, Protein 29g

Pork Chops and Peas

Prep Time: 12 mins, Cook time: 10 mins, Servings: 4

Ingredients:

1 tbsp. olive oil
4 pork chops
1 medium onion, chopped

1 cup peas
½ tsp. salt
1 tsp. curry powder

Instructions:

1. Coat the Instant Pot with olive oil and set to Sauté setting.
2. Add the pork chops and sear for 3 minutes or until lightly browned.
3. Add the onion and sauté for 1 to 2 minutes or until soft.
4. Add peas, salt and curry powder and sauté for 3 to 5 minutes or until peas are tender.
5. Serve them warm on a large plate.

Nutritional info:

Calories 399, Carbs 6g, Fat 18g, Protein 51g

Herbed Sirloin Tip Roast

Prep Time: 5 mins, Cook Time: 1 hour 30 mins, Servings: 6

Ingredients:

2 tbsps. mixed herbs
1 tsp. garlic powder
3 lbs. sirloin tip roast
1¼ tsps. paprika

1 cup water
Salt and pepper, to taste

Instructions:

1. In the Instant Pot, combine all the ingredients. Stir to mix well.
2. Lock the lid. Set the pot to Meat/Stew mode and set the timer to 1 hour 30 minutes at High Pressure.
3. Once cooking is complete, use a natural pressure release for 10 minutes, then release any remaining pressure.
4. Carefully open the lid. Allow to cool for a few minutes. Transfer them on a large plate and discard the bay leaf, then serve.

Nutritional info:

Calories 394, Fat 25.4g, Carbs 1.6g, Protein 37.7g

Coconut Pork

Prep Time: 20 mins, Cook Time: 25 mins, Servings: 4

Ingredients:

1 tbsp. extra virgin olive oil
4 pork chops

1 tbsp. grated ginger
1 tsp. sea salt
2 cups coconut milk

Instructions:

1. Lightly coat the Instant Pot with olive oil and select the setting to Sauté.
2. Add and brown the pork chops for 3 minutes.
3. Add the remaining ingredients to the pot. Stir to combine well.
4. Lock the lid. Set the Manual mode and set the cooking time to 25 minutes at High Pressure.
5. Once cooking is complete, use a natural pressure release for 10 minutes, then release any remaining pressure.
6. Carefully open the lid. Allow to cool for a few minutes. Transfer them on a large plate and serve immediately.

Nutritional info:

Calories 607, Carbs 13g, Fat 38g, Protein 52g

Bell Pepper and Beef

Prep Time: 12 mins, Cook time: 30 mins, Servings: 4

Ingredients:

1½ lbs. beef tenderloin
1 tsp. sea salt
4 green bell peppers, deseeded and stems removed
1 tbsp. extra virgin olive oil
1 red onion, peeled and diced
1 cup water

Instructions:

1. On a clean work surface, cut the beef into 1-inch thick slices, sprinkle with salt
2. Cut the bell peppers into ¼-inch slices.
3. Set Instant Pot to Sauté setting, then add extra virgin olive oil and heat until hot.
4. Add the beef and cook for 4 to 5 minutes or until browned.
5. Add peppers and onion, and sauté for 2 minutes. Pour in the water.
6. Lock the lid. Set the Instant Pot to the Manual setting and set the timer at 30 minutes at High Pressure.
7. When the timer beeps, press Cancel, then use a quick pressure release.
8. Carefully open the lid and allow to cool for a few minutes. Serve warm.

Nutritional info:

Calories 355, Carbs 24g, Fat 10g, Protein 39g

Fried Rice with Sausage and Egg

Prep Time: 12 mins, Cook Time: 15 mins, Servings: 2

Ingredients:

1 tsp. butter
2 oz. chorizo sausage, thinly sliced
2 large eggs, beaten
2 cups cooked rice
1 red bell pepper, chopped
Salt and pepper, to taste

Instructions:

1. Press Sauté on the Instant Pot. Heat the butter in the pot until melted.
2. Add the sausage and sauté for 2 to 3 minutes per side to evenly brown.
3. Add the beaten eggs and sauté for 2 to 3 minutes to scramble.
4. Add the rice and bell pepper. Sprinkle with salt and pepper. Sauté for 5 minutes; serve warm.

Nutritional info:

Calories 145, Fat 6g, Carbs 17g, Protein 6g

Smokey and Spicy Pork Roast

Prep Time: 6 mins, Cook Time: 1 hour, Servings: 12

Ingredients:

1 tbsp. cayenne pepper flakes
5 tbsps. olive oil
Salt and pepper, to taste
2 tbsps. liquid smoke
4 lbs. pork butt
1 cup water

Instructions:

1. Place all ingredients in the Instant Pot. Stir to combine well.
2. Lock the lid. Press the Meat/Stew button and set the cooking time to 1 hour at High Pressure.
3. Once cooking is complete, perform a natural pressure release for 10 to 20 minutes, and then release any remaining pressure. Carefully open the lid.
4. Remove the pork from the pot and serve warm.

Nutritional info:

Calories 456, Carbs 0.7g, Protein 32.9g, Fat 39g

Super Beef Chili

Prep Time: 12 mins, Cook Time: 8 mins, Servings: 4

Ingredients:

1 lb. ground beef
1½ tsps. sea salt
1 medium onion, chopped
2 cups tomato purée
2 cups zucchini,
peeled and rinsed, cut into 1-inch bites
1 cup water
1 tsp. chili spice powder

Instructions:

1. Select the Instant Pot to Sauté setting. Coat the pot with olive oil and heat until shimmering.
2. Add the beef, salt and onion, then sauté for 4 minutes or until the beef is lightly browned.
3. Add the tomato purée, zucchini, water and chili spice powder. Stir to mix well.
4. Lock the lid. Set the Instant Pot to Manual setting and set the timer for 8 minutes at High Pressure.
5. Once cooking is complete, use a quick pressure release.
6. Carefully open the lid. Allow to cool for a few minutes. Transfer them on a large plate and serve immediately.

Nutritional info:

Calories 399, Carbs 6g, Fat 18g, Protein 51g

Pork with Jasmine Rice

Prep Time: 20 mins, Cook Time: 25 mins, Servings: 8
Ingredients:

1 tbsp. extra virgin olive oil	1 tsp sea salt
2 lbs. pork roast, sliced into 1-inch bites	1 cup Jasmine rice
	2 cups crushed tomatoes
	1 cup water

Instructions:
1. Lightly coat the Instant Pot with olive oil and set the setting to Sauté.
2. Add and brown the pork for 3 minutes.
3. Add the remaining ingredients. Stir to combine well.
4. Lock the lid. Set the Manual mode and set the cooking time for 20 minutes at Low Pressure.
5. Once cooking is complete, use a natural pressure release for 10 minutes, then release any remaining pressure.
6. Carefully open the lid. Allow to cool for a few minutes. Transfer them on a large plate and serve immediately.

Nutritional info:
Calories 492, Carbs 13g, Fat 25g, Protein 52g

Creamy Pork Pasta

Prep Time: 12 mins, Cook Time: 5 mins, Servings: 4
Ingredients:

1 tbsp. olive oil	4 eggplant, stem removed, rinsed, cut into 1-inch slices
1 lb. ground pork	
1½ tsps. salt	
6 garlic cloves, finely sliced	1 cup heavy cream

Instructions:
1. Set the Instant Pot to Sauté setting. Grease with olive oil and heat until shimmering.
2. Add the pork, salt and garlic. Sauté for 3 minutes or until the meat has browned.
3. Add the eggplant and heavy cream. Stir to mix well.
4. Lock the lid. Set the Instant Pot to Manual setting and set the timer for 5 minutes at High Pressure.
5. Once cooking is complete, use a quick pressure release.
6. Carefully open the lid. Allow to cool for a few minutes. Transfer them on a large plate and serve immediately.

Nutritional info:
Calories 399, Carbs 6g, Fat 18g, Protein 51g

Pork and Sweet Potato

Prep Time: 20 mins, Cook Time: 25 mins, Servings: 8
Ingredients:

2 tbsps. extra virgin olive oil	1 tsp. sea salt
2 lbs. pork tenderloin, slice into 1-inch bites	2 sweet potatoes, peeled and quartered
	4 cups beef broth

Instructions:
1. Lightly coat the Instant Pot with the olive oil and set the Sauté mode.
2. Add the pork along with salt and brown for 3 minutes on all sides.
3. Add sweet potatoes with beef broth to the pot.
4. Set the setting to Manual mode and set the cooking time for 25 minutes at High Pressure.
5. Once cooking is complete, use a quick pressure release.
6. Carefully open the lid. Allow to cool for a few minutes. Transfer them on a large plate and serve immediately.

Nutritional info:
Calories 492,Carbs 22g, Fat 25g, Protein 52g

Bacon and Peas

Prep Time: 12 mins, Cook time: 30 mins, Servings: 4
Ingredients:

1 tbsp. extra virgin olive oil	1 tsp. sea salt
1 lb. bacon slices, sliced into quarters	2 cups peas
	1 tsp. black pepper
	1 cup water

Instructions:
1. Set the Instant Pot to Sauté setting, then add the olive oil and heat until hot.
2. Add the bacon and sauté for 5 to 6 minutes or until browned on both sides.
3. Add the remaining ingredients.
4. Lock the lid. Select the Manual setting and set the timer at 30 minutes at High Pressure.
5. When the timer beeps, press Cancel, then use a quick pressure release.
6. Carefully open the lid and allow to cool for a few minutes. Serve warm.

Nutritional info:
Calories 226, Carbs 33g, Fat 8g, Protein 6g

Pork Potato Lunch

Prep Time: 12 mins, Cook Time: 25 mins, Servings: 4

Ingredients:

1 tbsp. olive oil	beef stock
1 onion, chopped	1 medium sweet
10 oz. fat removed pork neck	potato, chopped
3 cups low-sodium	Salt and pepper, to taste

Instructions:

1. Press the Sauté bottom on the Instant Pot. Grease the pot with the olive oil.
2. Add the onion and sauté for 2 minutes until translucent and softened.
3. Add the beef and sauté for 4 to 5 minutes to evenly brown.
4. Add the stock and potatoes. Sprinkle with salt and pepper. Stir to mix well.
5. Lock the lid. Press Manual. Set the timer to 20 minutes at High Pressure.
6. When the timer beeps, press Cancel, then use a quick pressure release.
7. Open the lid, transfer them in a large plate and serve warm.

Nutritional info:

Calories 278, Fat 18g, Carbs 12g, Protein 18g

Canadian Bacon

Prep Time: 12 mins, Cook Time: 55 mins, Servings: 8

Ingredients:

½ lb. peameal bacon, slice into 2-inch bites	4 cups zucchini
1 medium onion, minced	4 tbsps. tomato paste
	1 tsp. salt
	4 cups water

Instructions:

1. Set the Instant Pot to Sauté function.
2. Add the bacon and onion, then sauté for 6 minutes until bacon has lightly browned.
3. In the Instant Pot, add the remaining ingredients.
4. Lock the lid. Select the Instant Pot to the Manual setting and set the cooking time to 35 minutes at High Pressure.
5. Once cooking is complete, use a natural pressure release for 20 minutes, and then release any remaining pressure.
6. Carefully open the lid. Allow to cool for a few minutes. Transfer them on a large plate and serve immediately.

Nutritional info:

Calories 485, Fat 11g, Protein 28g, Carbs 7g

Spicy Pulled Pork

Prep Time: 6 mins, Cook Time: 8 hours 5 mins, Servings: 3

Ingredients:

1 lb. boneless pork shoulder	1 tsp. paprika
1 tbsp. cayenne pepper	Salt and pepper, to taste
1 tsp. garlic	1 cup water
	1 cup coconut milk

Instructions:

1. Place the pork shoulder, cayenne pepper, garlic, and paprika in the Instant Pot.
2. Sprinkle with salt and pepper and pour the water.
3. Lock the lid. Press the Slow Cook button and set the time to 8 hours at High Pressure.
4. Once cooking is complete, perform a natural pressure release. Carefully open the lid.
5. Remove the meat from the pot and shred with two forks.
6. Return the meat to the Instant Pot and pour in the coconut milk.
7. Lock the lid. Press the Meat/Stew button and set the cooking time to 5 minutes at High Pressure.
8. Once cooking is complete, perform a natural pressure release for 10 minutes, and then release any remaining pressure. Carefully open the lid.
9. Remove the pork from the pot and serve warm.

Nutritional info:

Calories 298, Carbs 3.1g, Protein 20.1g, Fat 23.6g

Pork with Turnip

Prep Time: 20 mins, Cook Time: 25 mins, Servings: 4
Ingredients:

1 tbsp. extra virgin olive oil
2 lbs. pork tenderloin
1 tsp sea salt
1 turnip, peeled and

diced
2 carrots, peeled and diced
1 cup water

Instructions:

1. Lightly coat the Instant Pot with olive oil and set the setting to Sauté.
2. On a clean work surface, rub the pork with salt, slice into 1-inch slices, then add the pork to the pot and brown for 3 minutes.
3. Add the remaining ingredients.
4. Lock the lid. Set the pot to Manual and set the cooking time for 20 minutes at High Pressure.
5. Once cooking is complete, use a natural pressure release.
6. Carefully open the lid. Allow to cool for a few minutes. Transfer them on a large plate and serve immediately.

Nutritional info:
Calories 492, Carbs 13g, Fat 25g, Protein 52g

Garlic Prime Rib

Prep Time: 12 mins, Cook Time: 1 hour, Servings: 10
Ingredients:

2 tbsps. olive oil
10 garlic cloves, minced
4 lbs. prime rib roast

2 tsps. dried thyme
Salt and pepper, to taste
1 cup water

Instructions:

1. Press the Sauté button on the Instant Pot and heat the oil.
2. Add and sauté the garlic for 1 to 2 minutes until fragrant.
3. Add the prime rib roast and sear on all sides for 3 minutes until lightly browned.
4. Sprinkle with thyme, salt and pepper.
5. Pour in the water and remove the browning at the bottom.
6. Lock the lid. Set the pot to Meat/Stew mode and set the timer to 1 hour at High Pressure.
7. Once cooking is complete, use a natural pressure release for 10 minutes, then release any remaining pressure.

8. Carefully open the lid. Allow to cool for a few minutes. Transfer them on a large plate and serve immediately.

Nutritional info:
Calories 776, Fat 66.5g, Carbs 1.4g, Protein 40.6g

Easy Chinese Pork

Prep Time: 10 mins, Cook Time: 25 mins, Servings: 4
Ingredients:

4 tbsps. coconut oil
4 garlic cloves, minced
1 tbsp. fresh ginger
4 boneless pork

chops
2 tbsps. soy sauce
Salt and pepper, to taste
1 cup water

Instructions:

1. Press the Sauté button on the Instant Pot and heat the coconut oil until melted.
2. Add and sauté the garlic and ginger for 1 minutes or until fragrant.
3. Add the pork and sauté for 3 minutes or until lightly browned.
4. Pour in the soy sauce and water, then sprinkle salt and pepper for seasoning.
5. Lock the lid. Press the Meat/Stew button and set the cooking time to 20 minutes at High Pressure.
6. Once cooking is complete, perform a natural pressure release for 10 minutes, and then release any remaining pressure. Carefully open the lid.
7. Press the Sauté button and allow to simmer for 3 to 5 minutes or until the sauce has thickened. Keep stirring.
8. Allow to cool for a few minutes. Remove them from the pot and serve warm.

Nutritional info:
Calories 359, Carbs 1.5g, Protein 19.7g, Fat 41.6g

Pork Medallions and Mushrooms

Prep Time: 12 mins, Cook time: 8 mins, Servings: 4

Ingredients:

2 tsps. extra virgin olive oil	12 oyster mushrooms, quartered
4 pork medallions, rinsed and trimmed	1 onion, diced
1 tsp. salt	1 cup water

Instructions:

1. Set the Instant Pot to Sauté setting, then add the extra virgin olive oil and heat until the oil is shimmering.
2. Add the pork medallions and brown for 3 to 4 minutes.
3. Add the remaining ingredients.
4. Lock the lid. Select the Manual setting and set the timer to 8 minutes at High Pressure.
5. When the timer beeps, press Cancel, then use a quick pressure release.
6. Carefully open the lid. Allow to cool for a few minutes. Transfer them on a large plate and serve immediately.

Nutritional info:

Calories 624, Carbs 34g, Fat 44g, Protein 31g

Mustard Pork and Mushrooms

Prep Time: 6 mins, Cook Time: 35 mins, Servings: 6

Ingredients:

3 tbsps. butter	1 cup sliced mushrooms
2 lbs. pork shoulder	
3 tbsps. yellow mustard	Salt and pepper, to taste
1 cup water	

Instructions:

1. Press the Sauté button on the Instant Pot and heat the butter until melted.
2. Add the pork shoulder and mustard. Sauté for 3 minutes or until the pork is lightly browned.
3. Stir in water and mushrooms. Sprinkle salt and pepper for seasoning.
4. Lock the lid. Press the Meat/Stew button and set the cooking time to 30 minutes at High Pressure.
5. Once cooking is complete, perform a natural pressure release for 10 minutes, and then release any remaining pressure. Carefully open the lid.

6. Remove the pork from the pot and serve warm.

Nutritional info:

Calories 286, Carbs 0.3g, Protein 22.9g, Fat 20.8g

Gingered Beef Tenderloin

Prep Time: 12 mins, Cook Time: 1 hour, Servings: 8

Ingredients:

2 tbsps. olive oil	4 fillet mignon steaks
2 tbsps. minced garlic	¼ cup soy sauce
2 tbsps. thinly sliced ginger	Salt and pepper, to taste
	1 cup water

Instructions:

1. Press the Sauté button on the Instant Pot and heat the olive oil.
2. Sauté the garlic for 1 minute until fragrant.
3. Add the ginger and fillet mignon and allow to sear for 4 minutes or until lightly browned.
4. Drizzle with the soy sauce. Add salt and pepper to taste. Pour in a cup of water.
5. Lock the lid and select the Meat/Stew mode and set the timer to 1 hour at High Pressure.
6. Once cooking is complete, use a natural pressure release for 10 minutes, then release any remaining pressure.
7. Carefully open the lid. Allow to cool for a few minutes. Transfer them on a large plate and discard the bay leaf, then serve.

Nutritional info:

Calories 199, Fat 9.8g, Carbs 1.3g, Protein 24.8g

Instant Pot Rib

Prep Time: 6 mins, Cook Time: 8 hours, Servings: 3

Ingredients:

1 rack baby back rib
1 tbsp. smoked paprika
2 tbsps. olive oil
1 tbsp. onion powder
1 tbsp. garlic powder
Salt and pepper, to taste
½ cup water

Instructions:

1. Prepare a baking sheet. Lay on the ribs. Rub with paprika, olive oil, onion powder, garlic powder, salt, and pepper.
2. Place the well-coated rib in the Instant Pot. Pour in the water.
3. Lock the lid. Press the Slow Cook button and set the cooking time to 8 hours at High Pressure.
4. Once cooking is complete, perform a natural pressure release for 10 minutes, and then release any remaining pressure. Carefully open the lid.
5. Allow to cool for a few minutes. Remove the rib from the pot and serve warm.

Nutritional info:

Calories 1375, Carbs 6.4g, Protein 98.2g, Fat 104.7g

Mushroom and Beef Meal

Prep Time: 12 mins, Cook Time: 40 mins, Servings: 4

Ingredients:

1 lb. fat removed beef ribs
Salt, to taste
3 cups low-sodium beef stock
1 bacon slice, chopped
2 cups button mushrooms slices

Instructions:

1. On a clean work surface, rub the beef ribs with salt.
2. Add the ribs and stock to the Instant Pot. Stir to combine well.
3. Lock the lid. Press Manual. Set the timer to 30 minutes at High Pressure.
4. When the timer goes off, press Cancel, then use a natural pressure release for 10 minutes, and then release any remaining pressure.
5. Take out the beef and shred with a knife.
6. Put the shredded beef back to the pot, add the bacon and mushrooms; gently stir to combine.

7. Lock the lid. Press Manual. Set the timer to 7 minutes at High Pressure.
8. Once the timer goes off, press Cancel, then use a quick pressure release.
9. Open the lid, transfer them on 4 plates and serve.

Nutritional info:

Calories 318, Fat 27g, Carbs 3g, Protein 15g

Garlicky Beef

Prep Time: 12 mins, Cook time: 10 mins, Servings: 4

Ingredients:

1½ lbs. beef sirloin
1 tbsp. sea salt
1 tbsp. extra virgin olive oil
5 garlic cloves, chopped
1 cup heavy cream

Instructions:

1. On a clean work surface, rub the beef with salt.
2. Set the Instant Pot to Sauté mode. Add the olive oil and heat until shimmering.
3. Add the beef and sear for 3 minutes until lightly browned.
4. Add garlic and sauté for 30 seconds or until fragrant.
5. Mix in the heavy cream.
6. Lock the lid. Set the pot to Manual setting and set the timer for 10 minutes at High Pressure.
7. When the timer beeps, press Cancel, then use a natural pressure release for 10 minutes, and then release any remaining pressure.
8. Carefully open the lid. Allow to cool for a few minutes. Transfer them on a large plate and serve immediately.

Nutritional info:

Calories 402, Carbs 14g, Fat 6g, Protein 29g

Indian Roasted Pork

Prep Time: 6 mins, Cook Time: 8 hours, Servings: 3

Ingredients:

1 tbsp. olive oil	roughly chopped
1 lb. pork loin	1 onion, sliced
1 tsp. cumin	Salt and pepper, to
2 garlic cloves,	taste

Instructions:

1. Coat the Instant Pot with olive oil and add the pork loin. Set aside.
2. In a food processor, place the remaining ingredients.
3. Pulse until smooth then pour the mixture over the pork loin.
4. Lock the lid. Press the Slow Cook button and set the cooking time to 8 hours at High Pressure.
5. Once cooking is complete, perform a natural pressure release for 10 minutes, and then release any remaining pressure. Carefully open the lid.
6. Allow to cool for a few minutes. Remove them from the pot and serve warm.

Nutritional info:

Calories 321, Carbs 0.6g, Protein 19.5g, Fat 26.5g

Eggplant Lasagna

Prep Time: 15 mins, Coo Time: 45 mins, Servings: 7

Ingredients:

4 English eggplants, rinsed and stem removed	1 tsp. salt
	¾ cup shredded Mozzarella cheese
2 tbsps. olive oil	8 cups tomato sauce
1 lb. ground pork	

Instructions:

1. Slice eggplants into 1-inch slices and douse them in a bowl of water, squeeze slices and set aside.
2. Set the Instant Pot on Sauté setting. Heat the olive oil in the pot until shimmering.
3. Add pork and salt and sauté for 3 minutes or until lightly browned, remove from the pot.
4. Place half of the eggplant on the bottom of pot, pour in half of the tomato sauce, half of the pork and half of the Mozzarella cheese.

5. Top with remaining eggplants, tomato sauce, pork, and cheese.
6. Lock the lid. Set the Instant Pot to the Manual setting and set the time to 45 minutes at High Pressure.
7. Once cooking is complete, use a quick pressure release.
8. Carefully open the lid. Allow to cool for a few minutes. Transfer them on a large plate and serve immediately.

Nutritional info:

Calories 257, Carbs 16g, Fat 16g, Protein 16g

Rosemary Lamb

Prep Time: 12 mins, Cook Time: 30 mins, Servings: 4

Ingredients:

1 tbsp. olive oil	beef broth
2 lamb shanks	2 rosemary sprigs
2 bay leaves	Salt and pepper, to
2 onions, chopped	taste
3 cups low-sodium	

Instructions:

1. Press Sauté on the Instant Pot. Grease the pot with the olive oil.
2. Add the lamb and sauté for 4 to 5 minutes to evenly brown.
3. Add the onions and sauté for 4 minutes until translucent and softened.
4. Add the remaining ingredients and stir well.
5. Lock the lid. Press Manual. Set the timer to 20 minutes at High Pressure.
6. When the timer beeps, press Cancel, then use a natural pressure release for 10 minutes, and then release any remaining pressure.
7. Carefully open the top lid, transfer them on 4 serving plates.
8. Remove the rosemary sprigs and bay leaves. Serve warm.

Nutritional info:

Calories 318, Fat 17g, Carbs 3g, Protein 37g

Pork with Coconut Meat

Prep Time: 12 mins, Cook Time: 6 mins, Servings: 4

Ingredients:

1 tbsp. olive oil
½ lb. ground pork
1 tsp. salt
6 garlic cloves
2 cups tomato sauce
1 cup water
2 cups coconut meat

Instructions:

1. Set the Instant Pot to Sauté function. Coat the pot with olive oil and heat until the oil is shimmering.
2. Add pork to Instant Pot along with salt and garlic, then sauté for 3 minutes until lightly browned.
3. Add the tomato sauce and water.
4. Lock the lid. Set the Instant Port to Manual function and set the cooking time for 6 minutes at High Pressure.
5. Once cooking is complete, use a natural pressure release for 10 minutes, then release any remaining pressure.
6. Carefully open the lid. Allow to cool for a few minutes. Transfer them on a large plate and serve with coconut meat on top.

Nutritional info:

Calories 144, Fat 9g, Protein 5g, Carbs 12g

Mexican Chili Pork

Prep Time: 6 mins, Cook Time: 35 mins, Servings: 6

Ingredients:

3 tbsps. olive oil
2 tsps. minced garlic
2 lbs. pork sirloin, sliced
2 tsps. ground cumin
1 tbsp. red chili flakes
1 cup water
Salt and pepper, to taste

Instructions:

1. Press the Sauté button on the Instant pot and heat the olive oil until shimmering.
2. Add and sauté the garlic for 30 seconds or until fragrant.
3. Add the pork sirloin and sauté for 3 minutes or until lightly browned.
4. Add the cumin and chili flakes.
5. Pour in the water and sprinkle salt and pepper for seasoning.
6. Lock the lid. Press the Meat/Stew button and set the cooking time to 30 minutes at High Pressure.

7. Once cooking is complete, perform a natural pressure release for 10 minutes, and then release any remaining pressure. Carefully open the lid.
8. Remove the pork from the pot and serve warm.

Nutritional info:

Calories 159, Carbs 0.8g, Protein 21.1g, Fat 16.8g

Pear and Pork Butt

Prep Time: 12 mins, Cook time: 50 mins, Servings: 12

Ingredients:

4 lbs. pork butt
2 tbsps. sea salt
3 tbsps. extra virgin olive oil
4 pears, peeled, stem
removed, deseeded, and cut into ½-inch chunks
1½ cups chicken broth

Instructions:

1. On a clean work surface, rub the pork butt with salt.
2. Set the Instant Pot to Sauté setting, then add and heat the olive oil.
3. Place pork in pot and brown for 5 minutes per side.
4. Add pears and chicken broth. Stir to mix well.
5. Lock the lid. Set the pot to Manual setting and set the timer for 45 minutes at High Pressure.
6. When the timer beeps, press Cancel, then use a quick pressure release.
7. Carefully open the lid and allow to cool for a few minutes. Serve warm.

Nutritional info:

Calories 503, Carbs 9g, Fat 31g, Protein 44g

Basic Pork Chops

Prep Time: 6 mins, Cook Time: 30 mins, Servings: 6

Ingredients:

3 tbsps. butter
3 garlic cloves, minced
6 boneless pork chops
½ cup heavy cream
½ cup chicken broth
Salt and pepper, to taste

Instructions:

1. Press the Sauté button on the Instant Pot.
2. Heat the butter until melted and add and sauté the garlic for 1 minute or until fragrant.
3. Add the pork chops and sear for 3 minutes on each side until lightly browned.
4. Add the heavy cream and broth. Sprinkle salt and pepper for seasoning.
5. Lock the lid. Press the Meat/Stew button and set the cooking time to 30 minutes at High Pressure.
6. Once cooking is complete, perform a natural pressure release for 10 minutes, and then release any remaining pressure. Carefully open the lid.
7. Allow to cool for a few minutes. Remove the pork from the pot and baste with the juice remains in the pot before serving.

Nutritional info:

Calories 439, Carbs 0.9g, Protein 26.7g, Fat 46.2g

Pork Vindaloo (Curry Pork)

Prep Time: 6 mins, Cook Time: 35 mins, Servings: 6

Ingredients:

¼ cup coconut oil
2 lbs. pork shoulder, sliced
1 tbsp. garam masala
3 tbsps. freshly
squeezed lemon juice
1 cup water
Salt and pepper, to taste

Instructions:

1. Press the Sauté button on the Instant Pot and heat the coconut oil until melted.
2. Add and sear the pork loin on all sides for 3 minutes or until lightly browned.
3. Add the garam masala and continue sauté for 2 more minutes.
4. Stir in the lemon juice and water. Sprinkle with salt and pepper.

5. Lock the lid. Press the Meat/Stew button and set the cooking time to 30 minutes at High Pressure.
6. Once cooking is complete, perform a natural pressure release for 10 minutes, and then release any remaining pressure. Carefully open the lid.
7. Remove the pork from the pot and serve warm.

Nutritional info:

Calories 322, Carbs 0.4g, Protein 23.9g, Fat 25.2g

Sausage and Peppers

Prep Time: 12 mins, Cook time: 20 mins, Servings: 4

Ingredients:

1 tbsp. olive oil
4 links sausage
3 red bell peppers, deseeded, stem removed, and
julienned
1 cup chicken stock
1 tsp. Himalayan salt
1 onion, chopped
1 cup water

Instructions:

1. Set Instant Pot to Sauté setting, Heat the olive oil in the pot until shimmering.
2. Add the sausage and sauté for 8 to 10 minutes or until lightly browned on all sides.
3. Add bell peppers to the Instant Pot and sauté for 2 minutes.
4. Add the remaining ingredients.
5. Lock the lid. Press the Manual setting and set the timer to 20 minutes at High Pressure.
6. When the timer beeps, press Cancel, then use a quick pressure release.
7. Carefully open the lid and allow to cool for a few minutes. Serve warm.

Nutritional info:

Calories 273, Carbs 23g, Fat 12g, Protein 8g

Super Stew

Prep Time: 20 mins, Cook Time: 30 mins, Servings: 8

Ingredients:

1½ lbs. pork tenderloin

1 tsp. oregano

1 tsp. sea salt

2 tbsps. extra virgin

olive oil

4 cups crushed tomatoes

1 cup water

Instructions:

1. On a clean work surface, massage the pork tenderloin with oregano and sea salt.
2. Lightly coat the Instant Pot with olive oil and set to Sauté mode.
3. Add the tomatoes and sauté for 5 minutes.
4. Place the tenderloin in the Instant Pot and sear for 2 minutes on each side.
5. Pour in the water.
6. Lock the lid. Set the setting to Manual and set the cooking time for 25 minutes at High Pressure.
7. Once cooking is complete, use a quick pressure release.
8. Carefully open the lid. Allow to cool for a few minutes. Transfer them on a large plate and serve immediately.

Nutritional info:
Calories 492, Carbs 13g, Fat 25g, Protein 52g

Asian Lemongrass Pork

Prep Time: 10 mins, Cook Time: 35 min, Servings: 6

Ingredients:

4 tbsps. coconut oil

6 garlic cloves

2 tbsps. lemongrass

2 lbs. pork shoulder

¼ cup fish sauce

Salt and pepper, to taste

1 cup water

Instructions:

1. Press the Sauté button on the Instant pot and heat the coconut oil until melted.
2. Add and sauté the garlic and lemongrass for 1 minutes or until fragrant.
3. Add and sauté the pork chunks for 3 minutes, or until all sides are seared.
4. Pour in the fish sauce. Sprinkle with salt and pepper, and pour in the water.
5. Lock the lid. Press the Meat/Stew button and set the cooking time to 30 minutes at High Pressure.

6. Once cooking is complete, perform a natural pressure release for 10 minutes, and then release any remaining pressure. Carefully open the lid.
7. Remove the pork from the pot and serve warm.

Nutritional info:
Calories 249, Carbs 0.8g, Protein 21.5g, Fat 23.3g

Pork Tenderloin with Celery

Prep Time: 12 mins, Cook Time: 25 mins, Servings: 4

Ingredients:

1½ lbs. pork tenderloin

2 tsps. sea salt

½ tsp. rosemary

1 cup heavy cream

4 celery stalks, rinsed, sliced into ½-inch pieces

1 cup water

Instructions:

1. On a clean work surface, rub the pork with salt and rosemary.
2. Slice the well-coated tenderloin into 1-inch thick slices.
3. Set the Instant Pot to Sauté setting.
4. Add the pork and brown for 3 minutes.
5. Add the celery, heavy cream, and water. Stir to combine well.
6. Lock the lid. Set the Instant Pot to Manual mode and set the timer for 20 minutes at High Pressure.
7. Once cooking is complete, use a natural pressure release for 10 minutes, then release any remaining pressure.
8. Carefully open the lid. Allow to cool for a few minutes. Transfer them on a large plate and serve immediately.

Nutritional info:
Calories 399, Carbs 6g, Fat 18g, Protein 51g

Asian Striped Pork

Prep Time: 6 mins, Cook Time: 20 mins, Servings: 2

Ingredients:

1 tbsp. avocado oil	½ cup water
2 garlic cloves	Salt and pepper, to
½ lb. pork sirloin,	taste
sliced	2 tbsps. sesame oil
1 tbsp. soy sauce	

Instructions:

1. Press the Sauté button on the Instant pot and heat the avocado oil.
2. Add and sauté the garlic for 1 minute or until fragrant.
3. Add the pork sirloin and sear on all sides for 3 minutes or until lightly browned.
4. Pour in the soy sauce and water, then sprinkle salt and pepper for seasoning.
5. Lock the lid. Press the Meat/Stew button and set the cooking time to 15 minutes at High Pressure.
6. Once cooking is complete, perform a natural pressure release for 10 minutes, and then release any remaining pressure. Carefully open the lid.
7. Allow to cool for a few minutes. Drizzle with sesame oil. Remove the pork from the pot and baste with the juice remains in the pot before serving.

Nutritional info:
Calories 251, Carbs 0.6g, Protein 12.1g, Fat 23.8g

Garlicky Pork Tenderloin

Prep Time: 6 mins, Cook Time: 8 hours, Servings: 10

Ingredients:

3 tbsps. extra virgin olive oil	3 lbs. pork tenderloin
¼ cup butter	1 cup water
1 tsp. thyme	Salt and pepper, to
1 garlic clove, minced	taste

Instructions:

1. Set the Instant Pot on Sauté. Heat the olive oil and butter until the butter is melted.
2. Add and sauté the garlic and thyme for 1 minute or until fragrant.
3. Add the pork tenderloin and sauté for 3 minutes or until lightly browned.
4. Pour in the water and sprinkle salt and pepper for seasoning.

5. Lock the lid. Press the Slow Cook button and set the cooking time to 8 hours at High Pressure.
6. Once cooking is complete, perform a natural pressure release for 10 minutes, and then release any remaining pressure. Carefully open the lid.
7. Allow to cool for a few minutes. Remove the pork from the pot and serve warm.

Nutritional info:
Calories 252, Carbs 0.2g, Protein 11.8g, Fat 35.6g

Paprika Pork Loin Roast

Prep Time: 6 mins, Cook Time: 50 mins, Servings: 9

Ingredients:

4 tbsps. olive oil	3 lbs. pork loin roast
4 garlic cloves	Salt and pepper, to
½ cup chopped	taste
paprika	1 cup water

Instructions:

1. Press the Sauté button on the Instant Pot. Coat the pot with olive oil.
2. Add and sauté the garlic and paprika for 1 minute or until fragrant.
3. Add the pork loin roast and sear on all sides for 3 minutes or until lightly browned.
4. Sprinkle salt and pepper for seasoning. Pour in the water.
5. Lock the lid. Press the Meat/Stew button and set the cooking time to 45 minutes at High Pressure.
6. Once cooking is complete, perform a natural pressure release for 10 minutes, and then release any remaining pressure. Carefully open the lid.
7. Allow to cool for a few minutes. Remove the pork from the pot and baste with the juice remains in the pot before serving.

Nutritional info:
Calories 273, Carbs 3.1g, Protein 20.7g, Fat 22.8g

Pine Nut Pork

Prep Time: 20 mins, Cook Time: 25 mins, Servings: 4
Ingredients:

1½ lbs. pork tenderloin
1 tsp. sea salt
1 tbsp. extra virgin olive oil
1 medium onion, finely sliced
½ cup pine nuts
1 cup pesto sauce

1. **Instructions:**
2. On a clean work surface, cut the pork tenderloin into 1-inch thick slices and rub with salt.
3. Place the olive oil in Instant Pot, then set to Sauté setting.
4. Add and brown the pork for 3 minutes, then add onion and sauté for a minute or until translucent.
5. Add the pine nuts and pesto sauce.
6. Lock the lid. Set the pot to Manual mode and set the timer to 20 minutes at High Pressure.
7. Once cooking is complete, use a natural pressure release for 10 minutes, then release any remaining pressure.
8. Carefully open the lid. Allow to cool for a few minutes. Transfer them on a large plate and serve immediately.

Nutritional info:
Calories 492, Carbs 13g, Fat 25g, Protein 52g

Pork Chops with Onions

Prep Time: 6 mins, Cook Time: 25 mins, Servings: 4
Ingredients:

3 tbsps. butter
4 boneless pork chops
3 onions, chopped
½ cup beef broth
Salt and pepper, to taste
¼ cup heavy cream

Instructions:

1. Press the Sauté button on the Instant Pot.
2. Heat the butter until melted and add the pork chops and onion.
3. Sauté for 3 minutes or until the pork is seared.
4. Stir in the broth and sprinkle salt and pepper for seasoning.
5. Lock the lid. Press the Meat/Stew button and set the cooking time to 20 minutes at High Pressure.

6. Once cooking is complete, perform a natural pressure release for 10 minutes, and then release any remaining pressure. Carefully open the lid.
7. Add the heavy cream. Press the Sauté button and allow to simmer for 5 minutes.
8. Allow to cool for a few minutes. Remove the pork from the pot and serve warm.

Nutritional info:
Calories 468, Carbs 8.4g, Protein 28.1g, Fat 35.2g

Pork Coconut Curry

Prep Time: 6 mins, Cook Time: 35 mins, Servings: 6
Ingredients:

3 tbsps. coconut oil
3 garlic cloves, minced
1 tbsp. garam masala
2 lbs. pork shoulders, sliced
1 cup freshly squeezed coconut milk
Salt and pepper, to taste

Instructions:

1. Press the Sauté button on the Instant Pot and heat the coconut oil until melted.
2. Add and sauté the garlic and garam masala until fragrant.
3. Add the pork and allow to sear on all sides for 3 minutes or until lightly browned.
4. Pour in the coconut milk. Sprinkle with salt and pepper.
5. Lock the lid. Press the Meat/Stew button and set the cooking time to 30 minutes at High pressure.
6. Once cooking is complete, perform a natural pressure release for 10 minutes, and then release any remaining pressure. Carefully open the lid.
7. Remove the pork from the pot and serve warm.

Nutritional info:
Calories 371, Carbs 1.8g, Protein 23.4g, Fat 28.7g

Pork with Paprika and Mushrooms

Prep Time: 6 mins, Cook Time: 8 hours, Servings: 3
Ingredients:

4 tbsps. olive oil	mushrooms
1 lb. pork loin	Salt and pepper, to
1 tbsp. thyme	taste
2 tbsps. paprika	½ cup water
1 cup sliced cremini	

Instructions:
1. Press the Sauté button on the Instant Pot and heat the olive oil until shimmering.
2. Add and sear the pork loin on all sides for 3 minutes or until lightly browned.
3. Add the thyme, paprika, and mushrooms.
4. Sprinkle with salt and pepper, then add the water.
5. Lock the lid. Press the Slow Cook button and set the time to 8 hours at High Pressure.
6. Once cooking is complete, perform a quick pressure release. Carefully open the lid.
7. Remove the pork from the pot and serve warm.

Nutritional info:
Calories 245, Carbs 1.3g, Protein 17.3g Fat 19.8g

Sunday Pork Roast

Prep Time: 12 mins, Cook Time: 15 mins, Servings: 12
Ingredients:

4 lbs. pork roast	rinsed, stem
1 tbsp. sea salt	removed, and cut
4 tbsps. extra virgin	into ¼-inch slices
olive oil	1 cup chicken stock
4 Chinese eggplants,	

Instructions:
1. On a clean work surface, rub the pork with salt.
2. Set the Instant Pot to Sauté mode. Add the olive oil to Instant Pot and heat until shimmering.
3. Add pork and brown for 3 minutes on all sides.
4. Add eggplant and stock.
5. Lock the lid. Set the pot to Manual setting and set the timer for 15 minutes at High Pressure.

6. Once cooking is complete, use a quick pressure release.
7. Carefully open the lid. Allow to cool for a few minutes. Transfer them on a large plate and serve immediately.

Nutritional info:
Calories 694, Carbs 66g, Fat 25g, Protein 49g

Tomato Chili Pork

Prep Time: 12 mins, Cook Time: 25 mins, Servings: 4
Ingredients:

1 tbsps. olive oil	1 lb. fat removed and
2 green chili peppers,	chopped pork neck
diced	Salt and pepper, to
2 yellow bell peppers,	taste
sliced	2 cups low-sodium
2 cups whole Roma	beef stock
tomatoes	

Instructions:
1. Press Sauté on the Instant Pot. Grease the pot with the olive oil.
2. Add the peppers and sauté for 3 to 4 minutes.
3. Add the tomatoes and sauté for 4 to 5 minutes.
4. Add the pork neck and sauté for 3 minutes or until lightly browned.
5. Season with salt and pepper, then mix in the stock.
6. Lock the lid. Press Manual. Set the timer to 15 minutes at High Pressure.
7. Once the timer goes off, press Cancel, then use a quick pressure release.
8. Carefully open the lid. Allow to cool for a few minutes, then divide them into 4 plates and serve warm.

Nutritional info:
Calories 178, Fat 10g, Carbs 9g, Protein 13g

Chapter 8 Soups and Stews Recipe

Asian Egg Drop Soup

Prep Time: 6 mins, Cook Time: 9 mins, Servings: 3
Ingredients:

1 tsp. grated ginger	Salt and pepper, to
3 cups water	taste
2 cups chopped kale	2 eggs, beaten
3 tbsps. coconut oil	

Instructions:
1. Place all ingredients, except for the beaten eggs, in the Instant Pot.
2. Lock the lid. Set the Manual mode and set the timer to 6 minutes at High Pressure.
3. When the timer goes off, perform a natural pressure release for 5 minutes, then release any remaining pressure.
4. Carefully open the lid. Press the Sauté button and bring the soup to a simmer.
5. Gradually pour in the beaten eggs and allow to simmer for 3 more minutes.
6. Pour the soup in a large bowl and serve warm.

Nutritional info:
Calories 209, Carbs 1.7g, Protein 6.5g, Fat 20.3g

Thai Coconut Shrimp Soup

Prep Time: 6 mins, Cook Time: 6 mins, Servings: 2
Ingredients:

6 oz. shrimps, shelled and deveined	Juice of 3 kaffir limes
2 cups water	1½ cups coconut milk
	1 cup fresh cilantro

Instructions:
1. In the Instant Pot, add all the ingredients excluding cilantro.
2. Lock the lid. Set on the Manual mode and set the timer to 6 minutes at Low Pressure.
3. When the timer goes off, perform a quick release.
4. Carefully open the lid. Garnish with the fresh cilantro and serve immediately.

Nutritional info:
Calories 517, Carbs 15.4g, Protein 21.9g, Fat 44.6g

Swiss Chard and Leek Soup

Prep Time: 12 mins, Cook Time: 6 mins, Servings: 4
Ingredients:

8 cups chopped Swiss chard	1½ cups chicken stock
3 leeks, chopped	1 cup coconut milk
Salt, to taste	

Instructions:
1. In the Instant Pot, mix the chard with leeks, salt, stock and coconut milk, stir to combine well.
2. Lock the lid. Select the Manual mode, then set the timer for 6 minutes at High Pressure.
3. Once the timer goes off, do a quick pressure release.
4. Carefully open the lid. Allow to cool for a few minutes, then pour the soup in an immersion blender and process until smooth. Ladle the soup into bowls and serve.

Nutritional info:
Calories 142, Fat 4g, Carbs 6g, Protein 7g

Asparagus Soup

Prep Time: 55 mins, Cook Time: 55 mins, Servings: 4
Ingredients:

1 tbsp. ghee	taste
1 medium onion, chopped	2 lbs. halved asparagus
1 garlic clove, minced	Salt and pepper, to
1 cup diced ham	taste
Salt and pepepr, to	

Instructions:
1. Set the Instant Pot to Sauté and melt the ghee.
2. Add the onions and garlic and cook for about 5 minutes
3. Add the diced ham, salt and pepper, and let it simmer for 2 to 3 minutes.
4. Add the asparagus.
5. Lock the lid. Select the Soup mode, then set the timer 45 minutes at High Pressure.
6. Once the timer goes off, do a quick pressure release. Carefully open the lid..
7. Transfer the soup to a food processor and pulse until smooth.
8. Serve warm.

Nutritional info:
Calories 80, Fat 2g, Carbs 0.5g, Protein 6g

Bacon and Potato Soup

Prep Time: 40 mins, Cook Time: 20 mins, Servings: 6

Ingredients:

1 tbsp. olive oil	1½ lbs. potatoes, chopped
2 cups chicken stock	
½ cup sour cream	4 halved bacon slices
½ cup chopped onion	

Instructions:

1. Set the Instant Pot to Sauté and heat the olive oil.
2. Add the bacon and cook for about 8 minutes until crispy.
3. Drain the bacon in paper towels and then chop. Set aside on a plate.
4. Add the chopped onion and sauté for 2 minutes or until translucent.
5. Add the potatoes and stock. Stir well.
6. Lock the lid. Select the Manual mode, then set the timer for 10 minutes at High Pressure.
7. Once the timer goes off, do a quick pressure release. Carefully open the lid.
8. Transfer the soup to a blender and purée until smooth.
9. Stir in the sour cream. Top with the cooked bacon and serve.

Nutritional info:

Calories 195, Fat 9.6g, Carbs 20g, Protein 7.6g

Leek and Salmon Soup

Prep Time: 6 mins, Cook Time: 10 mins, Servings: 4

Ingredients:

1 lb. salmon, sliced	4 leeks, trimmed and chopped
1¾ cup coconut milk	
2 tbsps. avocado oil	Salt and pepper, to taste
3 garlic cloves, minced	

Instructions:

1. Place all ingredients in the Instant Pot. Stir to combine well.
2. Lock the lid. Select the Manual mode and cook for 10 minutes at Low Pressure.
3. When the timer goes off, perform a quick release.
4. Carefully open the lid. Allow to cool for a few minutes. Serve immediately.

Nutritional info:

Calories 535, Fat 40.9g, Carbs 19.5g, Protein 27.3g

Broccoli Cheddar Soup

Prep Time: 6 mins, Cook Time: 10 mins, Servings: 4

Ingredients:

2 heads fresh broccoli	Salt and pepper, to taste
4 cups chicken broth	
1 cup heavy whipping cream	2 cups shredded Cheddar cheese

Ingredients:

1. Add the trivet to the bottom of the Instant Pot along with broccoli and broth.
2. Lock the lid. Select the Manual mode, then set the timer for 10 minutes at High Pressure.
3. Once the timer goes off, do a quick pressure release. Carefully open the lid.
4. Remove the trivet and add the cream, salt and pepper. Whisk well.
5. Purée the soup with an immersion blender.
6. Add the cheese to the soup and keep stirring until melted.
7. Ladle into bowls and serve.

Nutritional info:

Calories 117, Fat 8g, Carbs 1.5g, Protein 3g

Fish Soup

Prep Time: 12 mins, Cook Time: 8 mins, Servings: 4

Ingredients:

1 lb. boneless, skinless and cubed white fish fillets	4 cups chicken stock
	Salt and pepper, to taste
1 carrot, chopped	2 cups heavy whipping cream
1 cup chopped bacon	

Instructions:

1. In the Instant Pot, mix the fish with carrot, bacon and stock. Sprinkle with salt and pepper. Stir to combine well.
2. Lock the lid. Set to Manual function and set the timer for 5 minutes at Low Pressure.
3. Once the timer goes off, press Cancel. Do a quick pressure release.
4. Carefully open the lid. Add the cream, stir, set the pot to Sauté, cook for 3 minutes more, ladle the soup into bowls and serve.

Nutritional info:

Calories 271, Fat 7g, Carbs 30g, Protein 5g

Carrot and Mushroom Soup

Prep Time: 30 mins, Cook Time: 15 mins, Servings: 4

Ingredients:

1 tbsp. olive oil
4 cups chicken stock
1 diced onion
2 sliced celery stalks

2 sliced carrots
¼ cup mushroom
Zest of 1 lemon, for garnish

Instructions:

1. Set the Instant Pot to Sauté and heat the olive oil.
2. Cook the onion, celery, carrots and mushroom for 5 minutes, stirring occasionally. Pour in the chicken stock and stir well.
3. Lock the lid. Select the Manual mode, then set the timer for 10 minutes at High Pressure.
4. Once the timer goes off, do a quick pressure release. Carefully open the lid.
5. Garnish with lemon zest and serve.

Nutritional info:

Calories 71, Fat 1.2g, Carbs 13.4g, Protein 2.9g

Cheesy Broccoli Soup

Prep Time: 12 mins, Cook Time: 10 mins, Servings: 8

Ingredients:

4 garlic cloves, minced
4 cups broccoli florets
3½ cups chicken stock
1 cup heavy whipping

cream
Salt and pepper, to taste
3 cups grated Cheddar cheese

Instructions:

1. Set the Instant Pot to Sauté, then add the garlic and sauté it for 1 minute until fragrant.
2. Add the broccoli, stock and cream. Sprinkle with salt and pepper. Stir to combine well.
3. Lock the lid. Select the Manual mode, then set the timer for 8 to 9 minutes at Low Pressure.
4. Once the timer goes off, do a quick pressure release.
5. Carefully open the lid. Add the cheese and stir until it melts, then ladle into bowls and serve.

Nutritional info:

Calories 291, Fat 20g, Carbs 8g, Protein 13g

Carrot Soup

Prep Time: 30 mins, Cook Time: 7 mins, Servings: 3

Ingredients:

1 tbsp. olive oil
1 onion, chopped
1 lb. carrots, cubed
3 cups vegetable broth
¼ tsp. smoked

paprika
¼ tsp. cumin powder
Salt and pepper, to taste
Cilantro, for garnish

Instructions:

1. Select the Sauté setting on the Instant Pot and heat the olive oil.
2. Add the onions and sauté for about 2 minutes until translucent.
3. Add the carrots, vegetable broth, paprika, and cumin powder to the pot and stir well.
4. Lock the lid. Select the Manual mode, then set the timer for 5 minutes at High Pressure.
5. Once the timer goes off, do a quick pressure release. Carefully open the lid.
6. Transfer the soup to a blender and blend until smooth.
7. Season with salt and pepper. Garnish with fresh cilantro and serve.

Nutritional info:

Calories 116, Fat 1.5g, Carbs 19.4g, Protein 6.6g

Coconut Seafood Soup

Prep Time: 6 mins, Cook Time: 8 mins, Servings: 5

Ingredients:

1 cup coconut milk
10 shrimps, shelled and deveined
1 thumb-size ginger, crushed

4 tilapia fillets
2 cups water
Salt and pepper, to taste

Instructions:

1. Place all ingredients in the Instant Pot. Stir to combine well.
2. Lock the lid. Set on the Manual mode, then set the timer to 8 minutes at Low Pressure.
3. When the timer goes off, perform a quick release.
4. Carefully open the lid. Allow to cool before serving.

Nutritional info:

Calories 238, Carbs 2.7, Protein 13.6g, Fat 28.8g

Cabbage Soup

Prep Time: 15 mins, Cook Time: 35 mins, Servings: 2

Ingredients:

1 onion, shredded
1lb. cabbage, shredded
1 tbsp. black pepper
2 tbsps. mixed herbs
1 cup low-sodium vegetable broth

Instructions:

1. Mix all the ingredients in the Instant Pot.
2. Lock the lid. Select the Soup mode, then set the timer for 35 minutes at High Pressure.
3. Once the timer goes off, do a quick pressure release. Carefully open the lid.
4. Serve warm.

Nutritional info:

Calories 60, Carbs 2g, Fat 2g, Protein 4g

Egg Drop Soup with Shredded Chicken

Prep Time: 10 mins, Cook Time: 15 mins, Servings: 6

Ingredients:

2 tbsps. coconut oil
1 onion, minced
1 celery, chopped
3 cups shredded chicken
4 cups water
Salt and pepper, to taste
4 eggs, beaten

Instructions:

1. Press the Sauté button on the Instant Pot and heat the oil.
2. Sauté the onion and celery for 2 minutes or until fragrant.
3. Add the chicken and water.
4. Sprinkle salt and pepper for seasoning.
5. Lock the lid. Press the Poultry button and set the cooking time to 10 minutes at High Pressure.
6. When the timer goes off, perform a natural pressure release for 5 minutes, then release any remaining pressure.
7. Carefully open the lid. Press the Sauté button and bring the soup to a simmer.
8. Gradually pour in the beaten eggs and allow to simmer for 3 more minutes.
9. Pour the soup in a large bowl and serve warm.

Nutritional info:

Calories 154, Carbs 2.9g, Protein 9.6g, Fat 12.8g

Chili Con Carne (Chili with Meat)

Prep Time: 15 mins, Cook Time: 35 mins, Servings: 2

Ingredients:

2 cups chopped tomatoes
3 tbsps. mixed seasoning
1lb. ground beef
3 squares dark chocolate
1 cup mixed beans

Instructions:

1. Mix all the ingredients in the Instant Pot.
2. Lock the lid. Select the Meat/Stew setting. Set the timer for 35 minutes at High Pressure.
3. Once cooking is complete, perform a natural pressure release for 10 minutes, then release any remaining pressure. Carefully open the lid.
4. Serve warm.

Nutritional info:

Calories 340, Carbs 16g, Fat 12g, Protein 46g

Beet Soup

Prep Time: 12 mins, Cook Time: 52 mins, Servings: 6

Ingredients:

1 cup water
8 cups peeled and chopped beets
3 cups chopped cabbage
1 yellow onion, chopped
¼ tsp. salt
6 cups chicken stock

Instructions:

1. Add a cup of water to the Instant Pot, then add the beets.
2. Lock the lid and set on Manual mode, then set the timer for 7 minutes at High Pressure.
3. Once the timer goes off, do a quick pressure release. Discard the water, then return the beets to the pot.
4. Add the cabbage, onion, salt and stock. Stir to combine well.
5. Lock the lid. Cook on Manual mode and set the timer for 45 minutes at High Pressure.
6. Once the timer goes off, do a quick pressure release.
7. Carefully open the lid. Ladle soup into bowls and serve.

Nutritional info:

Calories 152, Fat 6g, Carbs 6g, Protein 8g

Ginger Halibut Soup

Prep Time: 6 mins, Cook Time: 12 mins, Servings: 4

Ingredients:

1 tbsp. olive oil	ginger
1 large onion, chopped	1 lb. halibut, sliced
2 cups water	Salt and pepper, to taste
2 tbsps. minced fresh	

Instructions:

1. Press the Sauté button on the Instant Pot and heat the olive oil.
2. Sauté the onion for 3 minutes or until translucent.
3. Add the remaining ingredients. Stir to combine well.
4. Lock the lid. Set on the Manual mode, then set the timer to 10 minutes at Low Pressure.
5. When the timer goes off, perform a quick release.
6. Carefully open the lid. Allow to cool before serving.

Nutritional info:

Calories 259, Carbs 7.9g, Protein 10.9g, Fat 22.8g

Minestrone

Prep Time: 12 mins, Cook Time: 6 mins, Servings: 4

Ingredients:

27 oz. tomato paste	soup
15 oz. drained canned cannellini beans	1 cup cooked orzo pasta
2 cups vegetable	¼ cup grated Parmesan cheese

Instructions:

1. In the Instant Pot, mix the tomato paste with beans and vegetable soup, stir to combine well.
2. Lock the lid. Set to the Manual mode and set the timer for 6 minutes at High Pressure.
3. Once the timer goes off, do a natural pressure release for 10 minutes, then release any remaining pressure.
4. Carefully open the lid. Add the orzo pasta and stir, then ladle the soup into bowls and serve with Parmesan sprinkled on top.

Nutritional info:

Calories 254, Fat 2g, Carbs 12g, Protein 4g

Greek Veggie Soup

Prep Time: 30 mins, Cook Time: 17 mins, Servings: 4

Ingredients:

1 tbsp. olive oil	1 (15 oz) can roasted tomatoes
1 garlic clove, minced	
3 cups shredded cabbage	Salt and pepper, to taste
2 carrots, minced	Crumbled feta cheese, for topping
4 cups vegetable broth	

Instructions:

1. Set the Instant Pot to Sauté and heat the olive oil.
2. Add the garlic and cabbage and cook for 5 minutes, stirring occasionally.
3. Add the carrots and cook for 2 more minutes.
4. Pour in the broth and tomatoes. Season with salt and pepper.
5. Lock the lid. Select the Soup mode, then set the timer for 10 minutes at High Pressure.
6. Once the timer goes off, do a quick pressure release. Carefully open the lid.
7. Top with crumbled feta cheese and serve.

Nutritional info:

Calories 94, Fat 1.4g, Carbs 12.9g, Protein 6.8g

Potato Soup

Prep Time: 12 mins, Cook Time: 15 mins, Servings: 8

Ingredients:

3 lbs. potatoes, peeled and cubed	12 green onions, chopped
2 cups milk	1 cup shredded Cheddar cheese
¼ tsp. salt	

Instructions:

1. In the Instant Pot, mix the potatoes with milk and salt. Stir to combine.
2. Lock the lid. Select the Manual mode and set the timer for 12 minutes at High Pressure.
3. Once the timer goes off, do a quick pressure release. Carefully open the lid.
4. Add the Cheddar cheese and green onions, and stir to mix well.
5. Set the pot to Sauté and cook until the cheese melts, about 3 minutes.
6. Ladle the soup into bowls and serve.

Nutritional info:

Calories 314, Fat 12g, Carbs 17g, Protein 5g

Leftover Chicken Soup

Prep Time: 6 mins,
Cook Time: 12 mins,
Servings: 3

Ingredients:

1 tbsp. coconut oil
1 onion, chopped
8 garlic cloves, minced
2 cups shredded

leftover chicken meat
Salt and pepper, to taste
7 cups water

Instructions:

1. Press the Sauté button on the Instant Pot and heat the coconut oil.
2. Sauté the onions and garlic for 2 to 3 minutes until fragrant.
3. Add the chicken meat and sprinkle salt and pepper for seasoning.
4. Pour in the water. Season with more salt and pepper.
5. Lock the lid. Set on the Manual mode, then set the timer to 10 minutes at High Pressure.
6. When the timer goes off, do a natural pressure release for 10 minutes, then release any remaining pressure.
7. Carefully open the lid and serve warm.

Nutritional info:

Calories 356, Fat 32.1g, Carbs 2.5g, Protein 23.4g

Pumpkin Soup

Prep Time: 30 mins, Cook Time: 8 mins, Servings: 4

Ingredients:

1 tsp. garlic powder
2 cups chicken stock
1 onion, chopped
30 oz. pumpkin purée
2 cups chopped

sweet potato
Salt and pepper, to taste
Sour cream, for serving

Instructions:

1. Add all the ingredients, except for the sour cream, in the Instant Pot.
2. Lock the lid. Select the Manual mode, then set the timer for 8 minutes at High Pressure.
3. Once the timer goes off, do a quick pressure release. Carefully open the lid.
4. Transfer the soup into a blender and pulse until smooth.
5. Serve with sour cream on top.

Nutritional info:

Calories 186, Fat 1.4g, Carbs 41.7g, Protein 5.5g

Lemon Chicken Soup

Prep Time: 10 mins, Cook Time: 8 mins, Servings: 4

Ingredients:

2 tbsps. lemon juice
6 cups chicken stock
3 chicken breast fillets

1 tsp. garlic powder
1 diced onion
Salt and pepper, to taste

Instructions:

1. Put the chicken stock, chicken breast fillets, garlic powder, and onion in the Instant Pot and mix well.
2. Lock the lid. Select the Manual mode, then set the timer for 6 minutes at High Pressure.
3. Once the timer goes off, do a natural pressure release for 5 minutes, then release any remaining pressure. Carefully open the lid.
4. Remove the chicken and shred.
5. Put it back to the pot and set the Instant Pot to Sauté.
6. Whisk in the lemon juice. Season with salt and pepper. Serve immediately.

Nutritional info:

Calories 238, Fat 9.1g, Carbs 4.3g, Protein 33.2g

Low Carb Chicken Noodle Soup

Prep Time: 30 mins, Cook Time: 27, Servings: 2

Ingredients:

2 tsps. coconut oil
1 lb. skinless and boneless chicken thighs
1 cup celery

1 cup diced carrots
Salt, to taste
10½ oz. spiral daikon noodles

Instructions:

1. In the Instant Pot, add the coconut oil and chicken thighs.
2. Set the Instant Pot to Sauté and cook for 10 minutes or until cooked through.
3. Shred the chicken meat with a fork and add the celery and carrots.
4. Continue cooking for 2 minutes more and season with salt.
5. Lock the lid. Change the setting to Soup and set the cooking time for 15 minutes.
6. After the timer stops, add the daikon noodles and serve.

Nutritional info:

Calories 371, Fat: 22g, Carbs 6.5g, Protein 36g

Low Carb Ham and Bean Soup

Prep Time: 12 mins, Cook Time: 40 mins, Servings: 6
Ingredients:

2 smoked ham hocks	2 cups chopped ham
1 cup chopped onion	1 tsp. dried oregano
1 cup black beans, soaked in water for at least an hour	1 tsp. Louisiana hot sauce
4 garlic cloves, minced	1 cup chopped celery
	½ tsp. Salt
	6 cups water

Instructions:
1. Put the ham hocks, onion, black beans, ham, and garlic in the Instant Pot.
2. Add the dried oregano, Louisiana hot sauce, chopped celery, salt, and water. Stir to combine.
3. Lock the lid. Select the Manual mode, then set the timer for 30 minutes at High Pressure.
4. Once the timer goes off, do a quick pressure release. Carefully open the lid.
5. Remove the ham bone and shred the meat remaining on it back to the soup.
6. Use an immersion blender to purée the soup.
7. Serve hot.

Nutritional info:
Calories 111, Fat 1.9g, Carbs 4g, Protein 10g

Kidney Bean Stew

Prep Time: 15 mins, Cook Time: 15 mins, Servings: 2
Ingredients:

1 cup tomato passata	beans
3 tbsps. Italian herbs	1 cup low-sodium
1lb. cooked kidney	beef broth

Instructions:
1. Mix all the ingredients in the Instant Pot.
2. Lock the lid. Select the Bean/Chili mode, then set the timer for 15 minutes at High Pressure.
3. Once the timer goes off, do a natural pressure release for 10 minutes, then release any remaining pressure. Carefully open the lid.
4. Serve warm.

Nutritional info:
Calories 270, Carbs 16g, Fat 10g, Protein 23g

Vegetable and Lentil Soup

Prep Time: 30 mins, Cook Time: 20 mins, Servings: 5
Ingredients:

1 tbsp. olive oil	5 tbsps. mixed spices
6 cups chicken stock	Salt, to taste
1¼ cup green lentils	4 cups mixed vegetables
6 garlic cloves, minced	

Instructions:
1. Set the Instant Pot to Sauté and heat the olive oil. Cook the garlic for 2 minutes or until fragrant.
2. Add the vegetables and spices. Season with salt and cook for 5 minutes more.
3. Add the stock and lentils and stir well.
4. Lock the lid. Select the Manual mode, then set the timer for 12 minutes at High Pressure.
5. Once the timer goes off, do a natural pressure release for 10 minutes, then release any remaining pressure. Carefully open the lid.
6. Serve immediately.

Nutritional info:
Calories 257, Fat 1.7g, Carbs 44.9g, Protein 16.2g

Salmon Head Soup

Prep Time: 6 mins, Cook Time: 12 mins, Servings: 1
Ingredients:

1 tsp. coconut oil	3-inch ginger piece, slivered
1 onion, sliced	Salt and pepper, to taste
3 cups water	
1 salmon head	

Instructions:
1. Press the Sauté button on the Instant Pot and heat the coconut oil.
2. Sauté the onion for 3 minutes or until translucent.
3. Pour in the water, then add the salmon head and ginger.
4. Sprinkle salt and pepper for seasoning.
5. Lock the lid. Set on the Manual mode, then set the timer to 10 minutes at Low Pressure.
6. When the timer goes off, perform a quick release.
7. Carefully open the lid. Allow to cool before serving.

Nutritional info:
Calories 474, Carbs 1.8g, Protein 15.3g, Fat 54.4g

Calamari Stew

Prep Time: 12 mins, Cook Time: 32 mins, Servings: 3

Ingredients:

1 tbsp. olive oil	½ bunch parsley, chopped
1 lb. separated calamari	7 oz. tomatoes, chopped
¼ cup white wine	

Instructions:

1. Set the Instant Pot to Sauté and add the oil and calamari. Stir to combine well.
2. Lock the lid. Select the Manual mode, then set the timer for 9 minutes at Low Pressure.
3. Once the timer goes off, do a quick pressure release. Carefully open the lid.
4. Add the wine, tomatoes and half of the parsley, and stir well.
5. Lock the lid. Select the Manual mode, then set the timer for 25 minutes at High Pressure.
6. Once the timer goes off, do a quick pressure release. Carefully open the lid.
7. Sprinkle the remaining parsley on top. Divide the soup into bowls and serve.

Nutritional info:

Calories 160, Fat 4g, Carbs 7g, Protein 7g

Chicken and Quinoa Stew

Prep Time: 30 mins, Cook Time: 23 mins, Servings: 6

Ingredients:

1¼ lbs. chicken thigh fillets	butternut squash
4 cups chicken stock	1 cup chopped onion
4 cups chopped	½ cup uncooked quinoa

Instructions:

1. Put the chicken in the Instant Pot. Add the chicken thigh fillets, stock, squash and chopped onion.
2. Lock the lid. Select the Manual mode, then set the timer for 8 minutes at High Pressure.
3. Once the timer goes off, do a quick pressure release. Carefully open the lid.
4. Stir the quinoa into the stew.
5. Set the Instant Pot to Sauté and cook for about 15 minutes, stirring occasionally.
6. Serve the stew in a large serving bowl.

Nutritional info:

Calories 251, Fat 4.2g, Carbs 22.3g, Protein 31g

Chicken Tomato Stew

Prep Time: 12 mins, Cook Time: 30 mins, Servings: 8

Ingredients:

4 onions, chopped	4 cups low-sodium chicken stock
1 tbsp. olive oil	
10 oz. chicken breast	¼ cup water
1 cup diced tomatoes	

Instructions:

1. Press the Sauté bottom on the Instant Pot.
2. Add and heat the olive oil.
3. Add the onions and sauté for 1 to 2 minutes until turn translucent and softened.
4. Add the chicken and evenly brown for 4 to 5 minutes.
5. Add the tomatoes and sauté for 2 minutes or until soft.
6. Pour in the stock and water.
7. Lock the lid. Press Manual. Set the timer to 20 minutes at High Pressure.
8. Once the timer goes off, press Cancel. Do a quick pressure release.
9. Open the lid, transfer them in a large bowl and serve.

Nutritional info:

Calories 278, Fat 8g, Carbs 6g, Protein 38g

Turmeric Chicken Soup

Prep Time: 6 mins, Cook Time: 15 mins, Servings: 3

Ingredients:

3 boneless chicken breasts	2½ tsps. turmeric powder
1 bay leaf	4 cups water
½ cup coconut milk	

Instructions:

1. Place all the ingredients in the Instant Pot. Stir to combine well.
2. Lock the lid. Set to Poultry mode and set the timer to 15 minutes at High Pressure.
3. When the timer goes off, perform a natural pressure release for 10 minutes, then release any remaining pressure.
4. Carefully open the lid. Allow to cool for a few minutes, then serve immediately.

Nutritional info:

Calories 599, Carbs 3.8g, Protein 46.8g Fat 61.4g

Mushroom Chicken Soup

Prep Time: 12 mins, Cook Time: 20 mins, Servings: 4

Ingredients:

1 tbsp. olive oil	4 cups low-sodium
7 oz. chicken breast	chicken stock
1 onion, finely	Salt and pepper, to
chopped	taste
2 cups sliced button	¼ cup heavy
mushrooms	whipping cream

Instructions:

1. Press the Sauté bottom on the Instant Pot.
2. Add and heat the olive oil.
3. Add the chicken breast and sauté for 3 to 4 minutes to evenly brown.
4. Add the onions and sauté for 3 minutes or until translucent and softened.
5. Add the mushrooms and stock. Sprinkle with salt and pepper.
6. Lock the lid. Press the Manual bottom in the pot. Set the timer to 15 minutes at High Pressure.
7. Once the timer goes off, press Cancel. Do a quick pressure release.
8. Open the lid, mix in the cream, transfer them in a large bowl and serve.

Nutritional info:

Calories 284, Fat 9g, Carbs 7g, Protein 41g

Veal and Buckwheat Groat Stew

Prep Time: 12 mins, Cook Time: 50 mins, Servings: 4

Ingredients:

¼ cup buckwheat	3 cups low-sodium
groats	beef stock
1 tsp. olive oil	Salt and pepper, to
1 onion, chopped	taste
7 oz. veal shoulder	

Instructions:

1. Add the buckwheat and pour in enough water to cover the buckwheat in the Instant Pot. Stir the ingredients to combine well.
2. Lock the lid. Press Manual. Set the timer to 12 minutes at Low Pressure.
3. Once the timer goes off, press Cancel. Do a natural pressure release, then release any remaining pressure.
4. Drain water and set the buckwheat aside.
5. Press the Sauté bottom on the Instant Pot.
6. Add and heat the olive oil.
7. Add the onions and cook for 3 minutes until translucent.
8. Add the veal shoulder and sauté for 4 to 5 minutes to evenly brown.
9. Pour in the beef stock. Sprinkle with salt and pepper.
10. Lock the lid. Press Manual. Set the timer to 30 minutes at High Pressure.
11. Once the timer goes off, press Cancel. Do a natural pressure release for 8 to 10 minutes.
12. Open the lid, mix in the buckwheat and transfer them in a large bowl and serve.

Nutritional info:

Calories 134, Fat 4g, Carbs 10g, Protein 14g

Salmon Stew

Prep Time: 6 mins, Cook Time:13 mins, Servings: 9

Ingredients:

2 tbsps. olive oil	3 lbs. salmon fillets
3 garlic cloves,	Salt and pepper, to
minced	taste
3 cups water	3 cups spinach leaves

Instructions:

1. Press the Sauté button on the Instant Pot and heat the olive oil.
2. Sauté the garlic for a minute until fragrant.
3. Add the water and salmon fillets. Sprinkle salt and pepper for seasoning.
4. Lock the lid. Set on the Manual mode, then set the timer to 10 minutes at Low Pressure.
5. When the timer goes off, perform a quick release.
6. Carefully open the lid. Press the Sauté button and add the spinach.
7. Allow to simmer for 3 minutes.
8. Serve warm.

Nutritional info:

Calories 825, Carbs 2.1g, Protein 46.1g, Fat 94.5g

Slow-Cooked Cabbage and Chuck Roast Stew

Prep Time: 6 mins, Cook Time: 36 mins, Servings: 10
Ingredients:

2 tbsps. olive oil
2 onions, sliced
1 garlic clove, minced
3 lbs. chuck roast
6 cups water

Salt and pepper, to taste
1 small cabbage head, chopped

Instructions:

1. Press the Sauté button on the Instant Pot and heat the olive oil.
2. Sauté the onions and garlic for 2 minutes until fragrant.
3. Add the chuck roast and sauté for 3 minutes or until lightly browned.
4. Pour in the water and sprinkle salt and pepper for seasoning.
5. Lock the lid. Set on the Manual mode, then set the timer to 30 minutes at High Pressure.
6. When the timer goes off, do a natural pressure release, then release any remaining pressure.
7. Carefully open the lid. Press the Sauté button and add the cabbage.
8. Allow to simmer for 3 minutes.
9. Serve warm.

Nutritional info:

Calories 312, Carbs 6.3g, Protein 20.3g, Fat 15.6g

Onion Soup with Pork Stock

Prep Time: 12 mins, Cook Time: 25 mins, Servings: 4
Ingredients:

2 tbsps. olive oil
8 cups yellow onions, sliced
1 tbsp. balsamic vinegar

6 cups pork stock
2 bay leaves
2 thyme stems
Salt, to taste

Instructions:

1. Set the Instant Pot to Sauté and heat the olive oil.
2. Stir in the onions and cook until translucent, about 15 minutes.
3. Add the vinegar and stock, bay leaves, thyme, and salt to taste.
4. Lock the lid. Select the Manual mode, then set the timer for about 10 minutes at High Pressure.

5. Once the timer goes off, do a quick pressure release. Carefully open the lid.
6. Discard the thyme stems and bay leaves and then blend the soup using a blender or if you have an immersion blender, then you can blend it directly into the pot.
7. Serve immediately.

Nutritional info:

Calories 55, Fat 1.8g, Carbs 1g, Protein 3.3g

Poached Egg Chicken Bone Soup

Prep Time: 6 mins, Cook Time: 36 mins, Servings: 2
Ingredients:

1 lb. chicken bones
1 tsp. olive oil
2 cups water
2 whole eggs

1 romaine lettuce head, chopped
Salt and pepper, to taste

Instructions:

1. Place the chicken bones, olive oil, and water in the Instant Pot.
2. Lock the lid. Set to Poultry mode and the timer to 30 minutes at High Pressure.
3. When the timer goes off, do a natural pressure release for 10 minutes, then release any remaining pressure.
4. Carefully open the lid, then discard the bones with tongs.
5. Press the Sauté button and bring the soup to a simmer.
6. Carefully crack the eggs in the pot and simmer for 3 minutes.
7. Add the lettuce and season with salt and pepper.
8. Allow to simmer for 3 more minutes.
9. Serve warm.

Nutritional info:

Calories 443, Carbs 4.3g, Protein 58.3g, Fat 39.2g

Salmon Meatballs Soup

Prep Time: 2 hours, Cook Time: 10 mins, Servings: 5

Ingredients:

2 tbsps. melted butter

2 garlic cloves, minced

2 large eggs, beaten

1 lb. ground salmon

Salt and pepper, to taste

2 cups hot water

Instructions:

1. In a bowl, mix the butter, garlic, eggs and salmon. Sprinkle with salt and pepper..
2. Combine the mixture and use the hands to form the mixture into small balls.
3. Place the fish balls in the freezer to set for 2 hours or until frozen.
4. Pour the hot water in the Instant Pot and drop in the frozen fish balls.
5. Lock the lid. Select the Manual mode and set the timer to 10 minutes at Low Pressure.
6. When the timer goes off, perform a quick release.
7. Carefully open the lid. Allow to cool for a few minutes and remove the fish balls from the pot. Serve immediately.

Nutritional info:

Calories 199, Carbs 0.6g, Protein 13.3g, Fat 19.4g

Turkey with Ginger and Turmeric Soup

Prep Time: 6 mins, Cook Time: 17 mins, Servings: 4

Ingredients:

1 tbsp. coconut oil

2 celery stalks, chopped

1 thumb-size ginger, sliced

1 tsp. turmeric

powder

1 lb. turkey meat, chopped

3 cups water

Salt and pepper, to taste

Instructions:

1. Press the Sauté button on the Instant Pot and heat the coconut oil.
2. Add the celery, ginger, and turmeric powder and sauté for 3 minutes or until fragrant and the celery is tender.
3. Add the turkey meat and stir for another 3 minutes until lightly browned.
4. Pour in the water and sprinkle salt and pepper for seasoning.

5. Lock the lid. Set on the Manual mode, then set the timer to 15 minutes at High Pressure.
6. When the timer goes off, do a natural pressure release, then release any remaining pressure.
7. Carefully open the lid. Serve warm.

Nutritional info:

Calories 287, Carbs 0.8g, Protein 22.8g, Fat 24.3g

Simple Chicken and Kale Soup

Prep Time: 6 mins, Cook Time: 20 mins, Servings: 4

Ingredients:

1 tbsp. coconut oil

1 onion, diced

2 celery stalks, chopped

1 lb. boneless chicken

breasts

3 cups water

Salt and pepper, to taste

4 cups chopped kale

Instructions:

1. Press the Sauté button on the Instant Pot and heat the coconut oil.
2. Sauté the onions and celery for 2 minutes until soft.
3. Add the chicken breasts and sear for 2 minutes on each side or until lightly browned.
4. Pour in the water and sprinkle salt and pepper for seasoning.
5. Lock the lid. Set to Poultry mode and set the timer to 15 minutes at High Pressure.
6. When the timer goes off, do a natural pressure release for 10 minutes, then release any remaining pressure.
7. Carefully open the lid. Press the Sauté button and add the kale.
8. Allow to simmer for 3 minutes.
9. Serve warm.

Nutritional info:

Calories 303, Carbs 2.2g, Protein 20.8g, Fat 29.3g

White Bean and Kale Soup

Prep Time: 30 mins, Cook Time: 13 mins, Servings: 10

Ingredients:

3 tbsps. olive oil

1 (28 oz) can diced tomatoes

4 cups kale

1 white onion,

chopped

30 oz. white cannellini beans

4 cups vegetable stock

Instructions:

1. Set the Instant Pot to Sauté and heat the olive oil.
2. Sauté the white onion for 3 minutes, stirring occasionally.
3. Add the tomatoes, beans, and vegetable stock, and whisk well.
4. Lock the lid. Select the Manual mode, then set the timer for 10 minutes at High Pressure.
5. Once the timer goes off, do a quick pressure release. Carefully open the lid.
6. Stir in the kale.
7. Cover the pot and let rest for a few minutes until the kale is wilted. Serve warm.

Nutritional info:

Calories 206, Fat 0.5g, Carbs 39.2g, Protein 12.5g

Bean and Tomato Stew

Prep Time: 12 mins, Cook Time: 20 mins, Servings: 4

Ingredients:

1 tbsp. olive oil

1 large onion, chopped

2 large tomatoes, roughly chopped

1 lb. green beans

2 cups low-sodium chicken stock

Salt and pepper, to taste

¼ cup Parmesan cheese

Instructions:

1. Press the Sauté bottom on the Instant Pot.
2. Add and heat the olive oil.
3. Add the onions and sauté for 2 minutes until translucent and softened.
4. Add the tomatoes and sauté for 3 to 4 minutes or until soft.
5. Add the beans and stock. Sprinkle with salt and pepper.
6. Lock the lid. Press Manual. Set the timer to 15 minutes at High Pressure.

7. Once the timer goes off, press Cancel. Do a quick pressure release.
8. Open the lid, transfer them in a large bowl and serve with Parmesan cheese on top.

Nutritional info:

Calories 112, Fat 5g, Carbs 13g, Protein 5g

Beef Tomato Stew

Prep Time: 12 mins, Cook Time: 30 mins, Servings: 4

Ingredients:

2 tsps. olive oil

1 lb. lean beef stew meat

2 cups diced tomatoes

2 spring onions,

chopped

4 cups low-sodium beef broth

Salt and pepper, to taste

Instructions:

1. Press the Sauté bottom on the Instant Pot.
2. Add and heat the olive oil.
3. Add the meat and sauté for 3 to 4 minutes to evenly brown.
4. Add the tomatoes and onions, then sauté for 3 to 4 minutes or until soft.
5. Pour in the broth. Sprinkle with salt and pepper.
6. Lock the lid. Press Meat/Stew bottom. Set the timer to 20 minutes at High Pressure.
7. Once the timer goes off, press Cancel. Do a quick pressure release.
8. Open the lid, transfer them in a large bowl and serve.

Nutritional info:

Calories 231, Fat 6g, Carbs 7g, Protein 24g

Kale and Veal Stew

Prep Time: 12 mins, Cook Time: 35 mins, Servings: 6

Ingredients:

1 tbsp. olive oil	10 oz. fat removed
2 large onions, finely	and chopped veal
chopped	shoulder
1 small sweet potato,	1 lb. fresh kale,
diced	chopped
4 cups low-sodium	Salt and pepper, to
beef stock	taste

Instructions:

1. Press the Sauté bottom on the Instant Pot.
2. Add and heat the olive oil.
3. Add the onions and sauté for 3 minutes until turn translucent and softened.
4. Add the sweet potato and ¼ cup of stock. Sauté for 5 minutes or until soft.
5. Add the remaining stock, veal shoulder, and kale to the Instant Pot. Sprinkle with salt and pepper. Combine to mix well.
6. Lock the lid. Press Manual. Set the timer to 25 minutes at High pressure.
7. Once the timer goes off, press Cancel. Do a quick pressure release.
8. Open the lid, transfer them in a large bowl and serve

Nutritional info:

Calories 162, Fat 4g, Carbs 8g, Protein 13g

White Bean and Swiss Chard Stew

Prep Time: 15 mins, Cook Time: 10 mins, Servings: 8

Ingredients:

1 tbsp. olive oil	Salt and pepper, to
1 lb. Great Northern	taste
beans, rinsed, soaked	4 cups vegetable
and dried	stock
2 tsps. dried thyme	1 bunch Swiss chard,
28 oz. canned	chopped
roasted tomatoes	

Instructions:

1. Set the Instant Pot to Sauté and heat the olive oil.
2. Add the beans, thyme and tomatoes. Season with salt and pepper. Stir for 1 minute.
3. Pour in the broth and whisk to combine.

4. Lock the lid. Select the Bean/Chili function, then set the timer for 3 minutes at High Pressure.
5. Once the timer goes off, do a quick pressure release. Carefully open the lid.
6. Select the Sauté button.
7. Add the Swiss chard and cook for 3 minutes until tender. Transfer to a plate and serve.

Nutritional info:

Calories 241, Fat 0.8g, Carbs 44.5g, Protein 15.1g

Veggie Stew

Prep Time: 40 mins, Cook Time: 20 mins, Servings: 4

Ingredients:

1 tbsp. olive oil	20 oz. tomato sauce
1 onion, minced	2 tsps. Italian
1 package mixed	seasoning
frozen vegetables	Salt and pepper, to
4 cups vegetable	taste
broth	

Instructions:

1. Set the Instant Pot to Sauté and heat the olive oil.
2. Cook the onion for 1 minute until translucent. Add the frozen vegetables and cook for 5 minutes, stirring frequently.
3. Add the remaining ingredients and stir to combine.
4. Lock the lid. Select the Manual mode, then set the timer for 15 minutes at High Pressure.
5. Once the timer goes off, do a quick pressure release. Carefully open the lid.
6. Serve immediately.

Nutritional info:

Calories 138, Fat 2.5g, Carbs 22.1g, Protein 8.7g

Chicken and Tomato Soup

Prep Time: 30 mins, Cook Time: 17 mins, Servings: 6

Ingredients:

1 tbsp. olive oil	1 (28 oz) can crushed tomatoes
3 garlic cloves, minced	½ cup shredded Parmesan cheese, for garnish
1 lb. chicken breasts, cubed	
6 cups chicken broth	½ cup plain Greek yogurt, for serving
1 tsp. mixed garlic and onion powder	

Instructions:

1. Set the Instant Pot to Sauté and heat the olive oil.
2. Cook the garlic until fragrant, about 2 minutes.
3. Add the chicken breast cubes and sauté for 5 minutes until browned on both sides.
4. Pour in the remaining ingredients.
5. Lock the lid. Select the Manual mode, then set the timer for 10 minutes at High Pressure.
6. Once the timer goes off, do a natural pressure release for 10 minutes, then release any remaining pressure. Carefully open the lid.
7. Sprinkle the Parmesan cheese on top of the soup and serve with yogurt.

Nutritional info:
Calories 237, Fat 7g, Carbs 12g, Protein 30g

Creamy Broccoli Chicken Bone Soup

Prep Time: 6 mins, Cook Time: 34 mins, Servings: 5

Ingredients:

½ lb. chicken bones	into florets
4 cups water	1 small avocado, sliced
Salt and pepper, to taste	
2 heads broccoli, cut	1 tsp. paprika powder

Instructions:

1. Place the chicken bones and water in the Instant Pot.
2. Sprinkle salt and pepper for seasoning
3. Lock the lid. Set on the Manual mode, then set the timer to 30 minutes at High Pressure.
4. When the timer goes off, do a natural pressure release for 10 minutes, then release any remaining pressure.
5. Carefully open the lid, then discard the bones with tongs.
6. Add the broccoli.
7. Close the lid again and press the Manual button and cook for 4 minutes at Low Pressure.
8. When the timer goes off, do a quick pressure release.
9. Transfer the soup into a blender, then add avocado slices.
10. Pulse until smooth and set in a bowl.
11. Sprinkle with paprika powder.
12. Serve immediately.

Nutritional info:
Calories 118, Fat 10.3g, Carbs 1.9g, Protein 7.3

Chicken Soup

Prep Time: 12 mins, Cook Time: 10 mins, Servings: 2

Ingredients:

1 cup heavy whipping cream	2 packets skinned and deboned chicken breasts
¼ cup onions	
1 garlic cloves, minced	1 tbsp. ghee
	3 cups water

Instructions:

1. Combine all the ingredients, except for the heavy whipping cream, in the Instant Pot.
2. Lock the lid. Select the Manual mode, then set the timer for 6 minutes at High Pressure.
3. Once the timer goes off, do a natural pressure release for 5 minutes, then release any remaining pressure. Carefully open the lid.
4. Remove the chicken from the pot and transfer to a platter to shred it into pieces using forks.
5. Return it to the Instant Pot and add the heavy whipping cream to the soup. Stir to blend ingredients.
6. Serve warm.

Nutritional info:
Calories 150, Fat 4g, Carbs 1g, Protein 19g

Chapter 9 Snacks and Appetizers Recipe

Asian Wings

Prep Time: 10 minutes, Cook Time: 10 minutes, Servings: 4
Ingredients:

¼ cup brown sugar
¼ cup water
4 lbs. chicken wings

¼ cup honey
2 tbsps. black soy sauce

Instructions:

1. In the Instant Pot, mix the chicken wings with black soy sauce, honey, sugar and water, and stir to combine well.
2. Lock the lid. Select the Manual mode, then set the timer for 5 minutes at High Pressure.
3. Once the timer goes off, do a quick pressure release. Carefully open the lid.
4. Transfer the chicken wings to a baking sheet and broil for about 5 minutes until golden brown.
5. Divide the wings among four plates and serve.

Nutritional info:

Calories 221, Fat 3g, Carbs 10g, Protein 6g

BBQ Chicken Wings

Prep Time: 7 mins, Cook Time: 15 mins, Servings: 6
Ingredients:

¼ cup red wine
2 tbsps. olive oil
12 chicken wings
1 large onion,

chopped
18 oz. sweet BBQ sauce

Instructions:

1. Put the oil and onions in the Instant Pot and select the Sauté mode.
2. Sauté for 3 minutes and add chicken wings.
3. Sauté for 2 minutes on each side and add BBQ sauce and red wine. Whisk well.
4. Lock the lid. Select the Manual mode, then set the timer for 10 minutes on High Pressure.
5. Once the timer goes off, do a quick pressure release. Carefully open the lid.
6. Serve immediately.

Nutritional info:

Calories 491, Fat 21.2g, Carbs 19.3g, Protein: 52.9g

BBQ Square Ribs

Prep Time: 12 mins, Cook Time: 20 mins, Servings: 3
Ingredients:

1 cup BBQ sauce
1 tsp. liquid smoke
1 cup apple juice

1 rack pork spare ribs
1 onion, chopped

Instructions:

1. In the Instant Pot, mix the spare ribs with onion, apple juice, BBQ sauce and liquid smoke, Stir to mix well.
2. Lock the lid. Select the Manual mode, then set the timer for 20 minutes at High Pressure.
3. Once the timer goes off, do a natural pressure release for 10 minutes, then release any remaining pressure. Carefully open the lid.
4. Divide the ribs among three plates and drizzle BBQ sauce all over. Serve immediately.

Nutritional info:

Calories 300, Fat 8g, Carbs 12g, Protein 4g

Brussels Sprouts and Apples Appetizer

Prep Time: 12 mins, Cook Time: 6 mins, Servings: 4
Ingredients:

1½ cups water
1 lb. halved Brussels sprouts
1 cup dried cranberries

2 tbsps. canola oil
1 green apple, cored and roughly chopped
2 tbsps. lemon juice

Instructions:

1. Pour the water into the Instant Pot and arrange the steamer basket in the pot, then add Brussels sprouts.
2. Lock the lid. Select the Manual mode, then set the timer for 4 minutes at High Pressure.
3. Once the timer goes off, do a quick pressure release. Carefully open the lid.
4. Drain the Brussels sprouts and transfer to a bowl.
5. Clean the pot and set it to Sauté. Heat the oil and add Brussels sprouts, stir and cook for 1 minute.
6. Stir in apple, cranberries and lemon juice, and cook for 1 minute. Serve warm.

Nutritional info:

Calories 163, Fat 3g, Carbs 6g, Protein 3g

Broccoli and Bacon Appetizer Salad

Prep Time: 12 mins, Cook Time: 12 mins, Servings: 4

Ingredients:

1½ cups water
½ tbsp. apple cider vinegar
¼ cup chopped cilantro
2 tbsps. olive oil
1 head broccoli, cut into florets
4 bacon slices, chopped

Instructions:

1. Add the water and steamer basket to the Instant Pot. Arrange the broccoli florets in the basket.
2. Lock the lid. Select the Manual mode, then set the timer for 3 minutes at High Pressure.
3. Once the timer goes off, do a quick pressure release. Carefully open the lid.
4. Drain the broccoli and transfer to a bowl.
5. Clean the pot and set it to Sauté. Add the bacon, stir and cook for 4 minutes per side until it's crispy.
6. Roughly chop broccoli and return it to the Instant Pot. Stir and cook for 1 minute more.
7. Add the oil, cilantro and vinegar, and mix well. Remove from the heat to a plate and serve.

Nutritional info:

Calories 200, Fat 4g, Carbs 6g, Protein 4g

Chili Aioli

Prep Time: 6 mins, Cook Time: 2 mins, Servings: 6

Ingredients:

½ tsp. chili flakes
1 tbsp. lemon juice
1 egg yolk
2 garlic cloves, minced
¾ cup avocado oil

Instructions:

1. Put all ingredients in the Instant Pot and whisk vigorously.
2. Press the Sauté button and allow to heat for 2 minutes while stirring. Do not bring to a boil.
3. You can serve the chili aioli on top of the seafood or salad.

Nutritional info:

Calories 253, Carbs 0.7g, Protein 0.5g, Fat 28.1g

Baby Carrots Snack

Prep Time: 12 mins, Cook Time: 2 mins, Servings: 6

Ingredients:

¼ cup Chinese wine
1 tbsp. liquid smoke
1 lb. baby carrots
¼ cup vegetable soup
¼ cup soy sauce

Instructions:

1. In the Instant Pot, mix the baby carrots with soy sauce, Chinese wine, soup and liquid smoke. Stir to combine well.
2. Lock the lid. Select the Manual mode, then set the timer for 2 minutes at High Pressure.
3. Once the timer goes off, do a quick pressure release. Carefully open the lid.
4. Drain the carrots and transfer to a platter. You can serve them as a snack with a dip on the side.

Nutritional info:

Calories 176, Fat 3g, Carbs 4g, Protein 4g

Brussels Sprouts and Broccoli Appetizer Salad

Prep Time: 12 mins, Cook Time: 6 mins, Servings: 6

Ingredients:

1½ cups water
2 tsps. mustard
1 head broccoli, cut into florets
½ cup walnut oil
1 lb. halved Brussels sprouts
¼ cup balsamic vinegar

Instructions:

1. Put the water in the Instant Pot and arrange the steamer basket in the pot, then add broccoli and Brussels sprouts.
2. Lock the lid. Select the Manual mode, then set the timer for 4 minutes at High Pressure.
3. Once the timer goes off, do a quick pressure release. Carefully open the lid.
4. Drain the vegetables and transfer to a bowl.
5. Clean the pot and set it to Sauté. Heat the oil and add broccoli and Brussels sprouts. Stir and cook for 1 minute.
6. Drizzle with the vinegar and cook for 1 minute more, then transfer to a bowl.
7. Add the mustard and toss well. Serve immediately or refrigerate to chill.

Nutritional info:

Calories 200, Fat 6g, Carbs 8g, Protein 5g

Black Bean Salsa

Prep Time: 12 mins, Cook Time: 8 mins, Servings: 4

Ingredients:

2 red jalapeños, chopped
1 small white onion, chopped

1 tbsp. olive oil
8 oz. canned black beans, drained
2 tbsps. lime juice

Instructions:

1. Set the Instant Pot to Sauté and heat the olive oil.
2. Add the onion, stir and cook for 2 to 3 minutes until tender.
3. Add the black beans, lime juice and jalapeños, and stir to combine well.
4. Lock the lid. Select the Manual mode, then set the timer for 3 minutes at High Pressure.
5. Once the timer goes off, do a quick pressure release. Carefully open the lid.
6. Divide the salsa into bowls and serve warm.

Nutritional info:

Calories 172, Fat 3g, Carbs 6g, Protein 3g

Chunky Warm Salsa

Prep Time: 12 mins, Cook Time: 5 mins, Servings: 5

Ingredients:

2 tbsps. lime juice
2 peaches, roughly chopped
1 tbsp. olive oil

1 red onion, roughly chopped
1 red bell pepper, sliced

Instructions:

1. Set the Instant Pot to Sauté and heat the olive oil.
2. Add the onions, stir, and cook for 2 minutes until translucent.
3. Add the red pepper, peaches and lime juice, and stir to incorporate.
4. Lock the lid. Select the Manual mode, then set the timer for 3 minutes at High Pressure.
5. Once the timer goes off, do a quick pressure release. Carefully open the lid.
6. Remove from the pot to a bowl and serve.

Nutritional info:

Calories 152, Fat 2g, Carbs 4g, Protein 4g

Greek Meatballs

Prep Time: 12 mins, Cook Time: 12 mins, Servings: 10

Ingredients:

1 egg, whisked
¼ cup chopped mint
1 lb. ground beef

3 tbsps. olive oil
¼ cup white vinegar

Instructions:

1. In a bowl, mix the beef with mint and egg, and whisk well. Shape the beef mixture into 10 meatballs with your hands.
2. Set the Instant Pot to Sauté and heat the olive oil.
3. Add the beef meatballs and brown them for about 4 minutes on each side.
4. Add the vinegar and stir to mix well.
5. Lock the lid. Select the Manual mode, then set the timer for 4 minutes at High Pressure.
6. Once the timer goes off, do a quick pressure release. Carefully open the lid.
7. Divide the meatballs among plates and serve them with a yogurt dip on the side.

Nutritional info:

Calories 200, Fat 4g, Carbs 8g, Protein 10g

Cheesy Shrimp and Tomatoes

Prep Time: 12 mins, Cook Time: 4 mins, Servings: 6

Ingredients:

1 lb. shrimp, shelled and deveined
2 tbsps. butter
1 cup crumbled feta cheese

1½ cups chopped onion
15 oz. chopped canned tomatoes

Instructions:

1. Set the Instant Pot to Sauté and melt the butter.
2. Add the onion, stir, and cook for 2 minutes.
3. Add the shrimp and tomatoes and mix well.
4. Lock the lid. Select the Manual mode, then set the timer for 2 minutes at Low Pressure.
5. Once the timer goes off, do a quick pressure release. Carefully open the lid.
6. Divide shrimp and tomatoes mixture into small bowls. Top with feta cheese and serve.

Nutritional info:

Calories 201, Fat 3g, Carbs 7g, Protein 4g

Blue Cheese Dip

Prep Time: 12 mins, Cook Time: 4 mins, Servings: 6

Ingredients:

2 tbsps. chopped chives	Black pepper, to taste
4 tbsps. crumbled blue cheese	1 cup sour cream
	1½ tsps. chopped rosemary

Instructions:

1. In the Instant Pot, mix blue cheese with sour cream, rosemary and black pepper, and stir to combine well.
2. Lock the lid. Select the Manual mode, then set the timer for 4 minutes at High Pressure.
3. Once the timer goes off, do a quick pressure release. Carefully open the lid.
4. Scatter the chives all over and stir well. Serve immediately or refrigerate to chill until ready to serve.

Nutritional info:

Calories 200, Fat 7g, Carbs 7g, Protein 4g

Crunchy Brussels Sprouts Salad

Prep Time: 12 mins, Cook Time: 6 mins, Servings: 4

Ingredients:

2 tbsps. apple cider vinegar	½ cup chopped pecans
1 lb. halved Brussels sprouts	1 tbsp. brown sugar
1 tbsp. olive oil	1½ cups water

Instructions:

1. Place the water in the Instant Pot and arrange the steamer basket in the pot, then add Brussels sprouts.
2. Lock the lid. Select the Manual mode, then set the timer for 4 minutes at High Pressure.
3. Once the timer goes off, do a quick pressure release. Carefully open the lid.
4. Drain the Brussels sprouts and transfer to a bowl.
5. Clean the pot and set it to Sauté. Heat the olive oil and add Brussels sprouts and vinegar, stir and cook for 1 minute.
6. Add the sugar and pecans, stir, and cook for 30 seconds more. Remove from the pot to a plate and serve.

Nutritional info:

Calories 186, Fat 4g, Carbs 9g, Protein 3g

Chicken Dip

Prep Time: 12 mins, Cook Time: 15 mins, Servings: 6

Ingredients:

1 cup Greek yogurt	shredded chicken
4 oz. cream cheese	1 cup shredded
½ cup hot sauce	Mozzarella cheese
3 cups cooked and	

Instructions:

1. In the Instant Pot, mix chicken with cream cheese and hot sauce, and stir to combine well.
2. Lock the lid. Select the Manual mode, then set the timer for 15 minutes at High Pressure.
3. Once the timer goes off, do a natural pressure release for 10 minutes, then release any remaining pressure. Carefully open the lid.
4. Add the yogurt and Mozzarella cheese. Give the mixture a good stir. Let rest for about 8 minutes, then serve.

Nutritional info:

Calories 188, Fat 4g, Carbs 8g, Protein 4g

Steamed Asparagus with Mustard Dip

Prep Time: 7 mins, Cook Time: 8 mins, Servings: 4

Ingredients:

1 tsp. Dijon mustard	1 cup water
2 tbsps. mayonnaise	12 asparagus stems
Salt and black pepper, to taste	3 tbsps. lemon juice

Instructions:

1. Mix the Dijon mustard, mayonnaise, salt and black pepper in a bowl. Set aside.
2. Set trivet to the Instant Pot and add the water.
3. Place asparagus stems on the trivet and drizzle with lemon juice.
4. Lock the lid. Select the Manual mode, then set the timer for 8 minutes at High Pressure.
5. Once the timer goes off, do a quick pressure release. Carefully open the lid.
6. Dip the asparagus into mustard mixture.

Nutritional info:

Calories 42, Fat 2.7g, Carbs 3.9g, Protein 1.3g

Cumin Dip

Prep Time: 12 mins, Cook Time: 2 mins, Servings: 4
Ingredients:

1 tbsp. hot sauce
1 tbsp. lime juice
1 cup sour cream
1¼ tsps. ground cumin
⅓ cup mayonnaise

Instructions:
1. In the Instant Pot, mix sour cream with cumin and hot sauce, and stir to combine well.
2. Lock the lid. Select the Manual mode, then set the timer for 2 minutes at High Pressure.
3. Once the timer goes off, do a quick pressure release. Carefully open the lid.
4. Allow the dip to rest until cooled completely. Add the mayo and lime juice and stir well, then serve.

Nutritional info:
Calories 209, Fat 6g, Carbs 7g, Protein 7g

Kale and Wild Rice Appetizer Salad

Prep Time: 12 mins, Cook Time: 25 mins, Servings: 4
Ingredients:

1 tsp. olive oil
1 avocado, peeled, pitted and chopped
3 oz. goat cheese, crumbled
1 cup cooked wild rice
1 bunch kale, roughly chopped

Instructions:
1. Set the Instant Pot to Sauté and heat the olive oil.
2. Add the rice and toast for 2 to 3 minutes, stirring often.
3. Add kale and stir well.
4. Lock the lid. Select the Manual mode, then set the timer for 20 minutes at Low Pressure.
5. Once the timer goes off, do a natural pressure release for 10 minutes, then release any remaining pressure. Carefully open the lid.
6. Add avocado and toss well. Sprinkle the cheese on top and serve.

Nutritional info:
Calories 182, Fat 3g, Carbs 4g, Protein 3g

Ham and Cheese Dip

Prep Time: 12 mins, Cook Time: 12 mins, Servings: 4
Ingredients:

8 ham slices, chopped
2 tbsps. chopped parsley
8 oz. cream cheese
1 cup grated Cheddar cheese
1 cup Swiss cheese

Instructions:
1. Set the Instant Pot to Sauté and brown the ham for 3 to 4 minutes.
2. Add the Swiss, Cheddar and cream cheese, and stir to combine well.
3. Lock the lid. Select the Manual mode, then set the timer for 6 minutes at High Pressure.
4. Once the timer goes off, do a natural pressure release for 5 minutes, then release any remaining pressure. Carefully open the lid.
5. Scatter the parsley all over and divide into bowls to serve.

Nutritional info:
Calories 243, Fat 4g, Carbs 7g, Protein 4g

Pinto Bean Dip

Prep Time: 12 mins, Cook Time: 8 mins, Servings: 4
Ingredients:

2 tbsps. chopped tomatoes
1 (8 oz) can pinto beans, drained
3 tbsps. lemon juice
1¼ cup chopped parsley
4 rosemary sprigs, chopped

Instructions:
1. In the Instant Pot, mix pinto beans with rosemary and tomatoes.
2. Lock the lid. Select the Manual mode, then set the timer for 8 minutes at High Pressure.
3. Once the timer goes off, do a quick pressure release. Carefully open the lid.
4. Blend the mixture with an immersion blender. Add the parsley and lemon juice, and pulse until well combined.
5. Store in an airtight container in the fridge until ready to serve.

Nutritional info:
Calories 272, Fat 3g, Carbs 9g, Protein 8g

Creamy Broccoli Appetizer

Prep Time: 12 mins, Cook Time: 3 mins, Servings: 4
Ingredients:

1 cup water
2 tbsps. mayonnaise
1 tbsp. honey
½ cup Greek yogurt

1 head broccoli, cut into florets
1 apple, cored and sliced

Instructions:

1. In the Instant Pot, add the water. Arrange the steamer basket in the pot, then add the broccoli inside.
2. Lock the lid. Select the Manual mode, then set the timer for 3 minutes at Low Pressure.
3. Once the timer goes off, do a quick pressure release. Carefully open the lid.
4. Drain the broccoli florets and transfer to a bowl. Add the apple, mayo, yogurt and honey, and toss well. Serve immediately.

Nutritional info:

Calories 200, Fat 3g, Carbs 7g, Protein 3g

Lemony Endives Appetizer

Prep Time: 12 mins, Cook Time: 13 mins, Servings: 4
Ingredients:

3 tbsps. olive oil
½ cup chicken stock
Juice of ½ lemon

2 tbsps. chopped parsley
8 endives, trimmed

Instructions:

1. Set the Instant Pot to Sauté and heat the olive oil. Add the endives and cook them for 3 minutes.
2. Add lemon juice and stock, and whisk well.
3. Lock the lid. Select the Manual mode, then set the timer for 10 minutes at High Pressure.
4. Once the timer goes off, do a quick pressure release. Carefully open the lid.
5. Transfer the endives to a large bowl. Drizzle some cooking juices all over and sprinkle with the chopped parsley before serving.

Nutritional info:

Calories 120, Fat 2g, Carbs 12g, Protein 4g

Carrot and Beet Spread

Prep Time: 12 mins, Cook Time: 12 mins, Servings: 6
Ingredients:

1 bunch basil, chopped
8 carrots, chopped
¼ cup lemon juice

4 beets, peeled and chopped
1 cup vegetable stock

Instructions:

1. In the Instant Pot, combine the beets with stock and carrots.
2. Lock the lid. Select the Manual mode and set the cooking time for 12 minutes at High Pressure.
3. Once cooking is complete, do a quick pressure release. Carefully open the lid.
4. Blend the ingredients with an immersion blender, and add the lemon juice and basil, and whisk well. Serve immediately.

Nutritional info:

Calories 100, Fat 1g, Carbs 10g, Protein 3g

Cashew Spread

Prep Time: 12 mins, Cook Time: 6 mins, Servings: 8
Ingredients:

¼ cup nutritional yeast
¼ tsp. garlic powder
½ cup soaked and

drained cashews
10 oz. hummus
½ cup water

Instructions:

1. In the Instant Pot, combine the cashews and water.
2. Lock the lid. Select the Manual mode, then set the timer for 6 minutes at High Pressure.
3. Once the timer goes off, do a quick pressure release. Carefully open the lid.
4. Transfer the cashews to the blender, and add hummus, yeast and garlic powder, and pulse until well combined. Serve immediately.

Nutritional info:

Calories 180, Fat 2g, Carbs 4g, Protein 5g

Crab Spread

Prep Time: 12 mins, Cook Time: 15 mins, Servings: 4

Ingredients:

1 tsp. Worcestershire sauce
½ bunch scallions, chopped
½ cup sour cream
¼ cup half-and-half
8 oz. crab meat

Instructions:

1. In the Instant Pot, mix the crabmeat with sour cream, half-and-half, scallions and Worcestershire sauce, and stir to combine well.
2. Lock the lid. Select the Manual mode, then set the timer for 15 minutes at Low Pressure.
3. Once the timer goes off, do a quick pressure release. Carefully open the lid.
4. Allow the spread cool for a few minutes and serve.

Nutritional info:

Calories 241, Fat 4g, Carbs 8g, Protein 3g

Creamy Avocado Spread

Prep Time: 12 mins, Cook Time: 2 mins, Servings: 4

Ingredients:

1 cup coconut milk
2 pitted, peeled and halved avocados
Juice of 2 limes
½ cup chopped cilantro
¼ tsp. stevia
1 cup water

Instructions:

1. In the Instant Pot, add the water and steamer basket. Place the avocados in the basket.
2. Lock the lid. Select the Manual mode and set the cooking time for 2 minutes at High Pressure.
3. Once cooking is complete, do a quick pressure release. Carefully open the lid.
4. Transfer the avocados to your blender, and add the cilantro, stevia, lime juice, and coconut milk, and blend, or until it reaches your desired consistency. Serve immediately or refrigerate to chill until ready to use.

Nutritional info:

Calories 190, Fat 6g, Carbs 10g, Protein 4g

Scallion and Mayo Spread

Prep Time: 12 mins, Cook Time: 3 mins, Servings: 6

Ingredients:

3 tbsps. chopped dill
1 cup sour cream
1 tbsp. grated lemon zest
½ cup chopped scallions
¼ cup mayonnaise

Instructions:

1. Set the Instant Pot to Sauté and add the scallions. Stir and cook for 1 minute.
2. Add the sour cream and stir to combine well.
3. Lock the lid. Select the Manual mode, then set the timer for 2 minutes at High Pressure.
4. Once the timer goes off, do a quick pressure release. Carefully open the lid.
5. Leave this mixture to rest until cooled completely. Add the mayo, dill, and lemon zest, and stir well. You can serve this with tortilla chips on the side.

Nutritional info:

Calories 222, Fat 4g, Carbs 8g, Protein 4g

Simple Egg Spread

Prep Time: 12 mins, Cook Time: 5 mins, Servings: 4

Ingredients:

1 tbsp. olive oil
4 eggs
1 cup water
Salt, to taste
½ cup mayonnaise
2 green onions, chopped

Instructions:

1. Grease a baking dish with olive oil and crack the eggs in it.
2. Add the water and trivet to the Instant Pot. Place the baking dish on the trivet.
3. Lock the lid. Select the Manual mode, then set the timer for 5 minutes at High Pressure.
4. Once the timer goes off, do a natural pressure release for 3 to 5 minutes. Carefully open the lid.
5. Cool eggs down and mash them with a fork. Sprinkle with salt, mayo, and green onions. Stir well and serve immediately.

Nutritional info:

Calories 222, Fat 3g, Carbs 10g, Protein 4g

Special Ranch Spread

Prep Time: 12 mins, Cook Time: 10 mins, Servings: 12

Ingredients:

4 green onions, chopped

1 cup sour cream

1 lb. bacon, chopped

1 cup shredded Monterey Jack cheese

1 cup mayonnaise

Instructions:

1. Set the Instant Pot to Sauté and cook the bacon for about 4 minutes on each side until it is crispy.
2. Add the sour cream and green onions, and stir to mix well.
3. Lock the lid. Select the Manual mode, then set the timer for 6 minutes at High Pressure.
4. Once the timer goes off, do a natural pressure release for 5 minutes. Carefully open the lid.
5. Add the cheese and mayo and stir. Allow to cool for a few minutes and serve.

Nutritional info:

Calories 261, Fat 4g, Carbs 7g, Protein 4g

Zucchini Spread

Prep Time: 12 mins, Cook Time: 9 mins, Servings: 6

Ingredients:

½ cup water

1 tbsp. olive oil

1 bunch basil, chopped

1½ lbs. zucchinis, chopped

2 garlic cloves, minced

Instructions:

1. Set the Instant Pot to Sauté and heat the olive oil. Cook the garlic cloves for 3 minutes, stirring occasionally.
2. Add zucchinis and water, and mix well.
3. Lock the lid. Select the Manual mode, then set the timer for 3 minutes at High Pressure.
4. Once the timer goes off, do a quick pressure release. Carefully open the lid.
5. Add the basil and blend the mixture with an immersion blender until smooth.
6. Select the Simmer mode and cook for 2 minutes more.
7. Transfer to a bowl and serve warm.

Nutritional info:

Calories 120, Fat 2g, Carbs 7g, Protein 2g

Chicken Meatballs in Barbecue Sauce

Prep Time: 6 mins, Cook Time: 15 mins, Servings: 8

Ingredients:

24 oz. frozen chicken meatballs

½ tsp. crushed red pepper

12 oz. barbecue

sauce

¼ cup water

12 oz. apricot preserves

Instructions:

1. Add all the ingredients to the Instant Pot. Stir to mix well.
2. Lock the lid. Select the Manual mode, then set the timer for 5 minutes at High Pressure.
3. Once the timer goes off, do a quick pressure release. Carefully open the lid.
4. Serve the meatballs on a platter.

Nutritional info:

Calories 347, Fat 11.1g, Carbs 47.7g, Protein: 14.6g

Goat Cheese Mushrooms

Prep Time: 12 mins, Cook Time: 10 mins, Servings:8

Ingredients:

1½ cups water

½ cup chopped, drained and roasted sweet red peppers

½ cup crumbled goat cheese

4 tsps. olive oil

24 baby Portobello mushrooms

White pepper, to taste

Instructions:

1. Add the trivet and water to the Instant Pot.
2. Place mushroom caps in a greased baking pan and top with cheese and red pepper.
3. Sprinkle with white pepper and drizzle with olive oil.
4. Place the baking pan on the trivet.
5. Lock the lid. Select the Manual mode, then set the timer for 10 minutes at High Pressure.
6. Once the timer goes off, do a quick pressure release. Carefully open the lid.
7. Allow to cool before serving.

Nutritional info:

Calories 90, Fat 3g, Carbs 9.6g, Protein 9.6g

Chili Endives Platter

Prep Time: 12 mins, Cook Time: 7 mins, Servings: 4

Ingredients:

¼ tsp. chili powder
1 tbsp. butter
4 trimmed and

halved endives
1 tbsp. lemon juice
Salt, to taste

Instructions:

1. Set the Instant Pot to Sauté and melt the butter. Add the endives, salt, chili powder and lemon juice to the pot.
2. Lock the lid. Select the Manual mode, then set the timer for 7 minutes at High Pressure.
3. Once the timer goes off, do a quick pressure release. Carefully open the lid.
4. Divide the endives into bowls. Drizzle some cooking juice over them and serve.

Nutritional info:

Calories 90, Fat 4g, Carbs 12g, Protein 3g

Green Olive Pâté

Prep Time: 12 mins, Cook Time: 2 mins, Servings: 4

Ingredients:

½ cup olive oil
2 anchovy fillets
1 tbsp. chopped capers

2 cups pitted green olives
2 garlic cloves, minced

Instructions:

1. In a food processor, process the olives with anchovy fillets, garlic, capers and olive oil, then transfer to the Instant Pot.
2. Lock the lid. Select the Manual mode, then set the timer for 2 minutes at Low Pressure.
3. Once the timer goes off, do a quick pressure release. Carefully open the lid.
4. Remove from the pot and serve warm.

Nutritional info:

Calories 118, Fat 2g, Carbs 5g, Protein 4g

Fish and Carrot Balls

Prep Time: 12 mins, Cook Time: 10 mins, Servings: 16

Ingredients:

¼ cup cornstarch
1 carrot, grated
1½ cups fish stock
3 egg whites

1½ lbs. skinless, boneless and ground pike fillets

Instructions:

1. In a bowl, mix the fillets with egg whites, cornstarch and carrot. Form the mixture into equal-sized balls with your hands.
2. Put the stock and fish balls into the Instant pot.
3. Lock the lid. Select the Manual function and cook for 10 minutes at Low Pressure.
4. Once cooking is complete, do a quick pressure release. Carefully open the lid.
5. Drain the fish balls and arrange them on a platter and serve.

Nutritional info:

Calories 162, Fat 3g, Carbs 8g, Protein 4g

Cheesy Broccoli Appetizer Salad

Prep Time: 12 mins, Cook Time: 4 mins, Servings: 4

Ingredients:

1½ cups water
2 tbsps. balsamic vinegar
4 oz. cubed Cheddar cheese

1 cup mayonnaise
1 head broccoli, cut into florets
⅛ cup pumpkin seeds

Instructions:

1. Put the water into the Instant Pot and arrange the steamer basket in the pot, then add the broccoli.
2. Lock the lid. Select the Manual mode, then set the timer for 3 minutes at High Pressure.
3. Once the timer goes off, do a quick pressure release. Carefully open the lid.
4. Drain the broccoli and chop, then transfer to a bowl.
5. Add the cheese, pumpkin seeds, mayo and vinegar, and toss to combine. Serve immediately.

Nutritional info:

Calories 182, Fat 4g, Carbs 7g, Protein 4g

Grated Carrot Appetizer Salad

Prep Time: 12 mins, Cook Time: 3 mins, Servings: 4

Ingredients:

1 lb. carrots, grated
¼ cup water
Salt, to taste
1 tbsp. lemon juice
1 tsp. red pepper flakes
1 tbsp. chopped parsley

Instructions:

1. In the Instant Pot, mix the carrots with water and salt.
2. Lock the lid. Select the Manual mode, then set the timer for 3 minutes at High Pressure.
3. Once the timer goes off, do a quick pressure release. Carefully open the lid.
4. Drain the carrots and cool them in a bowl.
5. Add the lemon juice, pepper flakes and parsley to the bowl, and toss well. Serve immediately.

Nutritional info:

Calories 152, Fat 3g, Carbs 4g, Protein 3g

Creamy Endives Appetizer Salad

Prep Time: 12 mins, Cook Time: 18 mins, Servings: 3

Ingredients:

1 cup vegetable soup
3 big endives, roughly chopped
3 tbsps. heavy cream
2 tbsps. extra virgin olive oil
½ yellow onion, chopped

Instructions:

1. Set the Instant Pot to Sauté and heat the olive oil. Add the onion, stir and cook for 4 minutes until tender.
2. Add the endives, stir and cook for 4 minutes more. Pour in the stock and whisk to combine.
3. Lock the lid. Select the Manual mode, then set the timer for 10 minutes at High Pressure.
4. Once the timer goes off, do a quick pressure release. Carefully open the lid.
5. Stir in the heavy cream and cook for 1 minute. Remove from the pot and serve in bowls.

Nutritional info:

Calories 253, Fat 4g, Carbs 12g, Protein 15g

Green Beans Appetizer Salad

Prep Time: 12 mins, Cook Time: 2 mins, Servings: 4

Ingredients:

1 tbsp. red wine vinegar
1 lb. green beans
½ cup water
2 sliced red onions
1 tbsp. olive oil
1 tbsp. Creole mustard

Instructions:

1. In the Instant Pot, mix green beans with water.
2. Lock the lid. Select the Manual mode, then set the timer for 2 minutes at High Pressure.
3. Once the timer goes off, do a quick pressure release. Carefully open the lid.
4. Drain the green beans and transfer to a bowl. Add the onion slices, mustard, vinegar, and oil, and gently toss to combine. Serve immediately.

Nutritional info:

Calories 121, Fat 4g, Carbs 6g, Protein 4g

Kale and Carrots Salad

Prep Time: 12 mins, Cook Time: 7 mins, Servings: 4

Ingredients:

1 tbsp. olive oil
3 carrots, sliced
1 red onion, chopped
10 oz. kale, roughly chopped
½ cup chicken stock

Instructions:

1. Set the Instant Pot to Sauté and heat the olive oil.
2. Add the onion and carrots, stir, and cook for 1 to 2 minutes.
3. Stir in stock and kale.
4. Lock the lid. Select the Manual mode, then set the timer for 5 minutes at High Pressure.
5. Once the timer goes off, do a quick pressure release. Carefully open the lid.
6. Divide the vegetables among four bowls and serve.

Nutritional info:

Calories 128, Fat 2g, Carbs 8g, Protein 4g

Minty Kale Salad with Pineapple

Prep Time: 12 mins, Cook Time: 3 mins, Servings: 4

Ingredients:

2 tbsps. lemon juice
2 tbsps. chopped mint
1 bunch kale, roughly chopped
1 tsp. sesame oil
1 cup chopped pineapple

Instructions:

1. Set the Instant Pot to Sauté and heat the oil.
2. Add kale, stir, and cook for 1 minute.
3. Add pineapple, lemon juice and mint, and stir well. Divide the salad among plates and serve.

Nutritional info:

Calories 121, Fat 1g, Carbs 4g, Protein 2g

Hummus

Prep Time: 20 mins, Cook Time: 30 mins, Servings: 6

Ingredients:

1 (15 oz.) can chickpeas
1 cup water
3 garlic cloves, minced
2 oz. sliced fresh jalapeño pepper
2 tbsps. lemon juice
½ tsp. ground cumin

Instructions:

1. Drain the chickpeas but reserve the liquid in a bowl.
2. Pour the water and chickpeas into the Instant Pot.
3. Lock the lid. Select the Manual mode, then set the timer for 35 minutes at High Pressure.
4. Once the timer goes off, do a quick pressure release. Carefully open the lid.
5. Transfer the chickpeas to a food processor.
6. Add the remaining ingredients to the food processor and pulse until smooth.
7. Serve with crackers, bread or vegetable strips.

Nutritional info:

Calories 23, Fat 0.2g, Carbs 4.5g, Protein: 1g

Watercress Appetizer Salad

Prep Time: 12 mins, Cook Time: 2 mins, Servings: 4

Ingredients:

1 bunch watercress, roughly torn
½ cup water
1 tbsp. lemon juice
1 cubed watermelon
1 tbsp. olive oil
2 peaches, pitted and sliced

Instructions:

1. In the Instant Pot, mix watercress with water.
2. Lock the lid. Select the Manual mode, then set the timer for 2 minutes at High Pressure.
3. Once the timer goes off, do a quick pressure release. Carefully open the lid.
4. Drain the watercress and transfer to a bowl. Add peaches, watermelon, oil, and lemon juice, and toss well. Divide the salad into salad bowls and serve.

Nutritional info:

Calories 111, Fat 3g, Carbs 5g, Protein 3g

Simple Red Pepper Hummus

Prep Time: 12 mins, Cook Time: 1 hour 30 mins, Servings: 4

Ingredients:

½ cup lemon juice
2 tbsps. sesame oil
1 tbsp. tahini paste
3 roasted red peppers
1 lb. chickpeas, soaked in water overnight

Instructions:

1. In the Instant Pot, mix chickpeas with water.
2. Lock the lid. Select the Manual mode, then set the timer for 1 hour and 30 minutes at High Pressure.
3. Once the timer goes off, do a quick pressure release. Carefully open the lid.
4. Drain the chickpeas and transfer to a food processor. Add the roasted peppers, sesame oil, lemon juice, and tahini paste to the chickpeas, and pulse until it reaches your preferred consistency.
5. Serve immediately or refrigerate to chill until ready to use.

Nutritional info:

Calories 162, Fat 4g, Carbs 7g, Protein 8g

Lettuce Wrapped Tofu

Prep Time: 12 mins, Cook Time: 5 mins, Servings: 4

Ingredients:

1 cup water
2 tbsps. tomato ketchup
4 lettuce leaves
1 tbsp. BBQ sauce
½ cup shredded Mozzarella cheese
2 blocks firmly pressed tofu

Instructions:

1. Add the trivet and water to the Instant Pot.
2. Wrap the tofu well in lettuce leaves along with a little rubbing of BBQ sauce and tomato ketchup.
3. Transfer the wrapped tofu on the trivet and top with Mozzarella cheese.
4. Lock the lid. Select the Manual mode, then set the timer for 5 minutes at High Pressure.
5. Once the timer goes off, do a quick pressure release. Carefully open the lid.
6. Serve hot.

Nutritional info:

Calories 68, Fat 3.3g, Carbs 4.7g, Protein 6.3g

Maple Brussels Sprouts with Orange Juice

Prep Time: 12 mins, Cook Time: 6 mins, Servings: 4

Ingredients:

2 tbsps. maple syrup
¼ cup orange juice
1 tbsp. butter
2 lbs. halved Brussels sprouts
1 tsp. orange zest

Instructions:

1. Set the Instant Pot to Sauté and melt the butter.
2. Add orange juice, orange zest and maple syrup, stir and cook for 1 to 2 minutes.
3. Add Brussels sprouts and stir well.
4. Lock the lid. Select the Manual mode, then set the timer for 4 minutes at High Pressure.
5. Once the timer goes off, do a quick pressure release. Carefully open the lid.
6. Serve the Brussels sprouts on a plate.

Nutritional info:

Calories 90, Fat 2g, Carbs 12g, Protein 3g

Mexican Corn on the Cob

Prep Time: 12 mins, Cook Time: 15 mins, Servings: 4

Ingredients:

4 ears of corn
¼ cup mayonnaise
1 tbsp. butter
¼ tsp. cayenne
pepper
1 cup water
¾ cup crumbled feta cheese

Instructions:

1. On a clean work surface, brush the corn generously with mayo and butter. Season with cayenne pepper.
2. Add the water and steamer basket to the Instant Pot. Arrange the corn in the steamer basket.
3. Lock the lid. Select the Manual mode, then set the timer for 15 minutes at High Pressure.
4. Once the timer goes off, do a quick pressure release. Carefully open the lid.
5. Transfer the corn to a large platter. Sprinkle the feta cheese all over and serve hot.

Nutritional info:

Calories 172, Fat 4g, Carbs 5g, Protein 3g

Mushroom Bacon Skewers

Prep Time: 12 mins, Cook Time: 20 mins, Servings: 12

Ingredients:

24 medium fresh mushrooms
12 bacon strips
½ cup BBQ sauce
¼ cup chilli sauce
¼ cup vinegar
1 cup water

Instructions:

1. Wrap each mushroom with a piece of bacon and secure with a toothpick.
2. Thread onto wooden skewers and brush with BBQ sauce, chilli sauce and vinegar.
3. Add the trivet and water to the Instant Pot. Place the skewers on the trivet.
4. Lock the lid. Select the Manual mode, then set the timer for 20 minutes at High Pressure.
5. Once the timer goes off, do a quick pressure release. Carefully open the lid.
6. Serve hot.

Nutritional info:

Calories 126, Fat 9.1g, Carbs 5.2g, Protein 5.2g

Prosciutto Wrapped Asparagus

Prep Time: 6 mins, Cook Time: 4 mins, Servings: 4

Ingredients:

1 cup water	3 tbsps. mustard
2 tbsps. honey	sauce
1 lb. thick asparagus	9 oz. prosciutto,
1 cup shredded	thinly sliced
Cheddar cheese	

Instructions:

1. In the Instant Pot, add the water and trivet.
2. Wrap the asparagus well in thin slices of prosciutto and rub with mustard sauce.
3. Place the wrapped asparagus on the trivet and top with honey and cheese.
4. Lock the lid. Select the Manual mode, then set the timer for 4 minutes at High Pressure.
5. Once the timer goes off, do a quick pressure release. Carefully open the lid.
6. Serve hot.

Nutritional info:

Calories 275, Fat 14.2g, Carbs 15.3g, Protein 22.9g

Southern Peanuts

Prep Time: 12 mins, Cook Time: 1 hour 15 mins, Servings: 4

Ingredients:

1 lb. peanuts	2 garlic cloves,
¼ cup sea salt	minced
1 tbsp. Cajun	1 jalapeño pepper,
seasoning	chopped

Instructions:

1. In the Instant Pot mix peanuts with sea salt, Cajun seasoning, garlic and jalapeño.
2. Add enough water to cover.
3. Lock the lid. Select the Manual mode, then set the timer for 1 hour and 15 minutes at High Pressure.
4. Once the timer goes off, do a quick pressure release. Carefully open the lid.
5. Drain the peanuts and transfer to bowls, then serve.

Nutritional info:

Calories 100, Fat 4g, Carbs 7g, Protein 2g

Chapter 10 Broths and Sauces Recipe

Béarnaise Sauce

Prep Time: 6 mins, Cook Time: 3 mins, Servings: 4

Ingredients:

2 tsps. freshly	4 beaten egg yolks
squeezed lemon juice	¼ tsp. onion powder
2 tbsps. fresh	⅔ lb. butter
tarragon	

Instructions:

1. Press the Sauté button on the Instant Pot and melt the butter.
2. Transfer the melted butter to a mixing bowl.
3. Slowly add the egg yolks to the bowl while whisking.
4. Continue stirring so that no lumps form.
5. Add the lemon juice, onion powder, and fresh tarragon, and whisk well.
6. Béarnaise sauce is suitable for many dishes, you can serve it with roasted beef chops, grilled pork chops, or chicken tenderloin.

Nutritional info:

Calories 603, Carbs 1.4g, Protein 3.5g, Fat 66.2g

Hollandaise Sauce

Prep Time: 6 mins, Cook Time: 5 mins, Servings: 4

Ingredients:

⅔ lb. butter	Salt and pepper, to
4 egg yolks, beaten	taste
2 tbsps. lemon juice	

Instructions:

1. Press the Sauté button on the Instant Pot.
2. Add the butter and heat to melt.
3. Whisk vigorously while adding the yolks. Cook for 1 minute.
4. Continue stirring and add the lemon juice, salt, and pepper.
5. You can serve the hollandaise sauce with poached or grilled fish or chicken.

Nutritional info:

Calories 606, Fat 66.8g, Carbs 2.2g, Protein 3.5g

Chimichurri Sauce

Prep Time: 6 mins, Cook Time: 3 hours, Servings: 6

Ingredients:

2 garlic cloves, minced
1 green chili pepper, chopped
1 lemon, juice and zest
2 tbsps. olive oil
½ yellow bell pepper, chopped
1 tbsp. white wine vinegar

Instructions:

1. Place all ingredients in the Instant Pot and stir to combine.
2. Lock the lid. Select the Slow Cook mode, then set the timer for 3 hours at High Pressure.
3. Once the timer goes off, do a quick pressure release. Carefully open the lid.
4. Allow to cool for 30 minutes and serve with grilled meats, steaks, or sausages.

Nutritional info:

Calories 326, Carbs 1.9g, Protein 0.3g, Fat 36.5g

Creamy Cheese Sauce

Prep Time: 6 mins, Cook Time: 4 hours, Servings: 4

Ingredients:

¼ cup cream cheese
¼ cup heavy whipping cream
2 tbsps. melted butter
Salt and pepper, to taste
½ cup grated Cheddar cheese

Instructions:

1. Put all the ingredients in the Instant Pot and stir to combine.
2. Lock the lid. Select the Slow Cook mode, then set the timer for 4 hours at High Pressure.
3. Once the timer goes off, do a quick pressure release. Carefully open the lid.
4. You can serve this cheese sauce with French fries, Nachos, chicken nuggets, or pretzels.

Nutritional info:

Calories 250, Carbs5.3g, Protein 10.9g, Fat 20.3g

Satay Sauce

Prep Time: 6 mins, Cook Time: 3 hours, Servings: 6

Ingredients:

⅓ cup peanut butter
1 red chili pepper, finely chopped
4 tbsps. soy sauce
1 cup coconut milk
1 garlic clove, minced

Instructions:

1. Place all ingredients in the Instant Pot and stir until everything is well combined.
2. Lock the lid. Select the Slow Cook mode, then set the timer for 3 hours at High Pressure.
3. Once the timer goes off, do a quick pressure release. Carefully open the lid.
4. Serve the satay sauce with beef kebabs or chicken skewers, or you can serve it as dipping sauce.

Nutritional info:

Calories 138, Carbs 6.9g, Protein 2.1g, Fat 12.3g

Caesar Salad Dressing

Prep Time: 6 mins, Cook Time: 3 hours, Servings: 6

Ingredients:

½ cup olive oil
1 tbsp. Dijon mustard
½ cup grated Parmesan cheese
⅔ oz. chopped anchovies
½ freshly squeezed lemon juice
¼ cup water
Salt and pepper, to taste

Instructions:

1. Place all the ingredients in the Instant Pot and stir to incorporate.
2. Lock the lid. Select the Slow Cook mode, then set the timer for 3 hours at High Pressure.
3. Once the timer goes off, do a quick pressure release. Carefully open the lid.
4. You can use the Caesar dressing to marinate the meat or dress the salad, or you can use it as a dipping sauce for crudités.

Nutritional info:

Calories 203, Carbs 1.5g, Protein 3.4g, Fat 20.7g

Spicy Thousand Island Dressing

Prep Time: 10 mins, Cook Time: 2 hours, Servings: 4

Ingredients:

1 tsp. tabasco
1 shallot, finely chopped
1 cup mayonnaise
4 tbsps. chopped dill pickles
1 tbsp. freshly squeezed lemon juice
¼ cup water
Salt and pepper, to taste

Instructions:

1. Place all the ingredients in the Instant Pot and whisk to combine.
2. Lock the lid. Select the Slow Cook mode, then set the timer for 2 hours at High Pressure.
3. Once the timer goes off, do a quick pressure release. Carefully open the lid.
4. You can use this dressing to serve the burgers, sandwiches, or salads.

Nutritional info:

Calories 85, Carbs 2.3g, Protein 1.7g, Fat 7.8g

Keto Gravy

Prep Time: 6 mins, Cook Time: 10 mins, Servings: 6

Ingredients:

2 tbsps. butter
1 white onion, chopped
2 cups chicken bone
broth
1 tbsp. balsamic vinegar
¼ cup coconut milk

Instructions:

1. Press the Sauté button on the Instant Pot.
2. Melt the butter and sauté the onions for 2 minutes.
3. Add the remaining ingredients. Stir constantly for 5 minutes or until slightly thickened.
4. You can serve the gravy on top of any roasted steaks, meats, or seafoods. You can even use it as a dressing for your salad.

Nutritional info:

Calories 59, Fat 6.3g, Carbs 1.1g, Protein 0.2g

Chicken Bone Broth

Prep Time: 12 mins, Cook time: 2 to 3 hours, Servings: 4

Ingredients:

1 lb. bones of one whole chicken
2 tbsps. apple cider vinegar
2 cloves garlic, minced
8 cups water
1 tsp. sea salt

Instructions:

1. Add all the ingredients to the Instant Pot.
2. Lock the lid. Select the Soup mode, then set the timer for 2 to 3 hours at High Pressure.
3. Once the timer goes off, do a natural pressure release for 10 to 20 minutes, then release any remaining pressure. Carefully open the lid.
4. Strain the liquid and transfer the broth to an airtight container to store in the refrigerator for up to 5 days. Bone soup is healthy and recommended for those with a leaky gut.

Nutritional info:

Calories: 100, Fat: 1g, Carbs: 0g, Protein: 20g

Ranch Dip

Prep Time: 6 mins, Cook Time: 2 mins, Servings: 8

Ingredients:

1 cup olive oil
Salt and pepper, to taste
1 cup beaten egg
whites
1 tsp. mustard paste
Juice of 1 lemon

Instructions:

1. In the Instant Pot, add all the ingredients and mix well.
2. Press the Sauté button and heat for 2 minutes while stirring. Do not bring to a simmer.
3. You can serve the ranch dip with chicken nuggets, French fries, or green salad.

Nutritional info:

Calories 258, Carbs 1.2g, Protein 3.4g, Fat 27.1g

Chapter 11 Beans, Grains and Legumes Recipe

Vegan Rice Pudding

Prep Time: 6 mins, Cook Time: 18 mins, Servings: 6

Ingredients:

⅔ cup Jasmine rice, rinsed and drained
¼ cup granulated sugar

3 cups almond milk
Salt, to taste
1½ tsps. vanilla extract

Instructions:

1. Add all the ingredients, except vanilla extract, to the Instant Pot.
2. Lock the lid. Select the Manual mode, then set the timer for 18 minutes at Low Pressure.
3. Once the timer goes off, do a natural pressure release for 10 minutes, then release any remaining pressure. Carefully open the lid.
4. Stir in the vanilla extract and cool for 10 minutes, then serve.

Nutritional info:

Calories 154, Fat 1.3g, Carbs 32.6g, Protein: 2g

Almond Arborio Risotto

Prep Time: 10 mins, Cook Time: 5 mins, Servings: 2

Ingredients:

½ cup Arborio rice
2 cups vanilla almond milk
1 tsp. vanilla extract

2 tbsps. agave syrup
¼ cup toasted almond flakes, for garnish

Instructions:

1. Add all the ingredients, except for the almond flakes, to the Instant Pot. Stir to mix well.
2. Lock the lid. Set to the Manual mode, then set the timer for 5 minutes at Low Pressure.
3. Once the timer goes off, perform a natural pressure release. Carefully open the lid.
4. Serve the risotto with almond flakes immediately.

Nutritional info:

Calories 116, Carbs 22.5g, Protein 2.0g, Fat 2.1g

Butternut Squash Arborio Risotto

Prep Time: 10 mins, Cook Time: 12 mins, Servings: 4

Ingredients:

1 tbsp. olive oil
2 garlic cloves, whole
1 sprig sage, leaves removed
½ butternut squash, diced

1 cup Arborio rice
½ tsp. freshly ground nutmeg
2 tbsps. white wine
1 tsp. sea salt
2 cups water

Instructions:

1. Grease the Instant Pot with olive oil.
2. Set the pot to Sauté mode, then add the garlic and sage. Sauté for 2 minutes or until fragrant.
3. Add the butternut squash and sauté for 5 minutes.
4. Add the remaining ingredients. Stir to mix well.
5. Lock the lid. Set to the Manual mode, then set the timer for 5 minutes at Low Pressure.
6. Once the timer goes off, perform a natural pressure release. Carefully open the lid.
7. Serve immediately.

Nutritional info:

Calories 323, Carbs 62.4g, Protein 5.3g, Fat 5.2g

Mixed Rice Meal

Prep Time: 6 mins, Cook Time: 20 mins, Servings: 4

Ingredients:

3 cups mixture of brown rice and white rice

1½ tsps. salt
4½ cups water
2 tbsps. olive oil

Instructions:

1. Add all the ingredients to the pot.
2. Lock the lid. Select the Multigrain mode, then set the timer for 20 minutes at Low Pressure.
3. Once the timer goes off, do a natural pressure release for 10 minutes, then release any remaining pressure. Carefully open the lid.
4. Check if the grains are soft and cooked well. If not, cook for 5 minutes more.
5. Fluff the mixture with a fork and serve.

Nutritional info:

Calories 126, Carbs 18g, Fat 5g, Protein 0g

Quinoa Risotto

Prep Time: 6 mins, Cook Time: 3 hours, Servings: 4
Ingredients:

¾ cup diced onion
1 garlic clove, minced
1 tbsp. butter
Salt and pepper, to taste

2½ cups chicken broth
1 cup rinsed quinoa
¼ cup shredded Parmesan cheese

Instructions:
1. Combine the onion, garlic, and butter in a microwave-safe bowl.
2. Microwave for 5 minutes, stirring every 90 seconds.
3. Put the mixture in the Instant Pot.
4. Add the salt, pepper, broth, and quinoa and stir to combine.
5. Lock the lid. Select the Slow Cook mode, then set the timer for 3 hours at High Pressure.
6. Once the timer goes off, perform a natural release for 10 minutes, then release any remaining pressure. Carefully open the lid.
7. Mix the Parmesan into the mixture. Taste and adjust the seasoning, if needed.

Nutritional info:
Calories 282, Fat 8.5g, Carbs 39.7g, Protein 12.1g

Raisin Butter Rice

Prep Time: 3 mins, Cook Time: 12 mins, Servings: 4
Ingredients:

3 cups wild rice, soaked in water overnight and drained

3 cups water
½ cup raisins
¼ cup salted butter
1 tsp. salt

Instructions:
1. Add all the ingredients to the Instant Pot.
2. Lock the lid. Select the Rice mode, then set the timer for 12 minutes at Low Pressure.
3. Once the timer goes off, perform a natural release for 8 to 10 minutes.
4. Carefully open the lid and use a fork to fluff the rice.
5. Serve warm.

Nutritional info:
Calories 271, Fat 3.0g, Carbs 58.1g, Protein 2.4g

Parmesan Risotto

Prep Time: 6 mins, Cook Time: 20 mins, Servings: 4
Ingredients:

4 cups chicken broth, divided
4 tbsps. butter
1 small onion, diced
2 garlic cloves, minced

1½ cups Arborio rice
Salt and pepper, to taste
¼ cup shredded Parmesan cheese

Instructions:
1. Set the Instant Pot to sauté and melt the butter.
2. Mix the onions in and let them cook for 2 minutes until they have become soft.
3. Add the garlic and rice and stir. Cook for 1 more minute.
4. Add 1 cup of broth and cook about 3 minutes, or until the broth is absorbed.
5. Add 3 cups of broth, salt, and pepper.
6. Sprinkle with Parmesan cheese.
7. Lock the lid. Select the Manual mode, then set the timer for 10 minutes at Low Pressure.
8. Once the timer goes off, perform a natural release for 5 minutes, then release any remaining pressure. Carefully open the lid.
9. Ladle the rice into bowls and serve.

Nutritional info:
Calories 359, Fat 18.4g, Carbs 39.9g, Protein 9.8g

Green Tea Rice Risotto

Prep Time: 6 mins, Cook Time: 20 mins, Servings: 4
Ingredients:

¼ cup lentils, rinsed
Salt, to taste
3 green tea bags

1 cup brown rice, rinsed
7 cups water

Instructions:
1. In the Instant Pot, add all ingredients and stir gently.
2. Lock the lid. Select the Manual mode, then set the timer for 20 minutes at Low Pressure.
3. Once the timer goes off, do a quick pressure release. Carefully open the lid.
4. Serve immediately.

Nutritional info:
Calories 123, Carbs 24.5g, Fat 1g, Protein 3g

Basmati Rice

Prep Time: 2 minutes; Cook Time: 6 mins, Servings: 4

Ingredients:

2 cups Indian basmati rice

2 cups water

Instructions:

1. Add the rice and water to the Instant Pot.
2. Lock the lid. Select the Rice mode, then set the timer for 6 minutes at Low Pressure.
3. Once the timer goes off, do a natural pressure release for 3 to 5 minutes. Carefully open the lid.
4. Use a fork to fluff the rice, then serve.

Nutritional info:

Calories 130, Fat 0.2g, Carbs 28.7g, Protein 2.4g

Mexican Rice

Prep Time: 6 mins, Cook Time: 10 mins, Servings: 4

Ingredients:

2 cups long-grain rice
2½ cup water
½ cup green salsa
1 cup cilantro

1 avocado
Salt and pepper, to taste

Instructions:

1. Add the rice and water to the Instant Pot.
2. Lock the lid. Select the Rice mode, then set the timer for 5 minutes at Low Pressure.
3. Once the timer goes off, do a natural pressure release for 3 to 5 minutes. Carefully open the lid.
4. Fluff rice and let it cool. Put the salsa, cilantro, and avocado in a blender.
5. Pulse the ingredients together until they are creamy and mix into the rice.
6. Mix everything together and season with salt and pepper.
7. Serve immediately.

Nutritional info:

Calories 250, Fat 1.3g, Carbs 25.8g, Protein 2.8g

Multigrain Rice

Prep Time: 2 mins, Cook Time: 20 mins, Servings: 6 to 8

Ingredients:

2 tbsps. olive oil
3¾ cups water
3 cups wild brown

rice
Salt, to taste

Instructions:

1. Combine the oil, water, and brown rice in the pot.
2. Season with salt.
3. Lock the lid. Select the Multigrain mode, then set the timer for 20 minutes on Low Pressure.
4. Once the timer goes off, do a natural pressure release for 5 minutes. Carefully open the lid.
5. Fluff the rice with a fork.
6. Serve immediately.

Nutritional info:

Calories 160, Fat 1.5g, Carbs 33.0g, Protein 5.0g

Basic Tomato Rice

Prep Time: 6 mins, Cook Time:5 mins, Servings: 4

Ingredients:

1 tbsp. extra virgin olive oil
2 cups white rice, rinsed and drained

4½ cups water
1 large, ripe tomato
Salt and pepper, to taste

Instructions:

1. Add olive oil, rice, and water to Instant Pot. Gently stir.
2. Place whole tomato, bottom-side up, in the middle.
3. Lock the lid. Select the Rice mode, then set the timer for 5 minutes at Low Pressure.
4. Once the timer goes off, do a natural pressure release for 3 to 5 minutes, then release any remaining pressure. Carefully open the lid.
5. Using a rice paddle, break up tomato while fluffing up rice. Season with salt and pepper.
6. Serve immediately.

Nutritional info:

Calories 183, Carbs 25.4g, Fat 5g, Protein 19g

Black Olives in Tomato Rice

Prep Time: 12 mins, Cook Time:5 mins, Servings: 4

Ingredients:

¼ tsp. balsamic vinegar

4½ cups water

¼ cup black olives in brine rings

1 cup ripe tomato,

deseeded and minced

2 cups Basmati rice, rinsed and drained

Salt and pepper, to taste

Instructions:

1. Pour all the ingredients into Instant Pot. Gently stir.
2. Lock the lid. Select the Rice mode, then set the timer for 5 minutes at Low Pressure.
3. Once the timer goes off, do a natural pressure release for 3 to 5 minutes, then release any remaining pressure. Carefully open the lid.
4. Using a rice paddle, fluff up rice.
5. Serve warm.

Nutritional info:

Calories 176, Carbs 23.4g, Fat 3.1g, Protein 13g

Chipotle-Style Cilantro Rice

Prep Time: 20 mins, Cook Time: 20 mins, Servings: 4

Ingredients:

2 cups brown rice, rinsed

4 small bay leaves

2¾ cups water

1½ tbsps. olive oil

½ cup chopped cilantro

1 lime, juiced

1 tsp. salt

Instructions:

1. Place the brown rice, bay leaves, and water in the Instant Pot.
2. Lock the lid. Select the Rice mode and cook for 20 minutes at High Pressure.
3. Once cooking is complete, do a natural pressure release for 10 minutes, then release any remaining pressure. Carefully open the lid.
4. Add the olive oil, cilantro, lime juice, and salt to the pot and stir until well combined. Serve warm.

Nutritional info:

Calories 394, Carbs 73.8g, Protein 7.3g, Fat 7.7g

Confetti Basmati Rice

Prep Time: 12 mins, Cook Time: 13 mins, Servings: 6

Ingredients:

1 tbsp. olive oil

1 onion, chopped

½ cup frozen peas

2 cups basmati rice

Salt and pepper, to

taste

3 cups water

1 carrot, grated

1 medium bell pepper, chopped

Instructions:

1. Set the pot to Sauté and add the olive oil to coat the pot.
2. Add the onion and sauté for 3 minutes or until it becomes soft.
3. Put the peas and rice into the pot. Season with salt and pepper, and mix well.
4. Add the water, carrots, and bell pepper and stir again.
5. Lock the lid. Select the Manual mode, then set the timer for 3 minutes at Low Pressure.
6. Once the timer goes off, perform a natural release for 1 minutes, then release any remaining pressure. Carefully open the lid.
7. Fluff with a fork and enjoy.

Nutritional info:

Calories 271, Fat 2.9g, Carbs 54.8g, Protein 5.5g

Israeli Couscous

Prep Time: 4 mins, Cook Time: 10 mins, Servings: 10

Ingredients:

2 tbsps. butter

2 cups couscous

2½ cups chicken broth

Instructions:

1. Set the Instant Pot to Sauté and melt the butter.
2. Add the couscous and broth to the pot. Whisk well.
3. Lock the lid. Select the Rice mode, then set the timer for 5 minutes at High Pressure.
4. Once the timer goes off, do a natural pressure release for 3 to 5 minutes. Carefully open the lid.
5. Use a fork to fluff couscous, then serve warm.

Nutritional info:

Calories 380, Fat 1g, Carbs 80g, Protein 12g

Cauliflower and Pineapple Rice

Prep Time: 20 mins, Cook Time: 20 mins, Servings: 4

Ingredients:

2 tsps. extra virgin olive oil

2 cups jasmine rice

1 cauliflower, florets separated and chopped

½ pineapple, peeled and chopped

4 cups water

Salt and ground black pepper, to taste

Instructions:

1. Mix all the ingredients in your Instant Pot and stir to incorporate.
2. Lock the lid. Select the Manual mode and cook for 20 minutes at Low Pressure.
3. Once cooking is complete, do a natural pressure release for 10 minutes, then release any remaining pressure. Carefully open the lid.
4. Using a fork to fluff the rice and serve in bowls.

Nutritional info:

Calories 441, Carbs 95.3g, Protein 7.6g, Fat 3.0g

Khichdi Dal

Prep Time: 4 minutes; Cook Time: 12 mins, Servings: 4

Ingredients:

1 tbsp. butter

2 cups water

¼ tsp. salt

1 tsp. Balti seasoning

1 cup khichdi mix

Instructions:

1. Set the Instant Pot to Sauté. Add the butter and heat to melt.
2. Mix in the Balti seasoning and cook for 1 minute.
3. Add the Khichdi mix, water, and salt to the pot.
4. Lock the lid. Select the Porridge mode, then set the timer for 10 minutes at High Pressure.
5. Once the timer goes off, do a natural pressure release for 3 to 5 minutes. Carefully open the lid.
6. Fluff the khichdi with a fork and serve warm.

Nutritional info:

Calories 242, Fat 0.4g, Carbs 53.4g, Protein 4.4g

Copycat Cilantro Lime Rice

Prep Time: 3 minutes; Cook Time: 10 mins, Servings: 2

Ingredients:

1¼ cups water

1 cup white rice

Salt, to taste

3 tbsps. fresh

chopped cilantro

1 tbsp. fresh lime juice

2 tbsps. vegetable oil

Instructions:

1. Mix the rice and water together in the Instant Pot and stir to combine. Season with salt.
2. Lock the lid. Select the Rice mode, then set the timer for 5 minutes at Low Pressure.
3. Once the timer goes off, do a natural pressure release for 3 to 5 minutes. Carefully open the lid.
4. Use a quick release to get rid of the remaining pressure. Use a fork to fluff up the rice.
5. Mix the lime juice, cilantro, and oil in a bowl.
6. Whisk well and mix into the rice. Serve immediately.

Nutritional info:

Calories 242, Fat 0.4g, Carbs 53.4g, Protein 4.4g

Chickpea and Tomato Rice

Prep Time: 12 mins, Cook Time: 25 mins, Servings: 4

Ingredients:

½ cup canned chickpeas

4½ cups water

1 cup deseeded and minced ripe tomato

Salt and pepper, to taste

2 cups rinsed and drained white rice

Instructions:

1. Pour all the ingredients into Instant Pot. Gently stir.
2. Lock the lid. Select the Rice mode, then set the timer for 5 minutes at Low Pressure.
3. Once the timer goes off, do a quick pressure release. Carefully open the lid.
4. Using a rice paddle, fluff up rice.
5. Serve immediately.

Nutritional info:

Calories 154, Carbs 23.5g, Fat 3g, Protein 16g

Couscous with Spinach and Tomato

Prep Time: 12 mins, Cook Time: 6 mins, Servings: 4

Ingredients:

1 tbsp. butter	½ cup chopped spinach, blanched
1 cup couscous	
1¼ cups vegetable broth	1½ tomatoes, chopped

Instructions:

1. Set the Instant Pot to Sauté mode, then add and melt the butter.
2. Add the couscous and sauté for 1 minute.
3. Pour in the vegetable broth. Stir to mix well.
4. Lock the lid. Set to the Manual mode, then set the timer for 5 minutes at High Pressure.
5. Once the timer goes off, perform a quick pressure release. Carefully open the lid.
6. Mix in the spinach and tomatoes, then serve warm.

Nutritional info:

Calories 130, Carbs 15.8g, Protein 2.9g, Fat 6.3g

Creamy Polenta

Prep Time: 1 mins, Cook Time: 8 mins, Servings: 2

Ingredients:

2 ⅓ cups milk, divided	½ cup polenta
½ tsp. salt	3 tbsps. butter

Instructions:

1. Set the pot to Sauté and add 2 cups of milk and bring it to a boil.
2. Add the salt and polenta into the milk.
3. Lock the lid. Select the Porridge mode, then set the timer for 8 minutes at High Pressure.
4. Once the timer goes off, do a natural pressure release for 5 minutes. Carefully open the lid.
5. Stir in the remaining milk and butter, then serve.

Nutritional info:

Calories 160, Fat 2.6g, Carbs 27.7g, Protein 7.3g

Honey Polenta with Toasted Pine Nuts

Prep Time: 13 mins, Cook Time: 15 mins, Servings: 4

Ingredients:

½ cup honey	Salt, to taste
5 cups water	¼ cup pine nuts, toasted
1 cup polenta	
½ cup heavy cream	

Instructions:

1. Stir together the honey and water in your Instant Pot.
2. Select the Sauté mode and bring the mixture to a boil, stirring occasionally.
3. Stir in the polenta and lock the lid. Select the Manual mode and set the cooking time for 12 minutes at High Pressure.
4. When the timer beeps, do a quick pressure release. Carefully open the lid.
5. Fold in the heavy creamy and stir until well incorporated. Allow the dish to rest for 1 minute.
6. Season with salt and give it a good stir. Serve topped with toasted pine nuts.

Nutritional info:

Calories 294, Carbs 48.5g, Protein 2.7g, Fat 11.6g

Wheat Berries

Prep Time: 6 mins, Cook Time: 30 mins, Servings: 4

Ingredients:

1 cup wheat berries	¼ tsp. salt
3 cups water	

Instructions:

1. Add all the ingredients to the Instant Pot.
2. Lock the lid. Select the Manual mode, then set the timer for 30 minutes at High Pressure.
3. Once the timer goes off, perform a natural release for 8 to 10 minutes. Carefully open the lid.
4. Drain the wheat berries and enjoy.

Nutritional info:

Calories 150, Fat 0.5g, Carbs 32g, Protein 6g

Peaches and Steel-Cut Oats

Prep Time: 12 mins, Cook Time: 3 mins, Servings: 2

Ingredients:

2 peaches, diced
1 cup steel-cut oats
1 cup coconut milk
½ vanilla bean,
scraped, seeds and pod
2 cups water

Instructions:

1. Put all the ingredients into the Instant Pot. Stir to mix well.
2. Lock the lid. Set to the Manual mode, then set the timer for 3 minutes at High Pressure.
3. Once the timer goes off, perform a quick pressure release. Carefully open the lid.
4. Serve immediately.

Nutritional info:

Calories 450, Carbs 52.2g, Protein 12.3g, Fat 32.3g

Strawberry and Rolled Oats

Prep Time: 10 mins, Cook Time: 10 mins, Servings: 2

Ingredients:

2 cups water
⅓ cup rolled oats
2 tbsps. frozen dried strawberries
⅔ cup whole milk
Pinch of salt
½ tsp. white sugar

Instructions:

1. Arrange the steamer rack in the Instant Pot, then pour in the water.
2. Combine the oats, strawberries, milk, and salt in a bowl. Stir to mix well.
3. Put the bowl on the steamer rack.
4. Lock the lid. Set to the Manual mode, then set the timer for 10 minutes at High Pressure.
5. Once the timer goes off, perform a natural pressure release for 5 minutes, then release any remaining pressure. Carefully open the lid.
6. Remove the bowl from the pot, then sprinkle with sugar and serve.

Nutritional info:

Calories 105, Carbs 18.6g, Protein 5.4g, Fat 3.8g

Coconut Quinoa

Prep Time: 2 mins, Cook Time: 3 hours, Servings: 6

Ingredients:

1 tsp. sugar
1 cup rinsed quinoa
1 tsp coconut oil
1 can black beans
1 can coconut milk
2 tsps. garlic powder
Salt, to taste

Instructions:

1. Place all the ingredients in the Instant Pot.
2. Lock the lid. Select the Slow Cook mode, then set the timer for 3 hours at High Pressure.
3. Once the timer goes off, perform a quick release. Carefully open the lid.
4. Serve warm.

Nutritional info:

Calories 207, Fat 11.1g, Carbs 22.6g, Protein 5.9g

Quinoa Pilaf

Prep Time: 13 mins, Cook Time: 2 mins, Servings: 4

Ingredients:

1 tbsp. extra virgin olive oil
2 cloves garlic, minced
2 cups quinoa, rinsed
2 tsps. turmeric
2 tsps. ground cumin
Salt, to taste
3 cups water
1 handful parsley, chopped

Instructions:

1. Set the Instant Pot to Sauté mode, then add and heat the olive oil.
2. Add the garlic and sauté for a minute or until fragrant.
3. Add the quinoa, turmeric, cumin, salt, and water. Stir to combine well.
4. Lock the lid. Set to the Manual mode, then set the timer for 1 minutes at High Pressure.
5. Once the timer goes off, perform a natural pressure release. Carefully open the lid.
6. Spread the pilaf with parsley and serve.

Nutritional info:

Calories 389, Carbs 57.5g, Protein 12.9g, Fat 12.3g

Quinoa with Cranberry and Almond

Prep Time: 5 mins, Cook Time: 10 mins, Servings: 2

Ingredients:

1 cup quinoa, rinsed
2 cups water
¼ cup salted sunflower seeds
½ cup slivered almonds
1 cup dried cranberries

Instructions:

1. Pour the quinoa and water into the Instant Pot.
2. Lock the lid. Set to the Manual mode, then set the timer for 1 minutes at High Pressure.
3. Once the timer goes off, perform a natural pressure release. Carefully open the lid.
4. Mix in the remaining ingredients and serve immediately.

Nutritional info:

Calories 425, Carbs 63.2g, Protein 15.4g, Fat 13.3g

Quinoa with Vegetables

Prep Time: 13 mins, Cook Time: 2 mins, Servings: 4

Ingredients:

1½ cups rinsed quinoa
4 cups spinach, chopped
3 stalks celery, chopped
1 bell pepper, chopped
1½ cups chicken broth
¼ tsp. salt

Instructions:

1. Combine all ingredients in the Instant Pot. Stir to mix well.
2. Lock the lid. Set to the Manual mode, then set the timer for 2 minutes at High Pressure.
3. Once the timer goes off, perform a natural pressure release. Carefully open the lid.
4. Serve immediately.

Nutritional info:

Calories 254, Carbs 43.8g, Protein 10.8g, Fat 4.2g

Brothy Heirloom Beans with Cream

Prep Time: 15 mins, Cook Time: 45 mins, Servings: 4

Ingredients:

2 cups mixed dried heirloom beans, soaked overnight
8 cups chicken stock
4 sprigs thyme
Salt, to taste
½ cup heavy cream

Instructions:

1. Add the beans, chicken stock, thyme, and salt to the Instant Pot. Stir well.
2. Lock the lid. Select the Manual mode and set the cooking time for 45 minutes at High Pressure.
3. Once cooking is complete, do a quick pressure release. Carefully open the lid.
4. Set your Instant Pot to Sauté and stir in the heavy cream.
5. Allow to simmer for 5 minutes, then transfer to four bowls. Serve warm.

Nutritional info:

Calories 261, Carbs 24.6g, Protein 13.8g, Fat 11.5g

Simple Pinto Beans with Spices

Prep Time: 10 mins, Cook Time: 25 mins, Servings: 2

Ingredients:

1 cup dried Pinto beans
2 tbsps. garlic powder
1 tbsp. onion powder
1 tbsp. chili powder
1 tsp. oregano
½ tsp. salt
5 cups water

Instructions:

1. Add the beans, garlic powder, onion powder, chili powder, oregano, and salt to the Instant Pot. Pour in the water and stir to combine.
2. Lock the lid. Select the Manual mode and cook for 25 minutes at High Pressure.
3. Once cooking is complete, do a natural pressure release for 20 minutes, then release any remaining pressure. Carefully open the lid.
4. Taste and adjust the seasoning, if needed.

Nutritional info:

Calories 391, Carbs 72.5g, Protein 23.2g, Fat 1.9g

Simple Italian Flavor Cannellini Beans

Prep Time: 12 mins, Cook Time: 8 mins, Servings: 4

Ingredients:

1 cup cannellini beans, soaked overnight	4 cups water
	Dash of vinegar
1 clove garlic, smashed	1 tbsp. olive oil
	1 sprig mint
1 bay leaf	Salt and ground black pepper to taste

Instructions:

1. Put the beans, garlic, bay leaf, and water in the Instant Pot. Stir to mix well.
2. Lock the lid. Set to the Manual mode, then set the timer for 8 minutes at High Pressure.
3. Once the timer goes off, perform a natural pressure release for 5 minutes, then release any remaining pressure. Carefully open the lid. Discard the bay leaf.
4. Strain the beans, then drizzle with vinegar and olive oil. Sprinkle with mint, salt, and pepper. Mix and serve.

Nutritional info:

Calories 201, Carbs 31.0g, Protein 11.9g, Fat 3.9g

Black-Eyed Peas with Ham

Prep Time: 25 mins, Cook Time: 30 mins, Servings: 4

Ingredients:

½ lb. dried black-eyed peas	stock
	Salt and ground black pepper, to taste
3 oz. ham, diced	
3½ cups chicken	

Instructions:

1. Place the peas, ham, and chicken stock in the Instant Pot.
2. Lock the lid. Select the Manual mode and cook for 30 minutes at High Pressure.
3. Once cooking is complete, do a natural pressure release for 20 minutes, then release any remaining pressure. Carefully open the lid.
4. Season as needed with salt and pepper, then serve.

Nutritional info:

Calories 160, Carbs 13.2g, Protein 10.6g, Fat 7.1g

Creamy Corn Kernels with Cottage Cheese

Prep Time: 11 mins, Cook Time: 4 mins, Servings: 2

Ingredients:

2 ounces Cottage cheese, at room temperature	pepper flakes
	1 tablespoon butter, cut into pieces
1 cup corn kernels	1 cup water
⅓ cup double cream	Kosher salt and ground black pepper, to taste
⅓ teaspoon dried parsley flakes	
¼ teaspoon red	

Instructions:

1. Combine all the ingredients in the Instant Pot. Stir to mix well.
2. Lock the lid. Set to the Manual mode, then set the timer for 4 minutes at High Pressure.
3. Once the timer goes off, perform a natural pressure release. Carefully open the lid.
4. Serve immediately.

Nutritional info:

Calories 279, Carbs 19.8g, Protein 10.0g, Fat 19.3g

Cheesy Grits with Half-and-Half

Prep Time: 17 mins, Cook Time: 13 mins, Servings: 6

Ingredients:

2 tbsps. olive oil	4 oz. Cheddar cheese
2 cup stone-ground grits	2 tbsps. butter
	1½ tsps. salt
1 cup half-and-half	3 cups water

Instructions:

1. Set the Instant Pot to Sauté mode, then add and heat the olive oil.
2. Add the grits and sauté for 3 minutes.
3. Add the half-and-half, cheese, butter, salt, and water. Stir to combine well.
4. Lock the lid. Set to the Manual mode, then set the timer for 10 minutes at High Pressure.
5. Once the timer goes off, perform a natural pressure release for 5 minutes, then release any remaining pressure. Carefully open the lid.
6. Serve immediately.

Nutritional info:

Calories 230, Carbs 15.0g, Protein 6.9g, Fat 16.2g

Creamy Fig Millet

Prep Time: 15 mins, Cook Time: 10 mins, Servings: 4

Ingredients:

1¾ cups millet
2 cups water
1 cup almond milk
⅓ cup chopped dried figs
2 tbsps. coconut oil

Instructions:

1. Place all the ingredients in the Instant Pot and mix well.
2. Lock the lid. Select the Rice mode and set the cooking time for 10 minutes at High Pressure.
3. When the timer goes off, do a natural pressure release for 10 minutes, then release any remaining pressure. Carefully open the lid.
4. Using a fork to fluff the dish and serve on plates.

Nutritional info:

Calories 450, Carbs 74.5g, Protein 12.1g, Fat 11.8g

Ritzy Corn, Lentil, and Brown Rice Stew

Prep Time: 10 mins, Cook Time: 20 mins, Servings: 4

Ingredients:

½ tbsp. olive oil
1 medium carrot, sliced
⅓ cup dried lentils
½ cup fresh or frozen corn
1 medium tomato
3½ cups water
½ cup cooked brown rice
1 tbsp. soy sauce
Salt and pepper, to taste

Instructions:

1. Grease the Instant Pot with olive oil. Set the Instant Pot to Sauté mode.
2. Add the carrots and sauté for 5 minutes or until soft.
3. Add the lentils, corn, tomatoes, corn, and water to the pot.
4. Lock the lid. Set to the Manual mode, then set the timer for 15 minutes at High Pressure.
5. Once the timer goes off, perform a quick pressure release. Carefully open the lid.
6. Mix in the cooked brown rice and soy sauce. Sprinkle with salt and pepper before serving.

Nutritional info:

Calories 239, Carbs 47.4g, Protein 10.1g, Fat 1.5g

Refried Pinto Beans

Prep Time: 5 mins, Cook Time: 1 hour, Servings: 2

Ingredients:

1 cup pinto beans, drained and rinsed
3 cups water
1 tbsp. olive oil
1 onion, chopped
2 cloves garlic,
chopped
1 jalapeño pepper, chopped
1 bay leaf
1 tsp. salt

Instructions:

1. Put the pinto beans in the Instant Pot, then pour in the water.
2. Lock the lid. Set to the Manual mode, then set the timer for 40 minutes at High Pressure.
3. Once the timer goes off, perform a quick pressure release. Carefully open the lid.
4. Pat the beans dry with paper towels, then reserve the bean water.
5. Select the Sauté mode of the pot, then add the olive oil.
6. Add the onion, garlic, and jalapeño to the pot and sauté for 3 minutes or until fragrant.
7. Add the beans, reserved bean water, bay leaf, and salt to the pot. Stir to mix well.
8. Lock the lid. Set to the Manual mode, then set the timer for 20 minutes at High Pressure.
9. Once the timer goes off, perform a quick pressure release. Carefully open the lid. Discard the bay leaf.
10. Serve the beans on a plate immediately.

Nutritional info:

Calories 331, Carbs 29.0g, Protein 8.6g, Fat 21.1g

Chapter 12 Pasta and Side Dishes Recipe

Minty Carrots

Prep Time: 12 mins, Cook Time: 5 mins, Servings: 4
Ingredients:

16 oz. baby carrots
1 cup water
Salt, to taste
1 tbsp. butter
1 tsp. sweet paprika
1 tbsp. chopped mint

Instructions:

1. In the Instant Pot, mix the carrots with water.
2. Lock the lid. Select the Manual mode, then set the timer for 3 minutes at High Pressure.
3. Once the timer goes off, perform a quick release. Carefully open the lid.
4. Drain and transfer to a bowl.
5. Clean the pot and set it to Sauté. Add the butter and heat to melt.
6. Add the mint, stir and cook for 1 minute.
7. Add the carrots, salt and paprika, toss, divide between plates and serve as a side dish.

Nutritional info:
Calories 172, Fat 3g, Carbs 8g, Protein 4g

Kidney Beans and Corn Side Dish

Prep Time: 12 mins, Cook Time: 10 mins, Servings: 2
Ingredients:

½ tsp. chili powder
1½ cups chicken stock
1 cup cooked kidney
beans
½ cup corn
1 small red onion, chopped

Instructions:

1. In the Instant Pot, mix beans with corn, onion, chili powder and stock, stir.
2. Lock the lid. Select the Manual mode, then set the timer for 10 minutes at High Pressure.
3. Once the timer goes off, perform a quick release. Carefully open the lid.
4. Enjoy the side dish!

Nutritional info:
Calories 203, Fat 7g, Carbs 9g, Protein 2g

Simple Corn Side Dish

Prep Time: 12 mins, Cook Time: 12 mins, Servings: 4
Ingredients:

2 tbsps. butter
3 garlic cloves, minced
2 cups corn kernels
6 oz. cream cheese
⅓ cup milk

Instructions:

1. Set the Instant Pot to Sauté, add butter, melt it, add garlic, stir and cook for 2 minutes.
2. Stir in the corn and let cook for 2 additional minutes.
3. Add cream cheese and milk, stir.
4. Lock the lid. Select the Manual mode, then set the timer for 7 minutes at High Pressure.
5. Once the timer goes off, perform a quick release. Carefully open the lid.
6. Toss creamy corn one more time, divide between plates and serve as a side dish.

Nutritional info:
Calories 200, Fat 3g, Carbs 10g, Protein 3g

Pearl Onions Side Dish

Prep Time: 12 mins, Cook Time: 10 mins, Servings: 6
Ingredients:

1 lb. rainbow carrots, quartered
2 cups pearl onions
½ cup water
3 tbsps. butter
2 tbsps. chopped parsley
2 tbsps. balsamic vinegar

Instructions:

1. In the Instant Pot, mix carrots with onions and water.
2. Lock the lid. Select the Manual mode, then set the timer for 4 minutes at High Pressure.
3. Once the timer goes off, perform a quick release. Carefully open the lid.
4. Drain and transfer to a bowl.
5. Clean the pot and select the Sauté mode, add butter, melt it, add onions and carrots, vinegar and parsley, stir and sauté for 5 minutes.
6. Toss again, divide between plates and serve as a side dish.

Nutritional info:
Calories 162, Fat 4g, Carbs 12g, Protein 4g

Acorn Squash Side Dish

Prep Time: 12 mins, Cook Time: 15 mins, Servings: 4

Ingredients:

1 cup water	1 tbsp. brown sugar
2 acorn squash, halved and sliced into wedges	1 tsp. smoked paprika
4 tbsps. butter	3 tbsps. roasted pepitas

Instructions:

1. In the Instant Pot, add the water and steamer basket. Add acorn wedges in the basket.
2. Lock the lid. Select the Manual mode, then set the timer for 5 minutes at High Pressure.
3. Once the timer goes off, perform a quick release. Carefully open the lid.
4. Transfer to a bowl.
5. Clean the pot and select the Sauté mode, add butter, melt it, add acorn wedges, sugar, paprika and pepitas, stir and cook for 10 minutes.
6. Enjoy as a side dish.

Nutritional info:

Calories 128, Fat 4g, Carbs 6g, Protein 8g

Simple Spinach Side Dish

Prep Time: 12 mins, Cook Time: 5 mins, Servings: 3

Ingredients:

½ tsp. turmeric powder	½ cup vegetable soup
1 tsp. olive oil	½ tsp. garam masala
6 oz. spinach leaves	

Instructions:

1. Set the Instant Pot to Sauté and heat the olive oil. Add spinach, stir and toss for 1 to 2 minutes.
2. Add garam masala, turmeric and soup, stir.
3. Lock the lid. Select the Manual mode, then set the timer for 3 minutes at High Pressure.
4. Once the timer goes off, perform a quick release. Carefully open the lid.
5. Serve as a side dish!

Nutritional info:

Calories 100, Fat 3g, Carbs 6g, Protein 1g

Tasty Maple Acorn Squash Dish

Prep Time: 12 mins, Cook Time: 10 mins, Servings: 4

Ingredients:

2 tsps. sriracha sauce	3 tbsps. butter
¼ cup maple syrup	2 halved acorn squash
4 thyme sprigs, chopped	

Instructions:

1. Set the Instant Pot to Sauté, add butter, melt it, add acorn squash wedges, stir and cook for 1 to 2 minutes.
2. Add maple syrup, sriracha sauce and thyme, stir.
3. Lock the lid. Select the Manual mode, then set the timer for 8 minutes at High Pressure.
4. Once the timer goes off, perform a quick release. Carefully open the lid.
5. Toss squash wedges gently, divide between plates and serve as a side dish.

Nutritional info:

Calories 200, Fat 2g, Carbs 5g, Protein 4g

Green Beans and Cranberries Side Dish

Prep Time: 12 mins, Cook Time: 6 mins, Servings: 6

Ingredients:

¼ cup dried cranberries	¼ cup chopped almonds
½ cup water	¼ tsp. salt
2 lbs. green beans	3 tbsps. olive oil

Instructions:

1. Put the water and steamer basket in the Instant Pot. Arrange the green beans and cranberries in the basket.
2. Lock the lid. Select the Manual mode, then set the timer for 2 minutes at High Pressure.
3. Once the timer goes off, perform a quick release. Carefully open the lid.
4. Transfer to a bowl.
5. Clean the pot and select the Sauté mode. Heat the olive oil and toss in green beans, almonds, salt, and cranberries. Cook for 4 additional minutes.
6. Serve as a side dish.

Nutritional info:

Calories 130, Fat 3g, Carbs 7g, Protein 4g

Green Cabbage and Tomatoes Side Dish

Prep Time: 12 mins, Cook Time: 5 mins, Servings: 4
Ingredients:

15 oz. chopped canned tomatoes
3 tbsps. olive oil
½ cup chopped yellow onion

1 green cabbage head, chopped
2 tsps. turmeric powder

Instructions:
1. Set the Instant Pot to Sauté and heat the olive oil. Add onion, stir, and cook for 2 minutes.
2. Add cabbage, tomatoes and turmeric, stir.
3. Lock the lid. Select the Manual mode, then set the timer for 4 minutes at High Pressure.
4. Once the timer goes off, perform a quick release. Carefully open the lid.
5. Divide between plates and serve as a side dish.

Nutritional info:
Calories 152, Fat 5g, Carbs 9g, Protein 7g

Radishes Side Salad

Prep Time: 12 mins, Cook Time: 8 mins, Servings: 3
Ingredients:

2 chopped bacon slices
½ cup veggie stock
2 tbsps. sour cream

1 tbsp. chopped green onions
7 oz. halved red radishes

Instructions:
1. Set the Instant Pot to Sauté, add bacon, stir and cook for 6 minutes on both sides.
2. Add radishes and stock, stir.
3. Lock the lid. Select the Manual mode, then set the timer for 4 minutes at High Pressure.
4. Once the timer goes off, perform a quick release. Carefully open the lid.
5. Add sour cream and green onions, stir.
6. Lock the lid, then set the timer for 2 minutes.
7. Divide between plates and serve as a side dish.

Nutritional info:
Calories 187, Fat 6g, Carbs 10g, Protein 8g

Tomatoes Side Salad

Prep Time: 12 mins, Cook Time: 6 mins, Servings: 4
Ingredients:

¼ tsp. chopped parsley
1 tbsp. sherry vinegar
15 oz. drained

canned garbanzo beans
2 tbsps. olive oil
4 cups halved mixed cherry tomatoes

Instructions:
1. Set the Instant Pot to Sauté. Heat the olive oil and add garbanzo beans and tomatoes, stir and cook for 3 minutes.
2. Add parsley and vinegar, stir.
3. Lock the lid. Select the Manual mode, then set the timer for 3 minutes at High Pressure.
4. Once the timer goes off, perform a quick release. Carefully open the lid.
5. Enjoy as side dish!

Nutritional info:
Calories 132, Fat 3g, Carbs 7g, Protein 5g

Arborio Rice Side Salad

Prep Time: 12 mins, Cook Time: 4 mins, Servings: 4
Ingredients:

1 bunch basil, chopped
4 cups water
2 cups Arborio rice

¼ tsp. salt
1 cup pitted and sliced black olives in oil

Instructions:
1. In the Instant Pot, mix rice with water.
2. Lock the lid. Select the Manual mode, then set the timer for 20 minutes at Low Pressure.
3. Once the timer goes off, perform a natural release for 10 minutes, then release any remaining pressure. Carefully open the lid.
4. Drain and transfer to a salad bowl.
5. Add a pinch of salt, olives and basil, toss well, divide between plates and serve as a side salad.

Nutritional info:
Calories 120, Fat 4g, Carbs 5g, Protein 2g

Brown Rice Salad

Prep Time: 12 mins, Cook Time: 20 mins, Servings: 2

Ingredients:

½ cup mung beans
1 tsp. lemon juice
½ tsp. cumin seeds

½ cup brown rice
4 cups water

Instructions:

1. In the Instant Pot, mix mung beans with rice, water, lemon juice and cumin, stir.
2. Lock the lid. Select the Manual mode, then set the timer for 20 minutes at Low Pressure.
3. Once the timer goes off, perform a quick release. Carefully open the lid.
4. Enjoy the side dish!

Nutritional info:

Calories 170, Fat 6, Carbs 12g, Protein 4g

Delicious Green Beans and Blue Cheese

Prep Time: 12 mins, Cook Time: 7 mins, Servings: 4

Ingredients:

½ cup water
1½ lbs. green beans
2 tbsps. lemon juice
½ cup chopped

almonds
¼ cup olive oil
2 tbsps. crumbled blue cheese

Instructions:

1. Put the water and steamer basket in the Instant Pot, then add green beans inside.
2. Lock the lid. Select the Manual mode, then set the timer for 2 minutes at High Pressure.
3. Once the timer goes off, perform a quick release. Carefully open the lid.
4. Drain and transfer them to a bowl.
5. Clean the pot and select the Sauté mode. Heat the oil and add green beans, stir and cook for 3 minutes.
6. Add lemon juice and almonds, stir and cook for 2 minutes more.
7. Divide on plates, sprinkle blue cheese all over and serve as a side dish.

Nutritional info:

Calories 200, Fat 4g, Carbs 7g, Protein 4g

Haricots Verts Side Salad

Prep Time: 12 mins, Cook Time: 8 mins, Servings: 4

Ingredients:

4 oz. pancetta, chopped
Black pepper, to taste

½ cup chicken stock
½ cup sliced dates
2 lbs. haricot verts

Instructions:

1. Set the Instant Pot to Sauté, add pancetta, stir and cook for 3 minutes.
2. Add haricot verts, dates and black pepper, stir and cook for 2 minutes more.
3. Stir in the stock.
4. Lock the lid. Select the Manual mode, then set the timer for 3 minutes on High Pressure.
5. Once the timer goes off, perform a quick release. Carefully open the lid.
6. Set in serving bowls and enjoy as a side dish.

Nutritional info:

Calories 128, Fat 3g, Carbs 16g, Protein 4g

Sweet and Sour Side Salad

Prep Time: 12 mins, Cook Time: 7 mins, Servings: 8

Ingredients:

1 cup water
3 lbs. rainbow carrots, chopped
3 tbsps. vinegar

3 tbsps. honey
3 tbsps. butter
1 onion, chopped

Instructions:

1. Add the water to the Instant Pot, then add the carrots.
2. Lock the lid. Select the Manual mode, then set the timer for 3 minutes at High Pressure.
3. Once the timer goes off, perform a quick release. Carefully open the lid.
4. Drain and transfer to a bowl.
5. Clean the pot and select the Sauté mode, add butter, melt it, add onion, stir and cook for 2 minutes.
6. Stir in carrots, honey, and vinegar. Cook for 2 more minutes on High while covered.
7. Set in serving plates and enjoy as a side dish.

Nutritional info:

Calories 192, Fat 3g, Carbs 10g, Protein 3g

Brussels Sprouts Side Salad

Prep Time: 12 mins, Cook Time: 5 mins, Servings: 4

Ingredients:

2 tbsps. olive oil
1 lb. halved Brussels sprouts
½ cup chopped

pecans
3 tbsps. balsamic vinegar
2 tsps. Dijon mustard

Instructions:

1. Set the Instant Pot to Sauté. Heat the olive oil and add the Brussels sprouts to sauté for 2 minutes.
2. Add pecans, vinegar and mustard, toss
3. Lock the lid. Select the Manual mode, then set the timer for 3 minutes at High Pressure.
4. Once the timer goes off, perform a quick release. Carefully open the lid.
5. Divide Brussels sprouts mix on plates and serve as a side dish.

Nutritional info:

Calories 167, Fat 4g, Carbs 6g, Protein 4g

Tomatoes and Corn Side Salad

Prep Time: 12 mins, Cook Time: 7 mins, Servings: 6

Ingredients:

1½ cups water
3 oz. goat cheese, crumbled
6 sweet corn ears, shucked

¼ cup mint leaves
1 tbsp. olive oil
4 tomatoes, roughly chopped

Instructions:

1. Place the water in the Instant Pot, then add the corn.
2. Lock the lid. Select the Manual mode, then set the timer for 5 minutes at High Pressure.
3. Once the timer goes off, perform a quick release. Carefully open the lid.
4. Drain and transfer to a bowl.
5. Clean the pot and select the Sauté mode. Heat the olive oil and add corn and tomatoes, stir and cook for 2 minutes.
6. Add mint, stir, cook for 2 minutes more, divide between plates and serve with cheese on top.

Nutritional info:

Calories 122, Fat 3g, Carbs 6g, Protein 4g

Tasty Carrots and Walnuts Salad

Prep Time: 12 mins, Cook Time: 5 mins, Servings: 4

Ingredients:

2 lbs. baby carrots
1 cup water
2 tbsps. butter
3 oz. canned walnuts

1 tsp. syrup
Salt, to taste
1 tbsp. apple cider vinegar

Instructions:

1. In the Instant Pot, add the carrots and water.
2. Lock the lid. Select the Manual mode, then set the timer for 3 minutes at High Pressure.
3. Once the timer goes off, perform a quick release. Carefully open the lid.
4. Drain and transfer to a bowl.
5. Clean the pot and select the Sauté mode. Melt the butter and add carrots, stir and cook for 1 minute.
6. Add walnuts and syrup, salt and vinegar, toss, cook for 1 minute more, divide between plates and serve as a side dish.

Nutritional info:

Calories 172, Fat 3g, Carbs 10g, Protein 4g

Kale Sauté

Prep Time: 12 mins, Cook Time: 7 mins, Servings: 4

Ingredients:

1 tbsp. olive oil
3 garlic cloves
½ cup veggie stock

Juice of ½ lemon
1 lb. kale, trimmed

Instructions:

1. Set the Instant Pot to Sauté. Heat the oil and add garlic, stir and cook for 2 minutes.
2. Add kale, stock and lemon juice, stir a bit.
3. Lock the lid. Select the Manual mode, then set the timer for 5 minutes at High Pressure.
4. Once the timer goes off, perform a quick release. Carefully open the lid.
5. Stir and divide between plates and serve as a side dish.

Nutritional info:

Calories 132, Fat 3g, Carbs 8g, protein 2g

Tomatoes and Burrata Side Salad

Prep Time: 12 mins, Cook Time: 3 mins, Servings: 4

Ingredients:

4 tomatoes, diced	1 tbsp. water
2 tbsps. olive oil	5 oz. burrata cheese,
½ tsp. dried oregano	shredded

Instructions:

1. In the Instant Pot, mix tomatoes with oil, oregano and water, toss a bit.
2. Lock the lid. Select the Manual mode, then set the timer for 3 minutes at High Pressure.
3. Once the timer goes off, perform a quick release. Carefully open the lid.
4. Divide on plates, add burrata on top and serve an as a side dish.

Nutritional info:

Calories 111, Fat 2g, Carbs 3g, Protein 3g

Garlic Green Beans

Prep Time: 12 mins, Cook Time: 7 mins, Servings: 4

Ingredients:

1 cup water	minced
1½ lbs. green beans	½ tsp. red pepper
1 tbsp. shaved	flakes
Parmesan	3 tbsps. olive oil
4 garlic cloves,	

Instructions:

1. Put the water in the Instant Pot, arrange the steamer basket in the pot, add green beans inside.
2. Lock the lid. Select the Manual mode, then set the timer for 2 minutes at High Pressure.
3. Once the timer goes off, perform a quick release. Carefully open the lid.
4. Drain and transfer to a bowl.
5. Clean the pot and select the Sauté mode. Heat the oil and add garlic, stir and cook for 30 seconds.
6. Return green beans, also add pepper flakes, stir and sauté everything or 4 minutes more.
7. Divide green beans on plates, sprinkle shaved Parmesan on top and serve as a side dish.

Nutritional info:

Calories 172, Fat 3g, Carbs 6g, Protein 4g

Mixed Veggies

Prep Time: 12 mins, Cook Time: 10 mins, Servings: 4

Ingredients:

2 cups roughly	vinegar
chopped butternut	1 red bell pepper,
squash	chopped
1 red onion. chopped	1 tbsp. olive oil
2 tbsps. balsamic	1 cup water

Instructions:

1. In a bowl, mix squash with red onion, oil, bell pepper and vinegar and toss well.
2. In the Instant Pot, add the water and steamer basket, then add mixed veggies inside.
3. Lock the lid. Select the Manual mode, then set the timer for 10 minutes at High Pressure.
4. Once the timer goes off, perform a quick release. Carefully open the lid.
5. Divide mixed veggies between plates and serve as a side dish.

Nutritional info:

Calories 128, Fat 3g, Carbs 9g, Protein 8g

Collard Greens and Peas

Prep Time: 12 mins, Cook Time: 40 mins, Servings: 5

Ingredients:

1 smoked ham hock	1 onion, chopped
1 lb. collard greens,	1 lb. dried black-eyed
trimmed and roughly	peas
chopped	2 cups chicken stock

Instructions:

1. In the Instant Pot, mix peas with stock, onion and ham hock, stir.
2. Lock the lid. Select the Manual mode, then set the timer for 38 minutes at High Pressure.
3. Once the timer goes off, perform a natural release for 10 minutes, then release any remaining pressure. Carefully open the lid.
4. Add collard greens, stir.
5. Lock the lid, then set the timer for 2 minutes at High Pressure.
6. Once the timer goes off, perform a quick release. Carefully open the lid.
7. Divide collard greens and peas between plates and serve as a side dish.

Nutritional info:

Calories 271, Fat 4g, Carbs 12g, Protein 4g

Creamy Spinach

Prep Time: 10 minutes. Cook Time: 6 mins, Servings: 4

Ingredients:

Ground nutmeg
10 oz. spinach, roughly chopped

2 shallots, chopped
2 cups heavy cream
2 tbsps. butter

Instructions:

1. Set the Instant Pot to Sauté, add butter, melt it, add shallots, stir and cook for 2 minutes.
2. Add spinach, stir, and cook for 30 seconds more.
3. Add cream and nutmeg, stir.
4. Lock the lid. Select the Manual mode, then set the timer for 3 minutes at High Pressure.
5. Once the timer goes off, perform a quick release. Carefully open the lid.
6. Divide everything between plates and serve as a side dish.

Nutritional info:

Calories 200, Fat 3g, Carbs 15g, Protein 3g

Tasty Spinach and Salami

Prep Time: 12 mins, Cook Time: 6 mins, Servings: 4

Ingredients:

10 oz. baby spinach
½ cup chicken stock
3 garlic cloves, minced

3 tbsps. olive oil
3 salami slices, chopped

Instructions:

1. Set the Instant Pot to Sauté. Heat the oil and add garlic, stir and cook for 1 minute.
2. Add salami, stir, and cook for 2 minutes more.
3. Add spinach and stock, stir a bit.
4. Lock the lid. Select the Manual mode, then set the timer for 3 minutes at High Pressure.
5. Once the timer goes off, perform a quick release. Carefully open the lid.
6. Enjoy as a side dish.

Nutritional info:

Calories 172, Fat 3g, Carbs 12g, Protein 3g

Braised Collard Greens

Prep Time: 12 mins, Cook Time: 10 mins, Servings: 4

Ingredients:

1 tbsp. balsamic vinegar
2 tbsps. chopped tomatoes

1 bunch collard greens
½ cup chicken stock
2 tbsps. olive oil

Instructions:

1. In the Instant Pot, mix collard greens with stock, oil, tomatoes and vinegar, stir.
2. Lock the lid. Select the Manual mode, then set the timer for 10 minutes at High Pressure.
3. Once the timer goes off, perform a quick release. Carefully open the lid.
4. Divide kale mix on plates and serve as a side dish.

Nutritional info:

Calories 122, Fat 7g, Carbs 10g, Protein 4g

Chinese Mustard Greens

Prep Time: 12 mins, Cook Time: 7 mins, Servings: 4

Ingredients:

2 lbs. mustard greens, chopped
2 tbsps. vegetable oil
½ cup veggie stock

2 tsps. grated ginger
2 Chinese sausages, chopped

Instructions:

1. Set the Instant Pot to Sauté. Heat the oil and add ginger, stir and cook for 30 seconds.
2. Add Chinese sausages, stir and cook for 1 minute more.
3. Add mustard greens and stock, stir.
4. Lock the lid. Select the Manual mode, then set the timer for 4 minutes at High Pressure.
5. Once the timer goes off, perform a quick release. Carefully open the lid.
6. Enjoy as a side dish.

Nutritional info:

Calories 178, Fat 5g, Carbs 8g, Protein 9g

Chestnut Mushrooms

Prep Time: 12 mins, Cook Time: 10 mins, Servings: 4
Ingredients:

2 lbs. halved mushrooms
½ cup vegetable soup
1 tsp. Worcestershire sauce
1 cup halved jarred chestnuts
6 bacon slices, chopped

Instructions:
1. Set the Instant Pot to Sauté, add bacon, stir and cook for 5 minutes on both sides.
2. Stir in the chestnuts and sauté for 1 more minute.
3. Add mushrooms, Worcestershire sauce and soup, stir.
4. Lock the lid. Select the Manual mode, then set the timer for 8 minutes at High Pressure.
5. Once the timer goes off, perform a quick release. Carefully open the lid.
6. Enjoy as a side dish.

Nutritional info:
Calories 180, Fat 2g, Carbs 10g, Protein 2g

Cauliflower and Grapes

Prep Time: 12 mins, Cook Time: 5 mins, Servings: 4
Ingredients:

1 cup water
3 tbsps. olive oil
1 tsp. grated lemon zest
2 tbsps. capers
1 head cauliflower, cut into florets
1½ cups grapes

Instructions:
1. In the Instant Pot, add the water and steamer basket, then add cauliflower florets inside.
2. Lock the lid. Select the Manual mode, then set the timer for 1 minutes at High Pressure.
3. Once the timer goes off, perform a quick release. Carefully open the lid.
4. Drain and transfer to a bowl.
5. Clean the pot and select the Sauté mode. Heat the oil and return the cauliflower to the pot. Stir and cook for 2 minutes.
6. Add grapes, capers and lemon zest, stir, cook for 2 minutes more, divide between plates and serve as a side dish.

Nutritional info:
Calories 114, Fat 3g, Carbs 5g, Protein 2g

Tasty Carrots Mix

Prep Time: 12 mins, Cook Time: 10 mins, Servings: 6
Ingredients:

2½ lbs. baby carrots
1 tsp. thyme
2 tbsps. olive oil
1 cup water
3 shallots, chopped
¼ cup Greek yogurt

Instructions:
1. In a bowl, mix baby carrots with thyme and olive oil and toss.
2. Add the water to the Instant Pot, arrange the steamer basket in the pot, add carrots inside.
3. Lock the lid. Select the Manual mode, then set the timer for 5 minutes.
4. Once the timer goes off, perform a quick release. Carefully open the lid.
5. Transfer them to a bowl.
6. Clean the pot and set it to Sauté, add shallots and brown them for 1 to 2 minutes.
7. Add carrots, toss and heat them up.
8. Add yogurt, toss, divide between plates and serve as a side dish.

Nutritional info:
Calories 162, Fat 4g, Carbs 12g, Protein 5g

Delicious Shiitake Mushrooms Mix

Prep Time: 12 mins, Cook Time: 10 mins, Servings: 4
Ingredients:

2 tsps. ginger
1 cup veggie stock
1 lb. shiitake mushroom caps,
quartered
2 tbsps. butter
2 cups edamame

Instructions:
1. Set the Instant Pot to Sauté, add butter, melt it, add ginger, stir and cook for 30 seconds.
2. Add mushrooms, stir and cook for 1 to 2 minutes.
3. Add edamame and stock, stir.
4. Lock the lid. Select the Manual mode, then set the timer for 8 minutes at High Pressure.
5. Once the timer goes off, perform a quick release. Carefully open the lid.
6. Serve as a side dish.

Nutritional info:
Calories 164, Fat 3g, Carbs 8g, Protein 3g

Sweet Pearl Onion Mix

Prep Time: 12 mins, Cook Time: 5 mins, Servings: 4
Ingredients:

4 tbsps. balsamic vinegar
1 tbsp. sugar

1 lb. pearl onions
½ cup water
¼ tsp. salt

Instructions:
1. In the Instant Pot, mix pearl onions with salt, water, vinegar and sugar, stir.
2. Lock the lid. Select the Manual mode, then set the timer for 5 minutes on Low Pressure.
3. Once the timer goes off, perform a quick release. Carefully open the lid.
4. Toss onions again, divide them between plates and serve as a side dish.

Nutritional info:
Calories 130, Fat 2g, Carbs 7g, Protein 1g

Eggplant and Cashews Mix

Prep Time: 12 mins, Cook Time: 15 mins, Servings: 3
Ingredients:

1 tsp. lime juice
1 tbsp. coriander seeds
1 cup vegetable soup

2 tbsps. chopped cashews
4 baby eggplants, roughly chopped

Instructions:
1. In the Instant Pot, mix eggplants with stock and coriander, stir.
2. Lock the lid. Select the Manual mode, then set the timer for 10 minutes at High Pressure.
3. Once the timer goes off, perform a quick release. Carefully open the lid.
4. Add cashews and lime juice, stir, divide between plates and serve as a side dish.

Nutritional info:
Calories 170, Fat 4g, Carbs 7g, Protein 3g

Green Beans Fries

Prep Time: 12 mins, Cook Time: 9 mins, Servings: 4
Ingredients:

1 cup water
2 eggs, whisked
1½ lbs. green beans, trimmed

1 cup panko
Salt, to taste
½ cup grated Parmesan cheese

Instructions:
1. Place the water in the Instant Pot and arrange the steamer basket in the pot, then add green beans.
2. Lock the lid. Select the Manual mode, then set the timer for 5 minutes at High Pressure.
3. Once the timer goes off, perform a quick release. Carefully open the lid.
4. Transfer to a bowl.
5. In a bowl, mix panko with Parmesan and salt and stir.
6. Put the eggs in a separate bowl.
7. Dredge green beans in panko and then in eggs mix.
8. Set the pot to Sauté. Add green beans fries and cook them for 2 to 3 minutes on each side. Transfer them to plates and serve as a side dish.

Nutritional info:
Calories 174, Fat 3g, Carbs 7g, Protein 7g

Parmesan Zucchini Fries

Prep Time: 12 mins, Cook Time: 8 mins, Servings: 4
Ingredients:

½ cup grated Parmesan cheese
2 tbsps. chopped parsley
½ tsp. dried oregano

4 zucchinis, quartered
2 tbsps. olive oil
1 cup water

Instructions:
1. In a bowl, mix the Parmesan with parsley and oregano and toss.
2. In another bowl, mix the zucchini with the oil and toss well.
3. Dunk the oiled zucchini in the bowl of Parmesan mixture to coat well.
4. Put the water and steamer basket in the Instant Pot, then add zucchini inside.
5. Lock the lid. Select the Manual mode, then set the timer for 8 minutes at High Pressure.
6. Once the timer goes off, perform a quick release. Carefully open the lid.
7. Arrange on plates and serve as a side dish.

Nutritional info:
Calories 162, Fat 3g, Carbs 5g, Protein 4g

Red Onions and Apples Mix

Prep Time: 12 mins, Cook Time: 6 mins, Servings: 4

Ingredients:

3 tbsps. vegetable oil
3 tbsps. maple syrup
2 red onions, chopped
3 apples, cored and wedged
½ cup chicken stock

Instructions:

1. Set the Instant Pot to Sauté. Heat the oil and add onion and apple wedges, stir and cook for 2 to 3 minutes.
2. Add maple syrup and stock, stir a bit.
3. Lock the lid. Select the Manual mode, then set the timer for 4 minutes at High Pressure.
4. Once the timer goes off, perform a quick release. Carefully open the lid.
5. Enjoy as a side dish.

Nutritional info:

Calories 110, Fat 3g, Carbs 4g, Protein 2g

Flavored Parmesan Mushrooms

Prep Time: 12 mins, Cook Time: 10 mins, Servings: 4

Ingredients:

1½ lbs. cremini mushrooms, sliced
3 tbsps. olive oil
Salt, to taste
¼ cup lemon juice
¼ cup grated Parmesan cheese
1 cup water

Instructions:

1. In a bowl, mix mushrooms with oil, lemon juice, Parmesan and salt and toss well.
2. Add the water and steamer basket to the Instant Pot, then add mushrooms inside.
3. Lock the lid. Select the Manual mode, then set the timer for 10 minutes at High Pressure.
4. Once the timer goes off, perform a quick release. Carefully open the lid.
5. Serve as a side dish.

Nutritional info:

Calories 128, Fat 4g, Carbs 9g, Protein 4g

Tasty Mushrooms and Rosemary

Prep Time: 12 mins, Cook Time: 10 mins, Servings: 6

Ingredients:

½ cup white wine
3 lbs. mixed mushroom caps
3 rosemary sprigs,
chopped
4 garlic cloves, minced
¾ cup olive oil

Instructions:

1. Set the Instant Pot to Sauté, add oil, heat, add garlic and rosemary, stir and cook for 2 to 3 minutes.
2. Add mushroom caps and wine, stir.
3. Lock the lid. Select the Manual mode, then set the timer for 7 to 8 minutes at High Pressure.
4. Once the timer goes off, perform a quick release. Carefully open the lid.
5. Stir mushroom mix again, divide between plates and serve as a side dish.

Nutritional info:

Calories 172, Fat 3g, Carbs 17g, Protein 3g

Brussels Sprouts and Chestnuts

Prep Time: 12 mins, Cook Time: 5 mins, Servings: 5

Ingredients:

3 tbsps. olive oil
¼ cup vegetable soup
1 red vinegar splash
2 lbs. halved Brussels sprouts
1 cup halved jarred chestnuts

Instructions:

1. Set the Instant Pot to Sauté. Heat the oil and add Brussels sprouts, stir and cook for 2 minutes.
2. Add chestnuts, stock and vinegar, stir.
3. Lock the lid. Select the Manual mode, then set the timer for 3 minutes at High Pressure.
4. Once the timer goes off, perform a quick release. Carefully open the lid.
5. Enjoy the side dish.

Nutritional info:

Calories 182, Fat 3g, Carbs 6g, Protein 4g

Tasty Vidalia Onions Mix

Prep Time: 12 mins, Cook Time: 15 mins, Servings: 4

Ingredients:

2 tbsps. butter
4 Vidalia onions, sliced
1 tbsp. chopped sage
¼ cup chicken stock
½ cup cornbread stuffing cubes

Instructions:

1. Set the Instant Pot to Sauté, add butter, melt it, add onions and sage, toss a bit and cook for 3 minutes.
2. Add stock, stir.
3. Lock the lid. Select the Manual mode, then set the timer for 7 minutes at High Pressure.
4. Once the timer goes off, perform a quick release. Carefully open the lid.
5. Add cornbread stuffing cubes, set the pot in Sauté mode again, toss and cook everything for 3 to 4 minutes more.
6. Serve as a side dish!

Nutritional info:

Calories 146, Fat 4g, Carbs 8g, Protein 5g

Simple Buttery Potatoes

Prep Time: 12 mins, Cook Time: 6 mins, Servings: 4

Ingredients:

1 cup water
3 lbs. red potatoes, halved
¼ cup grated
Parmesan cheese
½ tsp. basil
Salt, to taste
2 tbsps. butter

Instructions:

1. Place the water in the Instant Pot, add potatoes.
2. Lock the lid. Select the Manual mode, then set the timer for 1 minutes at High Pressure.
3. Once the timer goes off, perform a quick release. Carefully open the lid.
4. Drain the potatoes and transfer to a bowl.
5. Clean the pot and select the Sauté mode, add butter, melt it, add potatoes, basil, salt and Parmesan, toss, cook for 5 minutes, divide between plates and serve as a side dish.

Nutritional info:

Calories 137, Fat 3g, Carbs 10g, Protein 3g

Measurement Conversion Chart

VOLUME EQUIVALENTS(DRY)

US STANDARD	METRIC (APPROXIMATE)
1/8 teaspoon	0.5 mL
1/4 teaspoon	1 mL
1/2 teaspoon	2 mL
3/4 teaspoon	4 mL
1 teaspoon	5 mL
1 tablespoon	15 mL
1/4 cup	59 mL
1/2 cup	118 mL
3/4 cup	177 mL
1 cup	235 mL
2 cups	475 mL
3 cups	700 mL
4 cups	1 L

VOLUME EQUIVALENTS(LIQUID)

US STANDARD	US STANDARD (OUNCES)	METRIC (APPROXIMATE)
2 tablespoons	1 fl.oz.	30 mL
1/4 cup	2 fl.oz.	60 mL
1/2 cup	4 fl.oz.	120 mL
1 cup	8 fl.oz.	240 mL
1 1/2 cup	12 fl.oz.	355 mL
2 cups or 1 pint	16 fl.oz.	475 mL
4 cups or 1 quart	32 fl.oz.	1 L
1 gallon	128 fl.oz.	4 L

TEMPERATURES EQUIVALENTS

FAHRENHEIT(F)	CELSIUS(C) (APPROXIMATE)
225 °F	107 °C
250 °F	120 °C
275 °F	135 °C
300 °F	150 °C
325 °F	160 °C
350 °F	180 °C
375 °F	190 °C
400 °F	205 °C
425 °F	220 °C
450 °F	235 °C
475 °F	245 °C
500 °F	260 °C

WEIGHT EQUIVALENTS

US STANDARD	METRIC (APPROXIMATE)
1 ounce	28 g
2 ounces	57 g
5 ounces	142 g
10 ounces	284 g
15 ounces	425 g
16 ounces (1 pound)	455 g
1.5 pounds	680 g
2 pounds	907 g

Made in the USA
Monee, IL
03 February 2021